FILM CENSORSHIP

FILM CENSORSHIP

by

GUY PHELPS

With an Introduction by
Alexander Walker

LONDON
VICTOR GOLLANCZ LTD
1975

In memory of
Martha Marietta Louise Wolf-Ferrari

MADE AND PRINTED IN GREAT BRITAIN BY
THE GARDEN CITY PRESS LIMITED
LETCHWORTH, HERTFORDSHIRE
SG6 1JS

CONTENTS

ACKNOWLEDGEMENTS

Many people have contributed to this book. The project could probably not have been undertaken at all without the assistance of an initial grant from the Centre for Mass Communication Research at Leicester University. For this and for his valuable comments on an early draft I owe a great debt to Professor James Halloran. Even more crucial in making the study possible were the parts played by Stephen Murphy and the British Board of Film Censors. In allowing me unrestricted access to the Board's files and to its viewing theatre over a period of two and a half years, Murphy overthrew all previous policy. Without the whole-hearted co-operation of the officers, examiners and administrative staff of the Board many parts of this book would have taken a very different, and less complete, form. I was also greatly helped by John Trevelyan who kindly filled in many gaps for me from the wealth of his experience and knowledge.

In addition many people were good enough to give their time to talk to me about their involvement in and attitudes toward censorship. In particular, local authority officials and politicians all over the country, film critics and representatives of pressure groups all gave valuable assistance. The unexciting task of typing the various drafts was undertaken by many fingers. To Lorna Hewitt, Nicky Hutchings, Jean Goddard, Enid Nightingale and Winnie Jefferson I am most grateful. Finally, it goes without saying that my wife, Liz,—sub-editor, critic, discussant, morale-booster and breadwinner—deserves far more thanks than any brief acknowledgement can possibly convey.

INTRODUCTION

by Alexander Walker

BETWEEN READING THE typescript of *Film Censorship* and
sitting down to write this introduction to it, I was steeling myself
for an experience hitherto unprecedented in English law. Namely
an appearance at the Central Criminal Court—the 'Old Bailey'—
as a witness for the defence in the trial of *Last Tango in Paris*,
which was being prosecuted under the Obscene Publications Act
of 1959—the first time the Act had been applied to a film being
shown in a public cinema.

The experience was so disorienting in a sense that Pirandello
would have relished that it is worth recording, I think, quite apart
from the guidelines it may establish if the Obscene Publications
Act is deemed to apply to such films. For, on this occasion, a
courageous Judge ruled that there was no case to answer. It would
appear that a film in such circumstances is 'published' to the licensee
of the cinema, not to the audience which pays to see it; and the
likelihood of the proprietor of the London cinema, where the film
had been showing for over a year, admitting that he had been
corrupted and depraved was regarded as remote. Since then, however, the Appeal Court has been asked to rule on the applicability
of the Act to films. 'Expert witnesses' such as the Act permits to be
called for the Defence may yet have a future; so, unfortunately,
may private prosecutions of the kind which was brought against
Last Tango in Paris by a former Salvation Army sergeant-major
in his seventies. What is more questionable is whether film censorship in such circumstances will have, or should have, any future.

So even though in November 1974 the case was closed before
the Defence needed to call any witnesses from among the film
critics, directors, playwrights, social historians, newspaper columnists
and actors who had volunteered, half out of duty, half out of
curiosity, to speak up for the film, we were all of us subjected to a
process of legal consultation that prompted reflections on how the
trial of a film might take place under the Act and how it would
differ from the trial, say, of a book.

In both cases, I imagine, witnesses go through a preliminary
canter with the lawyers that takes them into some strange territory.
What is at issue is a work of fiction, or so it seems at first. But the

process of the Law inexorably mounts its defence or prosecution
in a way that treats the characters and events in dispute as if they
were real people and actual incidents existing in a world as solid as
a judge's bench. To prepare myself for the trial I had to view
Last Tango in Paris five times; I wrote copious 'opinions' on it
running into several thousand words; I studied what is known as
the 'continuity script', which sets out scenes and dialogue as they
appear in the finished film; and I discussed, defended, interpreted
and debated the actions of two people called Paul and Jeanne for
the better part of ten hours. I assume that most of the other 'expert
witnesses' did much the same stint. The upshot was that after hours,
weeks and months of such opinion-sounding, Paul and Jeanne
(played in the film by Marlon Brando and Maria Schneider) had
become to me more life-like than the named defendants, United
Artists Corporation Ltd., who, in fact, were seldom mentioned in
discussions that came more and more to resemble the hair-splitting
glossaries of terms relating to sex, love and morality that must have
been familiar in the medieval Courts of Love and were now engag-
ing the attention, time and money of a platoon of people at the
Courts of Law.

Had I actually got as far as the witness box at the 'Old Bailey'
I should have looked around for Paul and Jeanne and assumed that
they had been prevented from actually appearing in person in the
dock to answer for their deeds, or misdeeds, by some fortuitous
circumstance that had put them beyond arrest, though possibly not
conviction.

The Law, in short, tends to treat fiction as if it were fact. In-
voluntarily or not, it gives flesh to the figures created on the screen
or the page; and, of course, where flesh is present, so is sin. A degree
of medical materialism is therefore added to the need for moral
justification, which can be shattering for many a witness who is
expecting to give evidence on artistic grounds—the Act specifically
excludes evidence on any other grounds, such as the tendency of the
work in question to deprave and corrupt, which are matters for
the jury alone—and then finds himself forced to consider acts like
rape, sodomy, masturbation and even putative bestiality *as if they
had actually taken place*. To justify such things as being 'for the
public good'—which is not the same as 'doing the public good'—it
is generally necessary to establish their artistic validity. But invariably that brings up the question of moral intention. And with
the Prosecution harping on the insalubrious medical reality of it
all, the witness may well wish himself back at his desk with the
soft option of film criticism facing him for the rest of his life.

It is perfectly feasible to speculate on what the different lines
of approach would have been had the *Last Tango in Paris* case
proceeded. The Defence would have been at pains to stress that

however flagrant, shocking, even loathsome the actions of Paul and Jeanne were, they are perfectly valid in the context of the film's intention and even reticently treated in the director's depiction of them. In short, 'artistic' and 'necessary'. The Prosecution, however, has an interest in stripping intention down to the bare bones and to the four-letter verbs and nouns. In short, 'carnal' and 'obscene'. Now a great deal of artistry on the part of a writer or film-maker lies in knowing what to leave out of his creation : the ambiguities and even the *lacunae* in morals and actions create a resonance in which the subtlety and audacity of the work can penetrate to the viewer. Unfortunately, such things also create a series of unguarded doors that can be kicked in by a well-shod Prosecution. Thus begins a deliberate process of repairing the film-maker's 'omissions' and spelling out his 'intentions' in order to conduct the artistic and moral defence of his characters. The latter have a far more 'complete' life thrust upon them as a result than they possess in the film. It is also, regrettably, a far less 'artistic' life. For it takes on the shape of a cast-iron alibi that will make good any striking character deficiencies and render their fleshly weaknesses less debatable and, it is to be hoped, less vulnerable.

At every step in every scene one is compelled to elucidate motivation, determine the degree of culpability (if any), establish innocence (if possible) and generally translate looks, words and even silences into their defensible moral correlatives.

For instance, there was the phrase 'holy family'. It is used by Paul in the course of what's come to be called 'the butter scene' in which he accompanies the act of buggering Jeanne by compelling her to repeat after him a string of denunciations. Does 'holy family' in this context mean the Biblical trinity of Jesus, Mary and Joseph? Or is it simply a social reference, to the bondage that the sacred institution of the family forces on individuals in the bourgeois society that Paul has rejected? I daresay these possible interpretations weren't unduly pondered by filmgoers watching such a scene; but they could be vital to sustaining a charge of blasphemy as well as buggery. And the scene itself raises a score more bristling problems for its defence. Is it absolutely essential to show it? Could the man not have made his point without driving it home in this unnatural fashion? Does it not leave the girl degraded? After one's been through the 'justification' for each thought and action, one is left with a sour feeling that more insidious damage has been done to the fabric of Bertolucci's film than the starkest accusation of depravity could entail. (Even now, I can never think of the film's most painful and piteous scene, where Paul compels the girl to humiliate him, without regretting the callous legalism of 'digital buggery' employed to identify it : my own suggestion of '*doigt du seigneur*' was regarded as injudiciously flippant.)

All this means giving a finite shape to relationships created out of one man's observation of the infinite variety of human nature : it is asking us to be the judges of fictitious figures as if they were subject to the same penalties as flesh-and-blood humans. It is hard to think an artist could ever create anything valuable and unique if he had to insert such prudent justifications for his characters' actions at every stage of his creation as would permit them to be defended against the charge of corruption and depravity in an English law-court.

Where the *Last Tango in Paris* trial would certainly have differed from, say, its notorious predecessor, the prosecution of *Lady Chatterley's Lover*—incidentally the same two QCs, Mr Jeremy Hutchinson and Mr Richard Du Cann, appeared for the Defence in each case, with Mr Gerald Gardiner QC as leading counsel in the 1960 trial—would have been in the difficulty it raised in judging the morality of a visual image by means of the printed word. I believe this to be a crucial test of any film brought to trial under a Statute which permits 'expert witnesses' to be called in its defence.

It is the continuity script of *Last Tango in Paris* that would have frequently formed the basis of question and cross-examination in court. Yet the script is only one part of a film and not necessarily its most important part, either. An inflection in Brando's voice, an expression on Maria Schneider's face, the subtlety of the light playing on and softening the crude physical contact of their bodies, the way Vittorio Storaro's colour photography adds an impressionistic dimension to the clinical detail : all are defensibly more vital parts of Bertolucci's film than a text whose spartan qualities look positively poverty-stricken in script form. Judge, jury and witnesses would have been repeatedly referred by counsel to a medium (the printed word) the affective quality of which is sometimes *in opposition to* the medium that carries the real message (the visual image). Moreover the qualifications that a jury would have to bring to the judgment of a movie, particularly one as elliptical and complex as *Last Tango in Paris*, would be even more exacting than the patience required to read *Lady Chatterley's Lover* in its unexpurgated Penguin edition. Though each encounter between man and girl has certain resemblances, each one actually advances their mutual knowledge (and ours of them) in subtle ways; and it would be asking a lot of people unaccustomed to viewing films, particularly films in which a lot of the dialogue is in French, to hold the scenes clearly enough in mind, as well as in sequence, that they can appraise their relevance to the charges.

In the case of a book, it's easy enough for counsel to quote a passage word for word, and a jury to turn to the appropriate page; but a film is in no sense a static document like a paragraph in a paperback. It touches the emotions and enters the mind through the ears as well as the eyes; and, short of providing the court (and the jury room) with a videotape recorder and a playback casette of the movie in dispute, I cannot see an easy solution to the problem of bringing a film to judgement. The Law will clearly have to allow for some transition in the nature of the evidence before the court if the Obscene Publications Act is found applicable to motion pictures shown in public theatres.

But no one who reads Dr Phelps's massively researched account of film censorship, lay as well as legal, can fail to sense that in the mid-1970s we are at a point of transition in our attitude to the position that the movies should hold in society as well as in court.

Whether the Law or the film censor plays the predominant part in controlling their freedom, it is too early to say; but the book strengthens the conviction I already hold, that the Law and the censor should not *both* exercise restraint over what an adult public wishes to see. No other art form today is so encumbered as the movies are by restraints on the public's access to it. The Customs, the film censor, the local authorities, the various parts of the Statutory and common law, and in recent years an ugly and dangerous growth of local pressure groups co-ordinated with some tactical skill to represent themselves as a genuine grass-roots movement : any or all of these can prove to be a tyrant. Dr Phelps narrates with wry understanding how the British Board of Film Censors' very timidity in certificating certain films, leaving the decision to the local authorities, actually awakened some of the latter to powers that their members never knew they possessed, so that pressure groups like the Festival of Light were able to forge a weapon by dint of repeated local lobbying and turn it against the B.B.F.C. The recent local government reconstruction has at least consigned a few of the more notable bigots to outer darkness, which no one will regret who reads this book's account of the councils-as-censors, the bizarre composition of film-viewing committees, the blackspots of local prejudice, the split decisions and the tight votes that irrationally meant freedom for a film in one town and the banning of it in another. The author has had access to the local weekly and daily Press, where such disgraceful if often ludicrous abuses of power are reported more fully than in national news-papers, and his book benefits from the map it includes of provincial as well as metropolitan censorship.

I regret, as I am sure he does, that the Greater London Council so narrowly failed at the beginning of 1975 to abolish film censor-ship for adults in its area, despite a recommendation from its film-viewing board. Had London allowed films to be shown uncensored to adults, it would have been a helpful test of public reaction to the very need for censorship. But the film industry would not, on the whole, welcome a move like this; and there are good grounds for believing it was this hint, passed along to the G.L.C. from Whitehall, that defeated the move by a few casting votes. Censorship has always been seen by the film Establishment as a protective, not a restrictive, measure. I have said elsewhere, but it bears repeating, that the censor is there to protect the public from the opportunism of the film industry and the industry from the intolerance of the public. I should like to add a third function. He is also there to ensure that the balance of profitability within the film industry is not unduly upset by some sudden rush to freedom by any section of it, in this case by the smaller and possibly less scrupulous film renters who would have benefited from the abolition of adult censorship to extend the lines they already do profitably in 'sexploitation' or soft-porn movies at the smaller and seedier cinemas in and out of London. Many such films are already severely truncated by the censor; others he rejects completely and they have to apply to the G.L.C. for a local certificate. Either way, censorship controls the flood of products that would pose an increasing threat to the box-office of the orthodox commercial cinema circuits in Britain or of those cinemas owned in London by the major renters. If the G.L.C. had been allowed to give the green light, so to speak, to any material that the smaller renters wished to put on the screen for adults—provided they took the risk of legal prosecution, and some would—more than the extremes of public opinion might have been upset.

The G.L.C.'s film-viewing board has commented : 'Analysis of [the views of exhibitors and distributors] indicates that their overriding interest is their desire for protection from legal action. Up till very recently, the industry has felt it could ensure this immunity by obtaining film certificates from the B.B.F.C. as required by the local licensing authority. The possibility of private prosecution under the Obscene Publications Act ... may alter this position. But it may also be queried whether the industry is entitled to such a degree of protection when the book publisher or play producer is not.' This view implies there is more 'immunity' in a censor's certificate than may actually be the case; nevertheless it is broadly correct in intimating that to get freedom for the film-maker it may be necessary to wrest it from the film distributor as well as from the film censor and the local authority.

In what I've written earlier about *Last Tango in Paris* I've drawn on my own experience to suggest the difficulties and risks that would follow from bringing films clearly within the jurisdiction of the Obscene Publications Act. But if it were possible to do this and simultaneously to abolish the need for adult censorship and withdraw from local authorities their statutory powers to censor films, then I would encourage the move as the lesser of two evils. I feel the risks inherent in seeing a film gets a 'fair trial' are less objectionable than the threats to the individual's freedom to see such a film from muddled or timorous censors, ignorant and bigoted councillors and stealthy and insidious pressure groups. Nor am I impressed by the argument of the film industry (and its censor) that the 'sampling' system of legal action against specific films is a more deplorable inconsistency than the present system of submitting all films to a process of secretive and often quite unnecessary cutting.

It is a valuable and, as far as I know, unprecedented feature of this book that its author was given access to some of the B.B.F.C.'s private files, in particular the examiners' reports. This is certainly to the retiring censor's credit; and one hopes that anyone appointed to follow him will take the hint. The use Dr Phelps has made of these is scrupulously fair and highly perceptive; but just reading the quoted excerpts fills one with misgivings about the extremely subjective and contentious way in which a film-maker's work is examined by those who have the power to determine the public's access to it in whole or part.

The abolition of censorship for adults, and the placing of films under the Law, would at the very least allow film-makers the same rights of access to their public that an author and publisher of a book already enjoy; and it would make for happier censors at the B.B.F.C. if their chief obligation was limited to classifying films for children.

Lastly, I am impressed by Dr Phelps's analysis of the role of the Press, T.V. and other media as active agents in elevating a film to controversial importance and, in some cases, actually influencing the degree of censorship which the censor felt compelled to inflict on it. This is an aspect of the media that seldom gets attention; one is not proud of it. I think in fairness, though, one should note the occasions when critics rallied to the defence of a controversial film before it had reached the censor, who was thereby heartened enough to ask for minimal cuts or none at all. Every street has two sides, even Fleet Street.

Film Censorship, to sum up, is a most important and long-awaited work. Along with Neville March Hunnings's account of *Film Censorship and the Law* and John Trevelyan's memoirs of his years at the B.B.F.C. in *What the Censor Saw*, it will become one of the standard reference books on its subject, widely and continuously quoted when censorship comes up for debate—which will be not infrequently, I imagine, in the months ahead.

May 1975

AUTHOR'S FOREWORD

The past may be a foreign country but time soon erodes the familiar contours of the present. This book is largely concerned with censorship of the cinema as it has been carried out in the last few years; recent history therefore, but history none the less. Even whilst revising the final draft of the manuscript I was made aware of the transience of 'current' events by hearing of the impending resignation of one of the major figures in this book, Stephen Murphy, Secretary of the British Board of Film Censors. Realising the impossibility of ever catching up with the present I have made no effort to take account of this development. For the purposes of this study 'now' must remain forever frozen at January 1975, a date already receding inexorably into the past.

Murphy, in any case, continues as censor until the summer. No doubt his successor will introduce some changes at the Board, but it is one of the themes of this study that individuals are tightly circumscribed by the forces of the social situation in which they find themselves. As Murphy found to his cost, the autonomy of even the apparently powerful is severely limited. It is an ironic fact that this book, appearing as it does at the time of his leaving office, represents one of the few surviving testaments to the policy of democratization and openness with which he approached the job.

The purpose of this book is to provide fact and information to contribute to the debate on censorship; a debate which too often has been bedevilled by ignorance and misapprehension. Ideally this implies that the author be objective, impartial and unbiased. Of course I am none of these. I can do no more than claim to have tried to control my opinions, and hope to arm the reader against my prejudices by making them explicit.

In theory I do not see the need for censorship for adults. I consider its potential 'dangers' to be greater than the 'protection' that it affords. But in practice it is clear that the nature of the mass media ensures that 'controls' will always exist. The commercial cinema with its enormous financial investment and oligopolistic distribution and exhibition structures will never be a vehicle for true freedom of expression. I cannot feel that official censorship is by any means the greatest barrier between the film-maker and his public—nor do I agree that the sort of changes recommended by many 'liberal' observers will necessarily improve the situation. It cannot be logical to argue, as some appear to, that on the one hand the Obscene Publications Acts are confusing and unworkable, and on the other that the cinema should be brought under these or similar statutes. I do not believe that the extension of such unsatisfactory laws would be advantageous—nor that it would inevitably lead to less restriction on the cinema. It can convincingly be argued that the industry's response to such a development would be extreme caution. The real need is for a radical reappraisal of the whole subject of obscenity law in this country. Until this is undertaken any 'improvements' in the censorship system, such as those discussed in the final chapter, cannot represent more than superficial cosmetics.

Meanwhile confusion continues to reign. The *Last Tango* case is to be considered by the Court of Appeal, while the successful prosecution of *More About the Language of Love*, in June, for indecency under common law is bound to lead to further such cases. As the law stands many films (irrespective of their artistic merit) may be condemned. Yet a Home Office paper, 'Vagrancy and Street Offences', has recommended that exhibitions such as film-shows to which the public gain admission by an act of will should be governed by the law of obscenity rather than that of indecent display—indecency, in legal terms, including a much wider range of behaviour.

The B.B.F.C. has continued to enjoy a period of relative calm. It was criticised for rejecting (on legal advice) *Ain't Misbehavin'* and for cutting Morrissey's *Flesh for Frankenstein* and *Blood for Dracula* and awaits censure over the banning of Makavejev's *Sweet Movie*. The new censor will undoubtedly face some difficult moments—Bertolucci's *1900*, Jewison's *Rollerball* and Jaekin's *The Story of O* all seem likely to present problems—but it must be hoped that he is allowed a quieter baptism than his predecessor.

I
CONTROVERSIAL PICTURE SHOW

THE MANAGER OF the Plaza cinema in London's West
End was reporting queues stretching for a quarter of a mile outside his premises, made up of film-goers anxious to see the
screen's latest controversy, a film that had been hailed by the
press as 'degrading, disgusting and offensive'. Although heavily
cut by the censors it was still able to provoke violent reactions :
Dilys Powell in the *Sunday Times* had called for a new 'D' for
'disgusting' certificate. It had even been discussed in the House
of Commons where the Prime Minister had been asked if he
would appoint 'a Royal Commission to investigate the standards
and methods of the British Board of Film Censors and to consider
the desirability of abolishing censorship altogether or of replacing
the present Board by a statutory body of impartial and educated
persons'. The Board of Trade was also questioned, its President
being asked if 'his attention had been drawn to the public indignation caused by the film and if no organization exists in
this country for assuring standards of decency and morality in
films shown in public cinemas'.

These anxieties were not shared by cinema audiences themselves. Questioned after seeing the film, not one of fifty people
condemned it, the general verdict being that 'it would not be
harmful to take even children to see it and that all that was
evil in the film was in the imagination of those who watched it'.
The Plaza received no complaints at all and continued to do
'abnormally good business'. The fact that 'never in the modern
history of show business in this country, has a film had such a
ruthlessly condemnatory press' served only to whet the public
appetite.

Official opinion was less sanguine however, and faced with
strong criticism from influential quarters the film censor was
forced to defend his decision to pass the film; but his argument
that he had insisted on many cuts was not sufficient to placate
his critics. Local authorities were soon intimating their desire to

see the film before allowing it to be exhibited in their areas. Surrey banned it immediately, and London insisted on amendments that removed a further eleven minutes from the version certificated by the censor.[1]

A cursory reading of this account might suggest that it concerned one of the 'shockers' of the seventies, but in fact the incident happened over a quarter of a century ago in 1948 and the film involved was an adaptation of James Hadley Chase's novel *No Orchids for Miss Blandish*. Despite the uproar, the case resulted in no sweeping changes in the system of film censorship in this country. The B.B.F.C. continued to apply its severe and rigid unwritten code, and no evidence was ever furnished that the exhibition of *No Orchids* had led to unforeseen outbreaks of reprehensible behaviour.

Yet, a generation later an almost identical pattern of events occurred over the film *Straw Dogs*, the chief protagonists no doubt unaware how closely they were following a well-worn path for, ever since the birth of the film industry, its products have been berated at frequent intervals. More often than not the 'blame' for the appearance of such films has been directed at the Board of Censors which has suffered almost unceasing opposition of varying intensity ever since its inception in 1912. Within five years, for example, a committee was calling for its replacement by a censor to be appointed 'by His Majesty in Council', and assisted by an Advisory Council 'representative of public interests'. Over half a century later similar suggestions are being put forward.

The problems that have exercised the minds of the censors and the public have also changed little. If it is thought that concern over violence, for instance, is a recent phenomenon, a study of past controversies will soon shatter this illusion. From its earliest days the cinema has consistently aggravated certain sections of the public by its awareness that themes of violence are particularly well-suited to the medium.

Philip French has noted how the American cinema has been regularly submitted to scrutiny on these grounds.[2] Thus, the outcry in the twenties led to the creation of the Production Code to regulate film content, while the gangster films of the following decade renewed the debate by contravening almost every section of that Code. Immediately after the war concern was expressed once more. One critic lamented the disappearance of the 'sophisticated attitude of American film-melodramas', commenting that 'instead we have the purposeless parade of violence for its own sake; physical violence unrelated to any known form of life and apparently catering for a supposed audience of sadistic school-children'.

Yet within ten years an article in *Sight and Sound* was asserting that 'the ferocity of American films has undeniably increased in the last few years'. This thesis was illustrated by an example supplied by the then film censor Arthur Watkins, who 'told me of a scene in an unspecified American film in which a man is forced to wear a deaf-aid while his tormentors put a radio which is blaring jazz next to the receiving end of the instrument and turned up the volume to an excruciating loudness. "It was horrible" he said, and so it sounds.'[3] It is hard to imagine such an episode arousing comment today.

French concluded that, at the time he was writing (in the mid-sixties), a fourth act of the continuing debate was in progress, stimulated in part by the James Bond films with their light-hearted amorality. Among his conclusions, 'the most apparent is that yesterday's excess is today's restraint. When the searing brutality of *Barabbas* struck London there were those who looked back to the good taste of *Quo Vadis?*, forgetting that it was from this film that many people, including a leading Labour M.P., had walked out in protest against its sadistic arena scenes'.

Recent years have seen further protest at film violence. Ironically at a time when a part of the United Kingdom itself is close to civil war, the debate has been renewed with more vehemence than ever.[4] Organizations have been formed specifically to combat certain developments in media content. Although initially dismissed as extremists, these groups have gained some degree of credibility and sustained pressure has been exerted on the various censoring bodies, at a time when they are also being heavily berated by others for being over-restrictive.

However it is not violence that these groups are worried about: their attention has been primarily focused on that other scourge of the censors—sex. Over the years sex has been the main preoccupation of both the censors and the alarmed sections of the public. As early as 1896 *The Kiss*, a fifty-foot film with an explanatory title, was a sensation in America where it came under attack. Three years later in England a travelling film exhibitor was taken to court by a parson who objected to a film entitled *Courtship* 'in which a lady was sitting on a seat in a garden while a gentleman came slyly up behind and kissed her'.[5] The

Catholic orientation of American censorship has generally led to more restriction on sexual matters than on violence, while obscenity laws are invariably more applicable to sex. In this country, too, censors have at all times been particularly concerned with sex. In 1917 the Board was working to a Code that was encapsulated in forty-three rules. Twenty of these related to sexual behaviour, including the specific banning of unnecessary exhibition of underclothing, indecorous dancing, scenes suggestive of immorality, situations accentuating delicate marital relations and, of course, nude figures.

In the fifties a writer commented that 'although the Board rightly claims that violence is what it abhors, sex is really the heart of the matter',[6] a comment that still has some validity today. The majority of cuts made are of a sexual nature, although this is largely a reflection of the sort of material that is dealt with. In addition, however, there is evidence that the public as a whole is still worried by the extent to which sex is dealt with by the mass media. Research by the television companies has indicated that sex and bad language are the main areas of concern, and that violence is particularly abhorrent only to a relatively small group of 'liberal intellectuals'.

The specific incidents and foci of attention may change with time but the battleground remains the same. Few would now hold that the cinema 'ministers to the lowest passions of children' or argue that its influence is 'wholly vicious' as the *Chicago Tribune* claimed in 1907, or support the judge who argued that the picture show 'indirectly or directly caused more juvenile crimes coming into this court than all other causes combined'.[7] Nevertheless, fear of the social impact of the cinema is world-wide; every country where films are shown has regulations restricting exhibition for children, and even where there is no censorship for adults, as in Belgium and Denmark, the obscenity laws still apply. Almost everywhere the cinema is more closely regulated than any comparable medium of communication.

The reasons are partly historical. The cinema was the first provider of mass entertainment. Books had for centuries been confined to a minority who were thought to be sufficiently educated and well-bred to be able to withstand corrupting influences. Significantly, as soon as mass literacy brought books within the reach of a wider public restrictions on publication began to appear. Newspapers had a wider appeal but were primarily organs of information and were, as such, protected by the freedom of the press. The cinema, with no such pretensions, was from the first considered to be purely a form of entertainment. Its early public was almost entirely working-class, consisting of those very people whom the better-educated and those in authority felt to be most open to corruption. The sort of paternalism on which censorship was founded was even apparent among those who opposed restriction as the following quotation, published as late as 1932, illustrates:

Even supposing there *were* little cinemas in the back streets of Rotherhithe showing filth to seamen, would England fall? If seamen want filth they know where to get it; the fact that so many of them frequent the decent pubs and mission-halls is an indication that the danger is not grave of the might of our Empire being undermined in this particular way. Supposing even family life in Lambeth was thus demoralized—as I don't believe for a moment it ever would be, for all the tendencies are in the other direction—would the rot spread through the whole fabric of society? Experience has taught us otherwise—that the moral tone of a nation, a family, a community is set from the top, not the bottom. We are most apt to ape our 'betters'. When courts have been profligate, nations have become debauched. The strict moral standards of England in the last century are well called Victorian, for it was the Head of State who set them; and while our Royal Family continues in its present high standard of conduct and demeanour, the nation stands in no need of Mrs Grundy's admonishing umbrella.[8]

Other commentators exhibited less faith in the power of the monarchy to ensure good behaviour and remained convinced that the cinema required strict control. It was rarely felt necessary to amplify this point of view, the common sense of which was generally thought to be self-evident. 'In an industry such as that dealing with films, it must be obvious even to the most unthinking, that some form of censorship was—and is—not only desirable, but necessary.'[9] The fact that, from its earliest days, the cinema was primarily a 'family' medium lay behind this assumption. Even now few people argue that children do not need extra protection and, in the days when censorship was introduced, unanimity on this point was greater still. Since it was taken for granted that nobody favoured a system that would

deny admittance to any film to any section of the public, every
production had to be of a standard suitable for children. No
distinction between adult and child was made or wanted for
many years.

In addition it was considered that films were more likely to
influence (and corrupt) their patrons than were books. It is true
that the size of the screen, the darkness and unfamiliarity of the
auditorium and the techniques available to the film-maker com-
bine to produce a particularly potent image. But there is no
evidence that a writer skilfully manipulating the almost unlimited
imagination of his reader cannot achieve as powerful an effect.
Indeed, as film-makers themselves have discovered, the hinted or
ambiguous can often be more suggestive than the visible reality.
In any case there are numerous books that many would consider
unsuitable for children which are not banned in any way; it is
the accessibility of the cinema which distinguishes it. Even today,
with age-graded classification and a cinema that is clearly no
longer a family medium, old ideas linger. Fear for the young
remains the prime motivation of many censors who grew up
with the cinema in its happier days, when the 'family film'
reigned supreme and the weekly, or bi-weekly, trip to the pictures
was the norm.

Another reason for the strict control exerted over the cinema
was noted twenty years ago by a writer who observed : 'One
reason for the severity of moral censorship in the cinema is the
attitude towards films of newspapers and other alleged sources
of public opinion. For many years they have more or less tacitly
expressed the feeling that the cinema is a rich but common
relation of the theatre, that it is a dangerous form of child's
play.'[10] This is perhaps less true today, but a suspicion of the
cinema remains and its status as anything more than a medium
of undemanding entertainment is often denied. The press is
now less guilty of this attitude (although it may contribute to
the maintenance of rigid censorship in other ways, as we shall
see). Unfortunately public opinion has changed more slowly.

Given that each newly discovered medium has in turn been
subjected to calls for control, it may appear strange that the
cinema is still one of the main objects of attack. One explanation
lies in the changed circumstances which have forced the cinema to
seek new material and new approaches. During its most successful
years the films that appeared on the screens of the many public
cinemas *were* little more than pure light entertainment with little

relevance to the lives of the audience. This had not always been so : before the First World War films had dealt extensively with working-class people in their own settings. The widening of the audience changed this emphasis as Lewis Jacobs has observed : 'Victorian preaching and didacticism began to fall back before the questioning attitudes and freer thinking of the more educated audiences. Having until now dealt mostly with the working man and his world, the camera turned towards the middle class. In the future it was to concentrate not on interpreting the working man's world, but on diverting him from it by showing the problems of the economically fortunate, which problems would interest him as entertainment rather than as sermons.'[11]

This function of providing escapism with material designed to take the viewer's mind off the worries and problems of his own life is now amply fulfilled by television with its constant, cheap and immediately available supply. The cinema has been forced to diversify from its traditional material, and one of its more succesful reactions to this competition has been the injection of greater realism into pictures. This has meant not only an increase in sex and violence, but also the attempt to deal with life itself in a more questioning manner. Modern films have more obvious implications for their audiences, and they also deal with more controversial matters. Indeed, a small but significant number discuss and even criticize and reject certain beliefs and institutions held by some to be the very corner-stones of our society and culture. The well-established conservatism of the cinema has now been challenged, and there is not likely to be a return to the days when all films could be confidently expected to support and reflect the *status quo*. This change has naturally aroused fierce opposition from those who would prefer the authorities to clip these newly spread wings. Although few overtly demand the imposition of political censorship, there is little doubt that some calls for stricter control, albeit couched in guardedly euphemistic terminology, amount to little less.

One crime with which the cinema is frequently charged is extraordinary by any standards. Time and again the industry is condemned for making money as a result of its production and exhibition of offensive films. The objection is frequently not so much to the material as to the profit, and cannot realistically be explained in terms of a fundamental dislike of capitalist society. The Longford Report, for instance, persistently made the point that 'pornography is business, and very big business' and that 'fortunes are being made out of pornography'.[12] In the subsequent Lords debate Lord Nugent reiterated that 'the objective in my opinion is the restraint of commercial exploitation of vice by pornographic material'.[13] The Protestant ethic, of course assumes that pecuniary benefit is one of the rewards for hard work and virtue, rather than for exploitation, but as Lord Birkett was quick to point out, 'half the great artists of the world have commercially exploited everything that they do. Most of our lives are devoted to commercial exploitation. Surely it is another word for earning your living.'[14]

As far as the cinema is concerned, the obstacles to making a profit are now formidable. The decline of the cinema audience[15] in the face of the challenge of television and other social changes associated with the greatly increased wealth of the nation has made investment in films almost as unattractive as investment in football—another entertainment medium that has suffered from the affluence of the working class. William Fadiman has commented that 'what was once a movie-going habit has become an occasion, which tends to benefit two kinds of films: those receiving extraordinary publicity through shrewd and expensive exploitation, and those of a highly libidinous or pornographic nature'.[16] The big American companies cling largely to the first formula, encouraged by the occasional *Love Story*, *Godfather* and *Exorcist*. Unfortunately the majors are now merely parts of huge conglomerate firms whose primary interests are real estate, chemicals and parking lots. Their concentration on finance above all else is an inevitable reaction to their ignorance of the industry, and results merely in the inability to make either good films or large profits. Bryan Forbes has described the frustrations of working for these 'faceless corporate men who were usually too busy jet-setting their way across the world in search of new acquisitions to actually view the films they made. What they couldn't understand they destroyed. What made them money, they squandered.'[17] All too often they are forced to turn to safe subjects that seem to offer a reasonable prospect of profit. Sex and violence figure prominently on an abbreviated list.

Even in this field they have largely failed. Attempts to make sex films by offering enormous budgets to men more accustomed to turning out pictures for a few thousand pounds, or by giving cash and facilities to young men who just *might* know how to appeal to the youth market, generally resulted in disaster, both financially and artistically. The successful sex films continue to to be made outside the major studios by independent producers working on a relatively small budget. Exploitation of violence has been more productive, and President Nixon's efforts to cleanse the screen of sex have led to further concentration on this ingredient.

Elsewhere the situation is little better. The British industry, never very lively, moves nearer an early grave. No sooner had part of Shepperton studios been saved from the property developers than the withdrawal of M.G.M. from most of its operations jeopardized the future of Elstree. But Britain is not the only sick man. The German film industry, of which there had been high hopes a short time ago, has sunk under a wave of unprepossessing sex 'comedies', only the cream of which ever come to grace the Charing Cross Road. The great reputations of directors like Truffaut, Godard, Bresson, etc. cannot hide the fact that the French industry also has profound problems. Even a record year in 1973 has not calmed the 'disquiet' felt by leading figures in France. In other countries a similar situation prevails.

In any case cultural differences, the structure of the exhibition system and censorship regulations ensure that only a tiny handful of foreign films are shown in Britain. The diet for film-goers in this country, therefore, largely consists of : American films, many of which are cut as a result of their violent content; British films which consist mostly of unambitious comedies and the occasional expensive costume drama; continental sex films, almost invariably reduced by various hands to a fraction of their original lengths; and a small but increasing number of European co-productions. Whereas in several countries admission statistics have at last shown an end to the decline, here there is, as yet, no indication of a similar trend.

The continuing crisis of the film industry in Britain is bound to influence the activities of the censors. On the one hand it is evident that too restrictive a policy could quickly lead to a situation in which the bulk of world production is not exhibitable here, thereby contributing to already severe problems. On the other hand too liberal a dispensation would, at best, alienate certain groups entirely from the cinema, at worst, cause a controversy leading to legislative changes resulting in greater and less flexible restriction. The Board of Film Censors must tread a narrow path between these two extremes. The ways in which it goes about this task and the measure of success that it achieves are among the main themes of this book.

THE ORIGIN AND DEVELOPMENT
OF FILM CENSORSHIP

PUBLIC FILM SHOWS in Britain date from 1896 and
concern about their contents arose almost immediately. The
first call for censorship was heard within two years following the
exhibition of a film in London. Using a microscope, Charles
Urban had filmed a study of 'life in a Stilton cheese', revealing
altogether too much for the British cheese industry which protested vigorously. Such complaints, however, failed to stir public
opinion and film censorship was eventually introduced as much
by accident as by design.

In those early days film shows were given in inadequate make-
shift premises which, in combination with the use of inflammable
nitrate stock and unsafe illuminants, made the danger of fire very
real, if not quite as inevitable as many contemporary commentators suggested. There was at this time a high level of public
and official awareness and fear of the fire hazard, as a result
of a number of large and fatal conflagrations in theatres throughout Europe during the nineteenth century, culminating in the
destruction of Vienna's Ring Theatre in 1881 with the loss of
450 lives, and the deaths of 186 people when the Theatre Royal,
Exeter, was burnt down in 1887. When in 1897 a small cinema
show in the annual Paris 'Bazar de la Charité' caught fire,
destroying the buildings and killing, among others, members of
the French aristocracy, the authorities became seriously alarmed
and introduced stringent (and occasionally over-zealous) regulations. In Britain the local councils, led by the London County
Council, were quick to pass fire regulations governing all premises licensed by them. This they were able to do as the music
which invariably accompanied film shows was deemed to bring
film within the compass of the Disorderly Houses Act of 1751
and thus subject to local authority licensing.

However the expansion of the industry led to the appearance,
early in this century, of 'picture-palaces' designed specifically for

the exhibition of films. As such, these lay beyond the scope of local authority regulations and their rapid proliferation soon made this a serious problem. The L.C.C. estimated that by 1907 there were about 170 unlicensed buildings in the city in which 'cinematograph exhibitions' were being given.

Worried by this apparent anomaly, the local authorities mounted a campaign to force the Home Secretary to take action to deal with these 'fire risks'. The film trade argued that the danger was being overestimated and sensationalized by the press, but although they had a reasonable case the individual members failed to take a firm or united stand against the introduction of legislation. From the very start the industry was unable to adopt a corporate policy for mutual protection. Foresight and clarity of vision were apparently no more characteristic of members of the trade then than now, for 'each adopted the attitude that his own products were harmless and that it was only a minority who were destroying the good name of the industry; the Act would deal with them and leave the others in peace. And so the opposition which might have killed the Bill was itself stifled in an orgy of self-congratulations; for the Home Secretary had on several occasions stated that he would not continue with the Bill if any opposition appeared.'[1]

The resulting Cinematograph Act of 1909 was intended solely to establish fire precautions. This is evident from its wording, from its full title, and from statements issuing from the Home Office.[2] However, to the dismay of the cinema exhibitors and the embryo distribution companies, local councils immediately began to interpret the law in a much broader way than that envisaged by its drafters. Their actions were supported by the courts which ruled that the Act was 'intended to confer on the County Councils a discretion as to the conditions which they will impose, so long as those conditions are not unreasonable'.[3]

As a result councils were free to impose conditions which were far removed from simple fire prevention measures. Hours of opening were fixed, 'barking' at the door was prohibited and licences were refused if the cinema was thought to be in a district that was 'unsuitable' or already had enough picture-houses. As early as 1910 conditions were introduced controlling the content of films. By the following year, inflamed by the press,[4] criticism of the cinema was becoming widespread. The industry was, by now, only too aware of the ramifications of the Act of 1909, but there was, by this time, little that it could do beyond

attempting to allay fears and disarm the critics. The major concern was the confusion and disruption of business that would
ensue from the activities of the 'many self-appointed guardians
of the public morals' as represented by the local authorities.

The best solution available seemed to be the appointment of
a trade censor, especially as the possibility of censorship was
already being canvassed. With this in mind, the trade organizations approached the Home Office early in 1912 but, while he
favoured the idea of trade censorship, the Home Secretary refused
to give active support, pointing out that the statutory powers lay
with the local authorities, and that only a further Parliamentary
Act could alter this situation. Despite the rebuff, and although
few authorities had yet actually introduced conditions regulating
film content, the industry was very concerned that continued
campaigns in the press and by religious groups would lead to
this form of control becoming general practice.

At a meeting of the exhibitors' association in July 1912 a
motion was passed that 'a censorship is necessary and advisable'
and plans for an examining board were drawn up. In November
the formation of the British Board of Film Censors was announced, to be under the Presidency of G. A. Redford who had much
experience as Examiner of Plays for the Lord Chamberlain. He
and his four examiners were to be 'a purely independent and impartial body, whose duty it will be to induce confidence in the
minds of the licensing authorities, and of those who have in
their charge the moral welfare of the community generally'.[5] The
Board started work on 1st January, 1913 and was able to
announce that all films released in Britain after 1st March would
bear the censor's certificate.

Since the submission of films to the Board was entirely voluntary this statement seems more optimistic than realistic, and,
indeed, many companies ignored the Board. A more important
weakness, however, remained the complete autonomy of the
local authorities. At first very few were inclined to recognize the
existence of the Board. By the end of 1915 only thirty-five
councils had adopted clauses stipulating that all films to be
shown must have the censor's certificate. The rest, including all
the important councils, retained their full powers. Indeed, the
existence of a board of censors seemed to stimulate many councils
to renewed censorial activity. When public criticism mounted
again, it became apparent to all that the present system was inadequate. Consequently, both the trade and the local authorities

made renewed efforts urging the Home Office to appoint an official censor. A new Home Secretary proved more sympathetic to these overtures than his predecessors had been, and indeed announced to a conference of local authorities in April, 1916 that 'I do not myself feel convinced that it is impossible to take steps along these lines'. He was evidently greatly impressed by the opinion of a number of chief constables, 'who declare with almost complete unanimity that the recent great increase in juvenile delinquency is, to a considerable extent, due to demoralizing cinematograph films', and was apparently aware of 'evidence with respect to films of other objectionable types, which leads to the conclusion that the present censorship arrangements are really not quite adequate'.[6]

Accordingly a scheme was drawn up for censorship by a Board with a Government-appointed President. The local authorities were generally satisfied with the proposals, for they retained their statutory powers, but the trade, which had assumed that local censorship would be abolished, was, for once, united in opposition. Protests, however, failed to impress the Home Office which in November 1916 announced that the new system would take effect from 1st January, 1917. Three weeks before this date, however, the Machiavellian intrigues of Lloyd-George brought about the downfall of Prime Minister Asquith and the appointment of a new Home Secretary whose disinterest in all matters pertaining to the film industry led him to cancel the scheme and reaffirm the powers of the local authorities. Thus narrowly was a development averted which would have changed the whole history of film censorship in this country.

Shortly afterwards an important document played a vital role in dampening criticism of the cinema. This was the Report of the Cinema Commission of Inquiry which had been set up by the National Council of Public Morals and which was published in October 1917. It cleared the film industry of most of the charges then being laid against it and reported favourably on the work of the B.B.F.C. With this support and under a new and vigorous President, T. P. O'Connor (Redford having died in 1916), the Board was able to consolidate its position. A real turning point was reached when, in 1920 and 1921 respectively, the influential Middlesex and London County Councils adopted the Board's certificate as a requirement for their licences. This development finally convinced the trade that the Board was a

viable proposition, and that with the full co-operation of members
it could be made to work.

The trade was, however, incensed at one item in the L.C.C.'s
new conditions. From the first the Board had issued two different
certificates. The 'U' Category (Universal) indicated that the film
was specially recommended for children's matinee performances,
while 'A' (Public) implied that the film was more suitable for
adults. The 'A' certificate did not in any way signify that the
film should not be shown to children : indeed an early B.B.F.C.
leaflet promised that 'no film subject will be passed that is not
clean and wholesome and absolutely above suspicion'. Now the
L.C.C. had radically changed this system, stipulating that 'no
young person shall be admitted to be present at any exhibition at
which films passed by the British Board of Film Censors for
"Public" but not for "Universal" exhibitions are shown, unless
accompanied by a parent or bona fide adult guardian of such
young person'.

The trade protested vigorously at the restriction of the audience
for 'A' films, but to no purpose, and the L.C.C.'s example was
soon followed by other authorities.[7] Indeed, in 1923 the Home
Office circulated to all authorities a recommendation that they
should adopt the L.C.C. rules, which by the end of 1924 most
of them had done. Finally, in November of that year, the L.C.C.
introduced a revised set of rules which demanded that :

(a) No cinematograph film shall be exhibited which is likely
to be injurious to morality or to encourage or incite to crime,
or to lead to disorder, or to be in any way offensive in the
circumstances to public feelings, or which contains any offensive
representations of living persons.

(b) No cinematograph film—other than photographs of current
events—which has not been passed for 'universal' or 'public'
exhibition by the British Board of Film Censors shall be
exhibited without the express consent of the Council.

(c) Immediately before the exhibition of each cinematograph
film . . . a reproduction of the certificate of the Board . . . shall
be exposed in such a manner that it shall be legible to all
persons attending the exhibition.

(d) No cinematograph film—other than photographs of current events—which has not been passed for 'universal' exhibition by the British Board of Film Censors shall be exhibited at
the premises without the express consent of the Council during

the time that any child under or appearing to be under the age of 16 years is therein, provided that this rule shall not apply in the case of any child who is accompanied by a parent or bona fide guardian of such child.

(e) Nothing in the foregoing shall be deemed to relieve the licensee of his personal responsibility for any cinematograph film shown which may, in the opinion of the Council, be detrimental to the public interest.[8]

These conditions were to form the basis for the censorship system. A few local authorities, most notably Manchester, refused to acknowledge it and applied their own rules, but in general it was accepted, and pressures for a radical revision have been rare. The Board itself was now in a position of much greater strength. All films except newsreels had to be submitted, although some years earlier the Board had refused to deal with 'propaganda' films, defined by O'Connor in his report for 1919 as 'produced for the purpose of enlisting public opinions or enlisting sympathy on certain subjects. Such films have included the effects of certain diseases, contracted and hereditary,[9] illegal operations, white slavery, race suicide, etc.' This list includes subjects that are now the staple diet of television documentary programmes and which are generally considered as a very important part of their coverage. In those days, however, the Board was of the opinion that such material was 'not suitable for exhibition in places maintained for the purpose of entertainment and recreation'. The Board had no doubt that this was the true and only aim of the cinema, and any educational or artistic aspects were strongly denied. As O'Connor remarked: 'My business is with the cinematograph manufacturer and the cinematograph proprietor who produces films for the purpose of profit, and I am a bit unwilling to enlarge my sphere.' This attitude prevailed throughout the twenties and thirties and was not seriously questioned within the Board until after the end of the war.

Throughout this period, the President was the dominant figure at the B.B.F.C. J. Brooke Wilkinson, who held the position of Secretary from 1912 until 1948, was very much a background figure, albeit one whose wealth of experience was invaluable to his Presidents. It seems that during his latter years in office he was almost totally blind, an indication of his relatively unimportant role in decision-making, although O'Connor also was unable to view films towards the end of his career as partial paralysis

32

prevented him from ascending the stairs to the projection theatre!
Nevertheless, until quite recently censorship was the personal
responsibility of the President, and the Secretary was his own
appointee with inevitable consequences for the relationship of
the two roles. From O'Connor (who had been a Member of
Parliament) onwards, the Presidency has always been held by
an ex-politician. Edward Shortt (1929–35) had in fact been
Home Secretary, while Lord Tyrrell (1935–47) had been in the
foreign service including a spell as Ambassador in Paris. Later
appointments have followed this tradition, and since 1929 the
appointment has always been subject to Home Office approval.

These facts have been held by some critics to demonstrate that
the Board is firmly under Government control. It is certainly
undeniable that in its early days the Board was very inclined to
defer to governmental pressure and that it was keen to support
the establishment and to offer protection to those in authority.
Of course the Board was in an invidious position. Although
nominally independent of the Government, its lack of statutory
powers and its openness to criticism and pressure, notably from
the local authorities who could, at any time, overturn its decisions, made it unlikely that the Board could steer a resolute autonomous course. Inevitably in need of outside support, the Board
was hardly in a position to ignore the 'official' point of view.

Moreover the early censors' definition of their role required
them to take close note of opinions from above. Their very broad
interpretation of their terms of reference identified the Board as
one of those institutions whose duty it was to protect the public.
They therefore inevitably saw themselves as a part of a paternalistic establishment. As John Trevelyan has commented: 'Up to
the last war the Board clearly considered itself the guardian
of public morality, allowing no departure from the accepted code
of conduct and behaviour, the protector of the establishment, the
protector of the reputation and image of Britain in other countries and the protector of cinema audiences from such dangerous
themes as those involving controversial politics.'[10]

There was little opposition to such a policy. The trade, which
might have been expected to object, remained silent, being re-
lieved to accept a system that offered a reasonable degree of
uniformity throughout the country. It was also well aware of
the low reputation that the cinema held amongst sections of the
population and was hopeful that censorship would help to raise
public regard for the cinema. The industry was proud to be able

to claim that 'the success of the cinematograph had been obtained by the fact that it was a clean and healthy entertainment, to which ladies and children could go with safety'. The Board was even able to assert that its policies originated in the industry's own attitudes. Thus a later President reviewing the early years noted that 'for the first 35 years the policy of the Board was based on the principle adopted by the trade that the cinema should provide for the family audience'.[11]

Nevertheless, the Board felt that its mission was to elevate the taste of certain material that was being produced, and early success was claimed in the annual report for 1914. 'There is reason to believe that [the Board's] influence is having the desired effect of eliminating certain subjects which are altogether unsuitable for British audiences, and further of raising the general standard of films exhibited in this country.' This policy was presented to the trade as in their best financial interest on the grounds that 'it is demonstrated by all the experience of the stage and the newspaper, as well as of the cinema, that among the peoples of these islands decency pays best in the long run'. The precise evidence for this optimistic appraisal was not made clear.

The course taken by the Board resulted not only from its low view of the nature of cinema but also from its low view of the cinema audience, which was assumed to include 'a not inconsiderable proportion of people of immature judgement'. The evidence submitted by the Board to the Cinema Commission of 1917 indicated that much account was taken of the 'immaturity' of a large part of the audience, and, in particular, its propensity to imitate bad behaviour seen on the screen. The Home Secretary's attribution to the cinema of a large part of the rise in crime among young people further fortified the censors who felt no qualms about their restrictive policies which were outlined to the Commission by one examiner in the following terms.

The examiners . . . have been guided by the broad principle that nothing should be passed which in their opinion was calculated to demoralize an audience or any section of it; that could be held to extenuate crime or to teach the methods of criminals; that could undermine the teachings of morality; that tended to bring the institution of marriage into contempt; that lowered the sacredness of family ties. They have refused their sanction to incidents which brought into contempt public characters acting in their capacity as such; i.e. officers wearing

H.M. uniform, ministers of religion, ministers of the crown, ambassadors and representatives of foreign nations, judges, etc. They have objected to subjects calculated to wound the susceptibilities of foreign peoples, or members of any religion. And, especially recently, they have rejected films calculated and possibly intended to ferment social unrest and discontent.[12]

Following this policy, the Board ensured that certain aspects of life were eliminated from the screen. Crime naturally presented an early problem and any film that suggested sympathy for or identification with the criminal received severe treatment 'as the Board cannot conceive anything more calculated to lower the standard of moral perception of the young than the constant exhibition of such unwholesome and unnatural stories'.[13] The censors' attitude was firmly expressed in the decision that no film 'in which crime is the dominant factor, and not merely an episode in the story, will be passed by the censor'. In 1925 a warning was issued to the industry concerning its tendency to show the criminal's point of view and to fail to show sufficient respect for the 'recognized authority of the law'.

Many aspects of sexual behaviour were also frowned upon and stories depicting 'manifestations of the pursuit of lust', 'indelicate sexual situations' and 'women leading immoral lives' were banned. 'Furthermore, drunkenness among women, brutality to women, fights between women, prostitution and procuration, "illegal operations", brothels, rape, confinements and puerperal pains were not just to be banned if "excessive" but were actually not to be mentioned at all. Girls were not made drunk or seduced, incest and the white slave trade did not exist.'[14] A Home Secretary, Sir William Joynson-Hicks, suggested one reason for the strictness and rigidity of these rulings : 'One side of this question, and one of terrible and far-reaching importance, is the effect of films produced either in America or in this country and exhibited in India and in the East, showing the white woman as an object of degradation. . . . It is undoubtedly essential that all nations which rule in Eastern countries should see to it that the pride and character of their womanhood is maintained unimpaired.'[15]

Such blatant racism, chauvinism and paternalism seems bad enough, but the Board's protective attitude towards authority had even wider implications. Direct political censorship is dealt with more fully elsewhere but it may be noted that among the many

items to which exception was taken were included the disparage-
ment of the institution of marriage, the ridiculing of British
social life, criticism of the police force and even stories casting
a bad light on nurses, dentists and workhouse officials. The 1921
report makes clear that the Board was always prepared and
even eager to ask for 'expert information when the need arises
—sometimes it is from public departments, sometimes from men
representative of social or religious opinion'. This advice was
considered to be 'an additional safeguard against the admission
to the film of any of the controversial themes and incidents that
are in opposition to the fundamental objection to the film being
used as agency for violent controversy in social or public life'.

Rachel Low has concluded that, in its efforts not to arouse
the censure of the powerful, the Board 'could be trusted to
come down on the side of the *status quo* on every political and
social issue'.[16] This policy was continued throughout the inter-
war years and resulted not only in the suppression of ideas but
also in the enfeebling of the British cinema itself. For while
home production was invariably denied the right to deal with
serious or controversial topics, foreign films that were now ventur-
ing into such territory were subjected to the same rigorous censorship as the trivial productions with which the Board was familiar
and which it helped to perpetuate. 'To some extent the very
poverty of imagination in British film production, and the early
contempt in which it was held, may have been due to the fact
that people simply did not know what could be done, and in
fact was being done abroad, with the film medium.'[17]

The situation had been further aggravated by the introduction
of sound in the late twenties. For some time the Board laboured
on without sound equipment, the examiners studying scripts
while the film was projected.[18] This deficiency was soon overcome
but no easy solution was available to the new problems posed
by sound film which presents technical obstacles to cutting.
For some time it seems that it was necessary to make a simple
decision between banning a film or passing it *in toto*. One consequence of lasting significance was the emergence of the practice
of studying scripts before production. This, of course, allowed
the Board an even greater degree of control than it had previously enjoyed. It is easier to insist on alterations to a project
that exists only on paper than to demand cuts in a finished film
representing huge financial investment. Naturally, it was particularly common for British scripts to be scrutinized before

shooting, thus penalizing the home industry at the expense of foreign productions. 'Producers themselves complain that the higher morality insisted on by the Board with regard to British films cramps them and inevitably makes them unreal, whereas much that is turned down in English scenarios is allowed when the Board suddenly finds itself face to face with the finished American products'.[19]

In 1932 local authority concern at the increasing number of horror films led to the introduction by the Board of the 'H' certificate, although this was no more than a warning to parents. There was no suggestion that children should be banned altogether from these films. Nevertheless, the Board's attitude towards them was made clear in the report for 1935 which restated the censors' continuing belief in their role as protectors of public morality, as a buffer between the public and a rapacious industry. 'Although a separate category has been established for these films, I am sorry to learn that they are on the increase, as I cannot believe that such films are wholesome, pandering as they do to the love of the morbid and horrible. . . . Some licensing authorities are already much disturbed about them, and I hope the producers and writers will accept this word of warning, and discourage this type of subject as far as possible.'

Shortt, who was President at this time, was much given to exhortations of this sort. On another occasion he complained bitterly that 'films are being produced in which the development of the theme necessitates a continuous succession of grossly brutal and sordid scenes, accompanied in the case of auditory films with sounds that accentuate the situation and nauseate the listener'.[20] His vehemence did tend to betray the fact that, as he once admitted, he 'was not enamoured' of the talkies.

The following year a warning note was sounded against other developments, together with an optimistic assertion that restriction was actually a guarantee of increased audiences and profits. 'Attention was drawn to a tendency to bring politics into films and to make films about scenes in hospitals. Both these tendencies were disparaged. . . . A continuing clean screen will lead to heights of popularity which we at the moment can hardly visualize.'

Throughout the thirties the situation regarding newsreels was much discussed. These, it will be remembered, had been specifically left outside the terms of reference of the B.B.F.C. in order to maintain the tradition of a free press. Nevertheless, local authorities made periodic attempts to impose restrictions on what could be exhibited, and as the political situation in Europe worsened, the Government took a closer interest. As early as 1934 the Home Secretary had revealed in the Commons that he had thought it his duty 'to see representatives of this branch of the industry and to point out that it rests with them so to handle their material as to make it unnecessary for the Government to consider the imposition of any censorship on newsreels'.[21]

On the outbreak of war film censorship came under the aegis of the Ministry of Information. In addition to the usual censorship which continued to be carried out by the B.B.F.C. and the local authorities, 'security censorship' was to be imposed. This made it an offence 'in any manner likely to prejudice the efficient prosecution of the war to obtain, possess or publish information on military matters' and was to apply to all films including newsreels. This operation was effected by the Board in co-operation with the Ministry which provided additional staff.

In 1940 the Board's offices in Carlisle Street, Soho, were destroyed with the loss of many records. Shortly after the end of the war both the President (Lord Tyrrell) and the Secretary (Brooke Wilkinson) died. With them passed the Board's role as public guardian, for post-war attitudes ensured that the old brand of paternalism would no longer be maintained. Change was slow, but it was inevitable.

The new officers, Sir Sidney Harris and Arthur Watkins, both had Home Office backgrounds, but under their charge the Board became gradually more independent of the Government. Traditional practices and policies gave way to a less paternalistic approach, and a new kind of working relationship was built up with the industry. Watkins' conception of the role of the Secretary differed markedly from that of his long-serving predecessor, and he assumed a much more central position in the running of the Board. During his period in office, the Secretary took over from the President as the key figure. Although Harris continued to affirm that he was chief censor, in practice the relationship between the two jobs was clearly changing.

Coincident with this change in Board personnel, it became clear that a major revision of the legislation upon which the whole system was based was necessary. The Cinematograph Act of 1909, intended purely as a safety measure, had made provision only for inflammable film. During the twenties and thirties technological advance had introduced non-inflammable stock which was not subject to local authority licensing rules. While inflammable film could be shown without restriction only in special circumstances (i.e. to a private audience in a private house, or at a trade show), non-inflammable film was subject to restriction only if it were shown in licensed premises or publicly exhibited to paying customers on a Sunday. As early as 1934 the Home Office was being urged by both the trade and the local authorities to close this ever-widening loophole, and in October of that year the Home Office announced that it was preparing new regulations. Progress appears to have been slow for nothing concrete had been done by 1939 when attention was diverted to more important matters.

The war had one important consequence in this respect, for it encouraged the use of 16mm non-inflammable films for instructional and propaganda purposes. This development encouraged several of the major distributors to begin handling 16mm as soon as the war was over. In response to this situation the Home Secretary, the Minister of Education and the Secretary of State for Scotland set up, in 1947, a committee under the chairmanship of Professor K. C. Wheare to consider the existing censorship machinery. By the time the committee reported in 1950 it was clear that, in a very short time, non-inflammable 35mm commercial film would be in universal use, rendering the 1909 Act impotent and removing licensing powers from the local authorities.

The Wheare Report recommended that non-inflammable film should be subject to the same conditions as inflammable, and that the licensing authorities should retain their powers. Rather surprisingly, the Home Office announced that it did not intend to legislate as a result of the report, but a change of Government the following year, accompanied by renewed pressures for action to be taken, finally led to the Cinematograph Act of 1952.

So well entrenched was the censorship system by this time that at no point during the parliamentary debates was it seriously suggested that any machinery other than that based on the local councils and the B.B.F.C. was possible or desirable. The Act did, however, make one major change in that it abolished all reference to 'safety and inflammability' and substituted 'regulation' as the key concept underlying censorship. This alteration introduced a new problem in that the many film societies that had grown up since the twenties had been exempted from censorship as a result of their use of non-inflammable 16mm prints. Now a new distinction was necessary if their existence was to be continued, and the rather more logical difference between commercial and non-commercial exhibitions was introduced. Uncertificated films could now be shown as long as either the public were not admitted, or they were admitted free, or the show was given by a non-profit-making organization. The Act received the Royal Assent in October 1952, but was not brought into operation until January 1955.

In the meantime Harris and Watkins had started to rethink the function of the Board. By 1950 the work of the Board had been encapsulated in three principles which were to guide all decisions :

(1) Was the story, incident or dialogue likely to impair the moral standards of the public by extenuating vice or crime or depreciating moral standards?
(2) Was it likely to give offence to reasonably minded cinema audiences?
(3) What effect would it have on children?[22]

Although couched in broad terms, open to widely differing inter-pretation, this formulation represented a considerable diminution of the Board's terms of reference.

The third principle was, of course, crucial at a time when no film could be passed that was not suitable for accompanied children (although some councils had, from time to time, barred children altogether from 'A' certificate films). The Wheare Report had recommended the introduction of 'a single category of films which should include the present "H" category from which children should be absolutely excluded'.[23] As a result the Board and most local authorities agreed to the implementation of an 'X' certificate which was effective from January 1951. Watkins made clear that the new category was not intended to cover 'merely sordid films dealing with unpleasant subjects, but films which, while not being suitable for children, are good adult entertainment and films which appeal to an intelligent public'.[24]

Eight films were passed that year in the 'X' category which limited the audience to those over sixteen years of age, and although a number of local authorities opposed the innovation, the majority acquiesced. Watkins was able to announce that the Board's 'general aim is, and will continue to be, the reduction of censorship for adults to the minimum'. Despite this apparently liberal policy, however, the Board continued to believe that 'it is performing a service both to the public and to the film industry if it removes offensive and distasteful material which cannot be regarded as entertainment and which if not excluded would in the long run do harm to the cinema's claim to that universal patronage on which its economy rests'.

This viewpoint seems to have been shared by the industry and the public, and the new category rapidly acquired a disreputable image. The industry was blithely unaware that the levelling off in admission statistics over the previous four or five years was to be the beginning of a disastrous, and continuing, downward trend. The main cinema circuits relied on the family audience and were convinced that the non-admission of children to any programme would not only lower receipts for that film, but would also, in the long run, disrupt the cinema-going habit. Thus 'X' film production was almost non-existent and 'X' films came to be confined to the smaller independent cinemas who were prepared to show 'daring' foreign pictures to minority audiences. 'X' and sex soon became associated in the public's mind. The big distributors avoided the new certificate, preferring to release a heavily cut 'A' version rather than an uncensored 'X' film. Since the Board retained strict standards even with 'adult' films, their attractions (and their profit-making capabilities) remained limited. The Rank circuit released only fourteen 'X' films throughout the nineteen-fifties, and A.B.C., although a little more adventurous in this respect, released only fifty during the decade, mostly in the last two or three years.

Meanwhile, almost for the first time, the Board had been forced to adjust its policy in the face of public opinion. Until this time there had been a strict veto on nudity that had only been relaxed for occasional European films. Now a number of American films purporting to celebrate the attractions of nudism appeared, challenging a long-held dogma. The Board at first refused to accept these films for public exhibition but was obliged to relent when the vast majority of local authorities failed to support its stand.[25]

As this incident indicates the Board remained essentially conservative, if less inflexible than in the past. Although the rule prohibiting nudity had been overturned it was immediately replaced by further rulings itemizing the degrees of nudity and the conditions under which they were permissible. On a number of occasions films rejected by the Board were passed locally: it was very much rarer for certificated films to be banned by local authorities.

Summarizing his years in office Watkins lamented a feature of the cinema which had been noted often before and remains a major pre-occupation. 'Without doubt a major problem with which the Board of Film Censors has been faced since the war has been the prevalence of scenes of violence and brutality in the films submitted for censorship.' Watkins had attempted to combat the inclusion of this material : 'A warning was addressed in May 1948, impartially to both British and American producers, that the Board would not in future be prepared to grant its certificate to any film in which the story depended in any marked degree on the violent or sadistic behaviour of the characters or to allow in any film any incident in which there was recourse to needless violence'.[26] A second warning followed in 1949, but there was little effect : 44 per cent of cuts made in films in the first seven months of 1955 came under the heading of violence.

Watkins resigned at the end of 1956. His most lasting achievement had been to change the way in which the Board was run. Trevelyan has summarized his achievements in this respect :

He took a direct interest in film production and got to know film-makers personally. He encouraged the submission of scripts to the Board before films went into production so that he could give personal advice to producers and directors. He visited studios, both in this country and overseas, and as a result film-makers began to feel that they were not dealing any more with an impersonal censorship board which was prepared to mutilate their films ruthlessly but with someone who understood their point of view as creative artists. . . . He was a brilliant and witty speaker and an admirable conversationalist. His company was enjoyed socially and he was accepted by the industry's 'inner circle'. All this gave prestige to the Board at a time when it was needed.[27]

Harris selected John Nicholls from the Cultural Section of the Foreign Office as the new Secretary. He seemed intent on following the path trodden by his predecessor, avoiding codification and showing particular concern for young people. 'Public opinion in matters of taste and behaviour changes with the times. The Board cannot therefore remain rigid; it must adapt its policy to such change. But it must also bear in mind one feature of the

cinema which has remained constant from its birth—it appeals
to young and old alike and unlike the theatre, it is the entertainment to which parents take their children; indeed adolescents
often form the major part of the audience. This fact governs the
approach of the Board to censorship questions.'[28]

However Nicholls's appointment was not a happy one. The
industry soon became fiercely critical of his approach. At a
meeting between the Board and the K.R.S. four main criticisms
were made :

(1) that there was 'arbitrary categorization of films irrespective of the wishes, known or apparent, of the renters';

(2) that 'decisions on category were now apparently being
taken by the examiners, whereas decisions had formerly been
taken by the Secretary';

(3) that the Board was taking no account of 'developments
in the type of material which was now considered admissible
on television and thus suitable for family consumption';

(4) and that the Board was operating 'artistic censorship' in
taking quality into account.[29]

It is not possible now to judge how far these criticisms were
fair, how much Nicholls's policies differed from those of his
predecessor, or whether the trade was simply hoping to take
advantage of the relative insecurity of a new Secretary in order
to weaken censorship. It is interesting to note that very similar
criticisms were made of Stephen Murphy within a few months
of his appointment.

Whatever the motivation of the industry, confidence in the
Board declined until it was clear that Nicholls could not continue
in office. The running of the Board was effectively taken over
by one of the examiners, John Trevelyan, pending Nicholls's
formal resignation. After this experience, the President was not
keen to elect a successor himself, and the new Secretary was
therefore appointed by a committee representing all sections of
the industry.

John Trevelyan thus became Secretary in a position of much
greater strength in relation to the President than his predecessors
had enjoyed. Since Sir Sidney was over eighty and taking a
decreasing part in the Board's affairs, it was clear that the Secretary was now entirely in control of the day-to-day affairs of
the Board. This situation was formalized by a statement from the

council of the K.M.A. in January 1960 that: 'It was the view of the Council that executive responsibility should rest with the Secretary of the Board and that, while the President should have a general responsibility to policy, his function should be primarily that of consultant.'[30]

Harris resigned in April of that year and was succeeded by Lord Morrison of Lambeth who, in Trevelyan's account, very much resented the decreased powers of the President. Trevelyan, however, had the support of the K.M.A. Council, and the elevation of the Secretary to the position of Chief Censor was firmly established. When Lord Harlech became President on Morrison's death in 1965 he was in full agreement that this was the only way the Board could work satisfactorily.

Trevelyan continued and broadened the policies of Watkins and relentlessly overturned the Board's tradition of maximum secrecy and minimum publicity. He also gradually introduced a more liberal approach into the Board's deliberations. However this was not a speedy evolution. Change was not introduced more quickly than the public (or the local authorities) would accept; more often the Board can be accused of reacting too slowly. In general Trevelyan's policies are characterized more by caution than by the swashbuckling liberalization with which he is sometimes credited.

At first his statements differed very little from those of previous censors. 'The Board's aim is to exclude from public exhibition anything likely to impair the moral standards of the public, by extenuating vice or crime or by depreciating social standards, and anything likely to give offence to any reasonably-minded members of the audience.'[31] Within a short time, however, the tenor of his remarks altered. References to 'offending and disgusting' which had hitherto been profuse in Board statements, disappeared, and a much more limited frame of reference was applied. 'The British Board of Film Censors cannot assume responsibility for the guardianship of public morality. It cannot refuse for exhibition to adults films that show behaviour which contravenes the accepted moral code, and it does not demand that "the wicked" should always be punished. It cannot legitimately refuse to pass films which criticize "the Establishment" and films which express minority opinions.'[32] And later: 'Censorship of the Arts may still be necessary, but it should exist only to stop what is dangerous and what could degrade and harm human personality.'[33] Such a statement, of course, is open to interpretation, and there is little doubt that Trevelyan continued to sound more liberal in discussion than he was in practice. In general, he reacted to changes in public attitudes rather than stimulating them.

Trevelyan took over at a time when the cinema was at last responding to the fast-falling admission statistics. Film-makers were forced to seek a new formula for success, and the most likely ingredient in the fight against television seemed to be realism. The 'X' certificate was finally losing its 'disastrous reputation', the turning point being the critical and commercial success of *Room at the Top* in 1958. The success of this film and others such as *Look Back in Anger, Saturday Night and Sunday Morning* and *A Kind of Loving* which followed, changed the situation whereby 'the film industry had made its reputation and its money, largely by presenting a fantasy world of unreal people'.[34] To deal with this new trend, the Board was forced to make a radical revision of its approach to cinema, and this Trevelyan was well-equipped to effect. Although early statements suggested that he had some sympathy with the traditional point of view that film was not the appropriate medium for discussing serious problems ('social comment and entertainment don't necessarily mix') as early as 1960 he was vigorously propounding a very different argument. When the critic Derek Hill accused the Board of being, in part, responsible for the British cinema's avoidance of 'worthwhile themes', Trevelyan countered :

> This is completely untrue, as many British film-makers would testify. If film-makers have not chosen themes of this kind, it is not because of censorship but because they, or possibly the distributors, have learned from experience that such films do not as a rule become box-office attractions. From the early days of the century the film was regarded as family entertainment and until recently it was the deliberate policy of the industry to maintain this. The industry did not want adult themes for the regular cinema audiences. It was, however, recognized by the Board that there was an audience that wanted adult films, and it was the Board that proposed the introduction of the 'X' certificate which made the way clear.[35]

Not all British film-makers were prepared to support Trevelyan on this point. Tony Richardson maintained that the Board continued to adopt a philistine approach to the medium.

I believe that the basis of the censor's attitude is that films must not be serious—that they must work within the limits of a formula. Over both the films that I made, Mr Trevelyan has insisted that these created problems for him—not because they themselves could possibly have corrupted anyone, but because (a) they were all too easy to be distorted in the press and in public out of context, and, more importantly, (b) because they were too 'real'. Audiences, it was implied, must not recognize their own world and must not relate what they see on the screens back to their social experience. It would be too disturbing.[36]

This analysis may well have been an accurate assessment of Board policies in the fifties, but it was certainly not a tenable position in the decade that followed, for the Board did gradually adapt itself to the greater realism being displayed in the cinema. The most important feature of this change was the introduction into the Board's deliberations of the concept of quality. We have seen that Watkins and Nicholls had made tentative movements in this direction. Trevelyan succeeded in following the course which Nicholls had failed to navigate, persuading the industry to accept that films of 'artistic quality and integrity' should be treated 'with respect'.

Trevelyan's position was sounder than that of his predecessor in one important respect. In 1959 the Obscene Publications Act was passed, ruling that a conviction could not be obtained against published material if it were proved that publication of the article in question 'is justified as being for the public good on the ground that it is in the interests of science, literature, art or learning, or of other objects of general concern'. This radical departure from tradition made possible the successful defence of the publication of *Lady Chatterley's Lover* the following year, and enabled the Board to argue that similar allowances should be made for the cinema.

There was a precedent for this new policy for, as we have seen, the Board had tended to allow more nudity in films produced abroad. This practice had been extended to cover sex in general, not necessarily because it was thought that these productions were of a higher quality and therefore deserving of leniency, but partly because they were aimed at a particular audience. Not only were more intellectual sections of the public less likely to be shocked or offended, they were also thought by the Board to be less corruptible. Defending his occasional habit of cutting sub-titles while allowing the original dialogue to remain, Trevelyan used to say that 'we regard anyone intelligent enough to under-stand the original as intelligent enough not to be harmed by its sentiments'.[37] Strong elements of paternalism remained in the Board's character.

Rather curiously in view of this increased leniency for films of quality, Trevelyan also tended to be fairly generous to pictures at quite the other end of the market. The proliferation of the production of sex films in Scandinavia, Germany, America and elsewhere was one of the major developments of the sixties. 'We were as reasonable as possible with these films, taking into account that there was a demand for them, and that since their publicity usually indicated what kind of films they were, the people who would object to them would probably not go to see them.'[38] Thus, it seems that, so long as films had a pre-selected audience, whether high or low-brow, the censor was able to be 'generous'. It was the films in the middle, which have always provided the basis of the industry, that suffered in comparison and, of course, it is just these films which have lost audiences to the most alarm-ing extent. It would hardly be fair to blame the censor for this, but it might reasonably be argued that he played a very minor role.

The reduction in the cutting of 'artistic' films can also be explained in terms of another aspect of Trevelyan's policy. As Robinson has pointed out, 'the fact that most films by Losey, Antonioni and many other "prestige" directors have remained uncut since this date is, however, possibly due more to pre-production script discussions with Trevelyan—an aspect of his work which he regards as one of the most important develop-ments of his term of office'.[39] We have seen how Arthur Watkins built up and encouraged the script-reading side of the Board's work. Trevelyan carried this a stage further and went out of his way to develop relationships with film-makers in order to forestall possible problems. Such action has obvious attractions for pro-ducers (who can be more sure of avoiding expensive troubles at a later stage) and for the censor (who can avoid the necessity for heavy cutting of the finished print) and some directors have found it a useful system. It does, however, have dangers, not least being the way in which it extends the scope of censorship. Some directors refused to submit scripts at all, feeling that the Board was more likely to be firm at script-stage than later, or that it would be strict with a finished film that differed markedly from the script previously vetted and accepted. Trevelyan has admitted that there was some truth in these fears.

Obvious problems arise when a censor, who can have an enormous influence on the commercial prospects of a film, becomes involved in its actual making, for there is frequently pressure exerted by financial backers and distributors on the director to accede to the wishes of the censor to ensure the certification of the film. The extent to which Trevelyan did concern himself in production can be gauged from the following quote from his memoirs.

If, for instance, we were discussing a sex-scene which could be more explicit than we would want, I might well suggest that the lighting should be dim, and that close-shots, except for heads and shoulders, should be avoided. Guidance could also be given about camera-angles, which could be important. With a scene of violence that would be acceptable in the United States and some other countries but too long and savage for Britain, I would suggest that the scene should be shot in a way that would enable a section or sections to be removed without loss of 'flow' or continuity. When there was some dialogue that I thought might be censorable, I would suggest that the camera should avoid front-face shots so that if necessary alternative lines could be dubbed on at a later stage without there being any problem of lip-movements.[40]

In the present state of the film industry many directors feel that they have too many non-creative advisers already. The addition of the censor to this list may not be wholly beneficial. As it is many producers can only obtain financial backing on the understanding that the script is approved by the censors before shooting begins. Thus British Lion agreed to finance Joseph Strick's *Ulysses* (1967) only if the script were cleared by the Board, forcing the director to revise the script in accordance with the Board's wishes. In setting up *Lolita* in 1962 Stanley Kubrick not only had to consult with Trevelyan and adjust his project accordingly but also had to have the approval of the American censors before bankers would agree to back him.[41]

There is also some risk of the censor becoming too closely involved with the film-maker and his problems. On the one hand friendship may incline him to be unconsciously lenient in his dealings with certain people; on the other he may stray beyond his terms of reference in discouraging others. There is some suggestion of this in Trevelyan's comment that 'my concern was that this producer should not be encouraged to make more films of this kind since I thought it likely that each film would be more salacious than its predecessor'.[42] It might well be questioned whether this is an appropriate concern of the B.B.F.C.

Nevertheless, although these reservations are important, there were many positive aspects of Trevelyan's approach. Some directors undeniably did find his way of working helpful. Joseph Losey, a committed opponent of censorship, has said that Trevelyan was 'a very beneficial influence and a very informed, knowledgeable and appreciative influence. And he has helped me in many pictures. I don't mean that I go to him to find out how to make them, but he helps to make it possible and he knows more about film-making than 99 per cent of the producers I deal with, and far more about film-making than 150 per cent of the distributors I deal with.'[43]

During the early sixties a new development in cinema exhibition appeared which had important consequences for censorship policy. This was the formation of commercial members-only cinema clubs, such as the Gala and Compton groups. By restricting admission to adult members such clubs avoided the licensing regulations and afforded outlets for films that would have been turned down or cut by the Board and the local authorities. Trevelyan supported this development, feeling that it would remove some of the Board's responsibility by offering exhibition opportunities for rejected films. Not that such films were entirely uncensored, for the clubs were still subject to common law rulings and distributors frequently cut their products in order to avoid the possibility of prosecution. At first these clubs showed films of some quality which had, for one reason or another, encountered censorship problems. Very soon, however, it became clear that profit lay in showing less demanding sex films, and this policy continues to be followed by groups such as the Tatler clubs. Nevertheless the emergence of these cinemas was significant for it denoted a change in the Board's activities, suggesting 'a restriction of the censorship function to that of protecting the mass indiscriminating cinema audience from unwelcome shock'.[44]

In 1965 the newly formed Greater London Council introduced a change in its licensing conditions that seemed likely to have wide repercussions. The council expressed the view that 'it would be wrong and illogical ... if the range of things prevented by the censors was greater than the range of things prohibited by law' and concluded, therefore, that 'the scope of censorship by the licensing authority should be restricted to preventing the kinds of harm which the law seeks to prevent in its provisions relating to the printed and spoken word'. The old criterion of 'offensiveness' was discarded on the grounds that 'the arts are sometimes intended to be disturbing rather than reassuring' and was to be replaced by the yardstick of legality. The new ruling denied exhibition only to a film which 'is likely to encourage or to incite to crime, or to lead to disorder, or to stir up hatred against any section of the public in Great Britain on grounds of colour, race or ethnic or national origins, or the effect of which is, if taken as a whole, such as to tend to deprave and corrupt persons who are likely to see it'.[45] Such a decision seemed certain to affect the B.B.F.C. which would have been forced to modify its policies or risk continuous reversals of its decision by the G.L.C., but the council in fact showed small inclination to implement its proposals, and the necessity for a complete reappraisal of censorship resulting from a confrontation between the Board and the G.L.C. never materialized.

Change was forthcoming, however, from another angle. Throughout the sixties the Board had felt increasing dissatisfaction with the limited classification categories at its disposal. The 'X', by admitting sixteen-year-olds, was not felt to be a truly adult category, while the 'A' allowed the admission of all ages, albeit accompanied in the case of juniors. As early as 1961 Trevelyan had proposed the introduction of an 'AA' certificate to lie between the 'A' and 'X', but no agreement had been reached with the trade and the local authorities. It was to be nine years before the classification system was finally revised. Then, after discussions between the Board, the trade associations, the local authorities and the Home Office, a new system was introduced which took effect from July 1970.[46] The age of admission to 'X' films was raised to eighteen and the 'AA' was added, indicating that only those aged fourteen or over were to be admitted. The 'A' certificate reverted to its original advisory status, no longer requiring children to be accompanied.

The new age limits brought Britain into line with the great majority of European countries, where cut-offs at ages twelve to fourteen and sixteen to eighteen are the norm.[47] It was rather naively hoped that the new, more adult 'X' certificate would enable the Board to pass almost all films, and that the cutting of films for adults would be very much reduced, but trends in the cinema both before and after this date made this a forlorn hope, in view of the Board's terms of reference.

This change was Trevelyan's last major act for in December 1970 he announced his intention to resign to make way for a younger man—he was now sixty-seven—adding also that he found the job less enjoyable than he had 'because I seem to see fewer good films than I used to'. His departure from the scene in July 1971 was marked by statements of regret and appreciation from all bodies in contact with the Board, who rightly acknowledged his achievements in altering the status and policies of the B.B.F.C. Following Arthur Watkins's lead, he had forged entirely new links between the Board and the film industry, transforming a relationship which had been distant and bureaucratic. He was eager to meet and communicate with members of the industry at every opportunity. Extrovert and hyperactive, he was well-equipped to proselytize for the Board and his frankness and informality in discussing problems led to greater knowledge and understanding of the Board's work. He became a frequent visitor at film studios, cutting tables, on location and in executives' offices where his wide knowledge of the industry inspired confidence and broke down many barriers.

Naturally this greater accessibility and openness supplied opponents of censorship with a great deal of evidence and ammunition. Here Trevelyan's control of public relations techniques stood him in good stead. Disarming critics with an apparently casual remark, he was able to ensure that what might have been a vituperative confrontation was never more than a civilized discussion. A master of debate he was always able to elude his pursuers. Yet reflection on his pronouncements often reveals that his was, in David Robinson's words, 'a beautiful conjuring trick, dazzling enough to distract us, most of the time at least, from the essential anomaly of the Board'.

Trevelyan was guilty of one practical error of some importance, for he adapted the machinery of the Board all too well to suit his own personality. He had made the office of Secretary pre-eminent, for not only had the President's power receded, but the status of the examiners remained low. They were encouraged to defer to the Secretary at all times, so that decisions of any consequence were invariably made by him. Sometimes decisions were effectively made before films had been seen by the examiners at all. While there are obvious advantages in keeping the examiners away from the public gaze and the attendant pressures, this policy was carried to extremes. This inevitably led to some demoralization among the examiners and Trevelyan himself has recorded that his relationships with his staff were not what he might have wished.

One difficulty was that one or two of the examiners were less than enthusiastic supporters of the rapid liberalization that characterized Trevelyan's last two or three years in office. Unfortunately, a situation had arisen when it would be true to say that the majority among the examiners were generally out of sympathy with the material with which they were being asked to deal. This arose largely as a result of the composition of the Board in terms of age for, although the Secretary can in theory dismiss his examiners at any time, such action would clearly be awkward and embarrassing in such a small body. In practice it does not happen. Unfortunately in Trevelyan's last years the Board was composed largely of examiners approaching retirement. In 1949 the average age had been estimated to be in the early forties; by 1969 this figure was nearer sixty. The rather aged nature of the Board may be gathered from Trevelyan's remark on the appointment of Lord Harlech in 1965, that he would bring 'a young approach to the job'. He was indeed the youngest person on the Board at that time (and incidentally, the first president to be appointed who had not passed the traditional retirement age of sixty-five),[48] but he was forty-seven years old, which in terms of the cinema-going audience is, at the very least, middle-aged.

But internal relations within the Board were only a small part of the problem that was to face Trevelyan's successor, and it is perhaps not surprising that a suitable person was not easy to find. Trevelyan had been searching for two years for a likely applicant without success and, although a leading film critic and a member of one of the trade associations had been tentatively linked with the job, it was not until Trevelyan's retirement had been formally announced that a strong candidate appeared.

3

PRESSURES ON THE BOARD

TREVELYAN'S RETIREMENT WAS followed almost immediately by an outburst of criticism of the Board from many quarters and a widespread loss of confidence in the censor's office. But this coincidence of events does not necessarily imply a causal relationship. In fact various pressures had been building up for a number of years, the arrival of a new and inexperienced censor being only one factor among many that preceded the eruption of controversy.

As in all matters connected with the film industry, developments in America cannot be overlooked. Ever since the First World War effectively stunted the emergent European cinema and gave Hollywood a primacy in world production that it was to hold for many years, a large proportion of the films seen in this country have originated on the other side of the Atlantic. Censorship emerged as quickly in America as it did in Britain and can be dated back to 1907, but not until the twenties did it become organized. Then criticism of the medium which was already being blamed for most of the ills of society was inflamed by a series of scandals in Hollywood.[1] As early as 1921, thirty-six States had been considering censorship legislation. Now the industry was forced to hire Will Hays, the Postmaster General, to try to create a better image for the 'picture-show'. He was put in charge of a new organization, the Motion Picture Producers and Distributors of America (later to become the Motion Picture Association of America, M.P.A.A.). Various efforts during the decade to discourage the inclusion of questionable material in films finally led, in 1930, to the drafting of the Production Code, which rigidly regulated what it was considered permissible to show on the screen. Significantly this document was the work of two Catholics, and it was Catholic pressure which was to make the Code the basis for a really effective regulatory system. For it very quickly became clear that the Code, a purely advisory document, was being frequently ignored by producers. In 1934 a committee of Catholic bishops formed the Legion of Decency to review and rate films, at the same time threatening a Catholic boycott of cinemas if the general moral tone of films did not improve. The result of this pressure led to the creation by the M.P.A.A. of the Production Code Administration (P.C.A.) with authority to withhold the seal of approval from any production which flouted the Code. The industry promised not to distribute or exhibit any picture that did not have the seal, and Joseph Breen became the first director of the P.C.A., a post which he held for twenty years.

The Code itself was developed from Hays's list of 'Don'ts and Be Carefuls' and consisted of three 'general principles' and a large number of more specific 'particular applications', including eight paragraphs of prohibitions under the heading of 'sex' and six dealing with crime. However, whereas the letter of the Code seemed to be extremely rigid, its interpretation was often more casual. The imprecision of the general principles allowed a certain amount of variation in translating the theory into practical terms, while Breen was not above inventing clauses that suited his purposes. Nevertheless this flexibility was relative, and by 1950 the Code appeared anachronistic. Many of its restrictions were based on principles that held little relevance in post-war America, and even increasing liberality in its interpretation could not prevent a number of confrontations between film-makers and the P.C.A.

Meanwhile a combination of events had changed the climate within which the P.C.A. operated. Since 1915 when the Supreme Court had ruled that films were not entitled to free speech under the First Amendment, prior censorship by state and municipality boards had been considered legal. *The Miracle* case of 1952, however, established that films were, after all, within the guarantees of the First and Fourteenth Amendments. 'In the wake of this decision the high court has steadily chipped away at standards used by state censorship bodies to bar certain motion pictures from public performance.'[2] Finally two cases in 1961 and 1965 were to show that while prior censorship was not itself unconstitutional, the boards established at that time did not have 'adequate safeguards against undue inhibition of expression' and this form of censorship virtually disappeared.

Of more immediate consequence for the P.C.A. was the success of a number of cinemas which, since the divorcement of exhibition and production following the anti-trust legislation of

1948, had begun to show foreign films without the Code's seal of approval. Hollywood was now beginning to feel the effects of competition from television, and was widening its horizons to include subjects of a more controversial nature. When, in 1953, Preminger's *The Moon is Blue*, a comedy about suspected adultery, was refused a seal and condemned by the Legion of Decency, United Artists resigned from the Association and released the film without a seal. The result was not the financial disaster that had been assumed, but a gross of $6 million on an investment of less than half a million. Three years later Preminger's *The Man with the Golden Arm* had a similar history (eventually forcing the alteration of Code regulations concerning the subject of drugs).

In 1954 Breen was succeeded by Geoffrey Shurlock, an Englishman of a more liberal persuasion. When he was accused of passing a film that 'teetered along the brink of suggestiveness from beginning to end' he responded that his policy was precisely that : to allow any production that didn't actually topple over.[3] Under his guidance the P.C.A. became less restrictive and greater latitude was allowed in the contentious fields of sex and religion : *Baby Doll*, *The Miracle*, *Lolita* and *The Nun's Story* were all passed. The Code had been revised in 1956, but even so the sixties brought many films that drove coaches-and-four through the spirit of the Code, and the general exhibition of which brought no signs of consternation from the public. As a result Jack Valenti, the new President of the M.P.A.A., introduced a revised Code 'designed to keep in closer harmony with the mores, the culture, the moral sense and the expectations of our society'. The new Code's standards were set out in fifteen sentences which allowed considerable room for manoeuvre. It also introduced the labelling of certain films as 'suggested for mature audiences', following the lead of Warner Brothers who had advertised *Who's Afraid of Virginia Woolf?* as S.M.A.

Even this device was insufficient to cover many films made in the succeeding years. As early as 1968 over half the pictures passed by the P.C.A. were designated S.M.A., and a deadlock situation arose over Antonioni's *Blow-Up*. M.G.M. had a considerable investment in the film to which the P.C.A. refused to grant a seal, but which the director refused to cut. The studio solved this problem by releasing the film through a subsidiary company which was not a specific signatory to the Code agreement. The discovery of this device inevitably presaged the demise

of the Code, although the decline of the film industry in the
face of television competition was a more basic cause. Valenti
was forced to rethink and complement the code with a classification system not dissimilar to that operated by the B.B.F.C.,
although with the major difference that no film can be banned
by the P.C.A. 'The new "code" has no specific restrictions or
regulations. The rating board weighs a film's theme, language and
visual treatment largely in secret, paying close attention to sex,
violence and drugs. Its members will not speak publicly about
their decision. . . . The seven board members in Hollywood and
four in New York arrive at a consensus decision on each film
after it has been viewed by most of the members.'[4]

The disappearance of the Code which had regulated American
films for so long indicated the weakness of the P.C.A. in face of
sustained pressure from the industry. In these years the major
film companies were lurching from one disaster to another. 1969
saw losses of $35 million by M.G.M., $37 million by 20th Century Fox and $52 million by Warner Brothers, while the follow-
ing year was no better with United Artists losing $45 million
and Fox a massive $77 million (including $12 million on one
film—*Hello Dolly*).[5] The total failure of the family musicals
made following the success of *The Sound of Music*, and the
relative success of 'X'-rated films, led many producers to concentrate on productions that featured the new magic ingredients,
sex and violence. With regard to sex the major companies could
not hope to compete with the pornographic films shown in small
cinemas in the larger cities, so there was a tendency to concentrate
on extremes of violence and sadism.

On another level it might be argued that screen violence was
no more than a reflection of the high level of violence in American
society. Whatever the cause it presented problems for the
B.B.F.C., suddenly confronted by material from America of a
very different kind from that with which it was accustomed to
deal. As Trevelyan observed as early as December 1968 :

Lord Harlech and I have become gravely concerned about
recent developments in film making in the United States. The
film industry has recently introduced a system of 'rating' films
on somewhat similar lines to our 'U', 'A' and 'X' categories,
but, since in that country there is likelihood of federal legislation on this matter, it has been introduced on a voluntary . . .
basis. We are afraid that this will have the effect of giving

certain film-makers the opportunity of going much further than they have done in scenes of sex and sexual perversion, since, with the protection of an 'X' category, they can shed personal responsibility.

Yet at this very time the Board was beginning to come under pressure from those who feared that the liberalization of the post-war years had been taken too far. Despite a flood of obscenity trials during the years 1953–5 the fifties were generally characterized by reform. The report of the Wolfenden Committee in 1957 which recommended the legalization of homosexual behaviour between consenting adults in private, and the Obscene Publications Act of 1959 which introduced the defence of publication being for the public good, were representative of the feeling of the time.

However, by the early sixties a reaction was beginning to become apparent. Sir Cyril Black, Conservative M.P. for Wimbledon, had formed the Moral Law Defence Association in 1960 and had gained the support of the Archbishop of Canterbury and the moderator of the Free Church Council. Another movement, Youth Impact, was founded in that year to combat 'increasing immorality', while a London Committee Against Obscenity was also established; but the influence of these groups was minor in comparison with that of the Women of Britain Clean-Up T.V. Campaign—later the National Viewers' and Listeners' Association (V.A.L.A.). Although dismissed at first as cranky and ineffectual, the campaign gathered force until by the latter sixties its voice was powerful enough to be influential even at the B.B.C.

On the publication front also there were indications that the liberal momentum had been halted. In 1961 the publisher of *The Ladies' Directory*—an advertising medium for prostitutes—was found guilty of, among other things, conspiring to corrupt public morals, under an old law that had long been thought defunct. In 1964 the Chief Metropolitan Magistrate upheld the seizure of copies of *Fanny Hill*, while two years later, *Last Exit to Brooklyn* was condemned by a magistrate, and found to be obscene by a jury, escaping on appeal only through a technicality, at a cost to the publishers of some £15,000. In 1968 a Brighton bookseller was convicted of having for sale a number of 'underground' magazines, paperbacks and posters, in a case which was to be only the first in a series of confrontations between the law and proponents of an 'alternative' society. Shortly afterwards material of a very different kind was deemed to be obscene. This was Walter's *My Secret Life*, an exhaustive account of a Victorian gentleman's sexual encounters, originally published in 1888. Witness by a number of distinguished social historians failed to convince the jury that the book was published 'for the public good'.

It became clear that the 1959 Act did not provide as sound a defence for serious books as many had assumed or hoped, and renewed efforts were made to organize support for those charged under the Act. A Free Art Legal Fund was set up to help meet the costs of such cases and the Defence of Literature and the Arts Society was founded with Stuart Hood as chairman. Not long afterwards an Arts Council working party recommended that the Obscene Publications Act should be repealed altogether for a trial period.

Meanwhile liberal opinion had been encouraged by the freeing of the theatre from prior censorship by the Theatres Act of 1968. This abolished the powers of the Lord Chamberlain and introduced similar measures to those specified in the Obscenity Act. The first serious tests of how the Act would be interpreted in relation to public theatrical performances came two years later. *Oh! Calcutta!*, a revue including nudity and simulated sexual behaviour, opened at the Roundhouse in July 1970. It aroused instant protest from many quarters, notably from Mary Whitehouse, David Holbrook, then a lecturer at Dartington Hall, the Dowager Lady Birdwood, founder of the London branch of the V.A.L.A., and Frank Smith, a non-conformist G.L.C. councillor. Despite their calls for action, however, the Director of Public Prosecutions declined to prosecute, while the Attorney-General refused permission for private proceedings.

This, however, was an isolated radical victory, for that same year brought a series of further defeats. In January the 'underground' magazine *International Times* (I.T.) was indicted for containing advertisements 'to induce readers to resort to the said advertisers for the purpose of homosexual practices and thereby to debauch and corrupt public morals'. A second charge alleged that the publishers had 'conspired to outrage public decency by inserting advertisements containing lewd, disgusting and offensive matter'. Regular calls on the I.T. offices did not prevent the police from pursuing other possible pornographers. On the day of the trial the London Arts Gallery was raided and a series of lithographs by John Lennon was seized. Some days later a party of thirty-two policemen descended on the Open Space Theatre, where Warhol and Morrissey's *Flesh* was being shown to club members following an initiative taken by John Trevelyan. The film, parts of the projector, the screen, names and addresses of those present, the club register and other records were all taken. In neither case did obsenity prosecutions follow, but the publicity arising from the cases forced the Home Secretary to comment that : 'There is a great deal of pornography about that is causing a great deal of concern to many people in this country. . . . Broadly speaking, I want the House to know that I shall support the police when they act in response to complaints from the public in investigating these matters. It may be that, on occasions, they will make mistakes of judgement, but I know perfectly well that the country as a whole is extremely alarmed at what is going on in these fields.'[6]

Caught in the cross-fire of the increasingly controversial and news-worthy pornography debate was the subject of sex education. The B.B.C.'s efforts to provide suitable material for transmission to schools had been frequently attacked by the V.A.L.A. and the debate was renewed by the sacking of a schoolteacher who had appeared in a sex education film made by Dr Martin Cole, a lecturer at Aston University.

The publicity surrounding this case raised further fears in the public mind that there was an increasing wave of 'pornography', an impression that was strengthened by the House of Lords debate of April 1971. This is remembered primarily for the announcement by Lord Longford of the setting up of his committee to investigate the subject. Of greater fundamental import, however, were the remarks of Lord Windlesham, Minister of State at the Home Office, who indicated that a circular had been sent to local authorities, 'reminding them of the powers they have concerning cinema licensing, and asking them to consider whether they were making adequate use of these powers, with particular reference to indecent or offensive advertisements for films.'[7]

The spring and summer of 1971 also saw three important obscenity trials which offered some comfort to the defendants, but rather more to those who had welcomed the prosecutions. In the first case, the publisher of *The Mouth and Oral Sex* by Paul Ableman was acquitted with regard to the book itself, but found guilty on charges relating to a publicity handout. Within a few months he was declared bankrupt. More important in its implications was the *Oz* trial. This was another 'underground' magazine, which in May 1970 had devoted an issue to the work of schoolchildren. The *Schoolkids' Oz* was very largely written and assembled by teenagers. Its title, however, was held to make it particularly likely to fall into the hands of young children, and heavy sentences were imposed on the publishers as a result, although they had been acquitted on the most serious charge of conspiracy. On appeal the Lord Chief Justice conceded that the judge had not directed the attention of the jury to the special definition of obscenity laid down by the Act and, therefore, quashed conviction on three charges. The fourth, however, was confirmed, although sentence was suspended. This was very much a Pyrrhic victory for the defence, for Lord Widgery took the opportunity to interpret the 1959 Act to imply that magazines should not be treated as a whole (i.e. one item is enough to render the whole obscene), and that expert witnesses must confine their remarks to the question of 'public good' and must not comment on whether they feel an article to be obscene or not.

The third case involved *The Little Red Schoolbook*, an English version of a Danish manual for children which set out to encourage a questioning rather than an accepting attitude on various issues. It included only a brief section on sex, but this was naturally the focus of attention. Expert witnesses were called by both sides, but the magistrate upheld the prosecution, concluding that the book was likely to corrupt a significant proportion of its readers, a decision that was confirmed on appeal to the Inner London Sessions.

Much encouraged by these events, the Christian pressure groups united under the banner of the Festival of Light and, taking their cue from the growing concern over ecology, sought to create public awareness of the 'moral pollution' that they saw as a greater danger. The Festival focused its challenge to 'permissiveness' almost entirely on the mass media. The cinema, forced, as we have observed, to concentrate on adult themes, represented a suitable, large and vulnerable target. Unlike the television companies, it had no spokesman to defend it, nor any mass public support to fall back upon. It was an ideal symbol of the ills in society which the Festival was now determined to expose and eradicate.

The censor was caught, unarmed, in the middle of this clash between a multi-million-dollar industry and a vigorous revivalist campaign. It was inevitable that he would be severely wounded by both sides. In the next chapter we will see how he narrowly survived, but first it will be useful to analyse more fully the legal intricacies of censorship, forming as they do the background to the action.

Obscenity first became a crime as recently as 1727 when the courts ruled that it was an offence at common law; i.e. an act pronounced criminal by the courts although not prohibited by any statute. The first statute did not appear until 1857 when an Obscene Publications Act was passed—often known as 'Lord Campbell's Act'. This Act was operationalized in 1868 in the Hicklin case where obscenity was defined in legal terms for the first time, and the test of whether the article was considered likely to deprave and corrupt was introduced. The extent to which this clarifies matters is, of course, debatable, and a large number of questions were left unanswered.

For over a century after 1857 obscenity was thus covered by the common law of obscene libel and by Lord Campbell's Act. All published matter whether it be in the form of books, pictures, films, or whatever, was included. The Obscene Publications Act of 1959 changed this. Its intentions were stated in the preamble —'an Act to amend the law relating to the publication of obscene matter; to provide for the protection of literature; and to strengthen the law concerning pornography'. A distinction was clearly intended between literature, which was to be given extra defence, and pornography which was to be attacked more severely. In practice it has not worked out quite like this.

The definition of obscenity employed is derived closely from the Hicklin judgement of Lord Chief Justice Cockburn: 'An article shall be deemed to be obscene if its effect or (where the article comprises two or more distinct items) the effect of any one of its items is, if taken as a whole, such as to tend to deprave and corrupt persons who are likely, having regard to all relevant circumstances, to read, see or hear the matter contained or embodied in it.'

The problem that immediately arises is to discover exactly what is covered by the Act. There are two subsections which attempt to explain. In the first, the word 'article' is defined as anything 'containing or embodying matter to be read or looked at or both, any sound record, and any film or other record of a picture or pictures'. This is clear enough, but a further subsection must be considered, for 'publication' is an essential requirement under the Act. The offence must involve 'publishing an obscene article' or 'having an obscene article for publication for gain'. It is over the definition of 'publication' that the complications arise.

Section 3 defines a publisher of an article as one who : '(a) distributes, circulates, sells, lets on hire, gives, or lends it, or who offers it for sale or for letting on hire; or (b) in the case of an article containing or embodying matter to be looked at or a record, shows, plays or projects it'. So far, so clear; films are undeniably included. But paragraph (b) has a proviso : 'Provided that paragraph (b) of this section shall not apply to anything done in the course of a cinematograph exhibition (within the meaning of the Cinematograph Act 1952), other than one excluded from the Cinematograph Act 1909, by subsection (4) of section seven of that Act (which relates to exhibitions in private houses to which the public are not admitted), or to anything done in the course of television or sound broadcasting.'

Thus paragraph (b) specifically excludes all films except those shown privately (which are therefore covered by the Act). The difficulty then arises of deciding whether the intention behind Section 3 was that only paragraph (b) was to refer to films, or whether paragraph (a) was designed to include film distribution. It was this problem of interpretation that lay behind the trial involving *Last Tango in Paris* in 1974. The case was brought under paragraph (a), the defendants being the distribution company, United Artists. At a magistrate's court on 7th January the Salvation Army social worker who had brought the prosecution argued that 'the film was a record of obscenities practised by Marlon Brando and Maria Schneider and was not a fictional event' and that 'copulation near the beginning was so gross and performed in such a way that very few human eyes had ever been called upon to look at'.[8]

The defence held that 'the provisions of the Obscene Publications Act did not apply to films properly shown in a licensed cinema. If the summons was good as it stood . . . the whole edifice of the public showing of films collapses'. After a hearing spread over three separate sessions between January and March, the magistrate concluded that there was a case to answer and committed United Artists for trial. This decision appeared to bring the cinema within the range of the Obscene Publications Act, particularly as it was upheld by Lord Widgery in May when he dismissed defence claims that the Act was inapplicable in these circumstances. However, at the Old Bailey in November Mr

Justice Kenneth Jones ruled otherwise, dismissing the case on the grounds that the Act does not apply to films shown in licensed cinemas, since film distributors hire only to the cinema manager and not to the public. It remains to be seen whether this is the final word.

Even if the 1959 Act does not apply to films the law still imposes a tight grip on the cinema. Two statutes clearly do apply to film. The Post Office Act of 1953 makes it an offence to send indecent or obscene films through the post, while the Customs Acts of 1896 and 1952 prohibit the importation of indecent or obscene photographs or other articles, which may be forfeited and destroyed. Until recently it was thought that the Vagrancy Acts of 1824 and 1838 could also be applied to the cinema. These state that anyone exposing an obscene print or picture, or any other indecent exhibition (note the almost interchangeable use of the epithets) in view of a public highway or public place may be imprisoned as a 'rogue or vagabond'. It was considered possible that cinemas might be classed as public places, but in February 1974 Cornish magistrates dismissed two summonses against *Last Tango* on the grounds that 'neither of these Acts are applicable' to licensed cinemas.

A similar decision was reached in London shortly afterwards. After the Director of Public Prosecutions had declined to take action against the G.L.C.-certificated *Blow Out*, Mary Whitehouse had summonsed the Curzon cinema under the Vagrancy Acts, only to be told that 'the Acts were not designed to prevent indecent exhibitions within the closed walls of a cinema'. However, the magistrate did offer Mrs Whitehouse more than a crumb of comfort when he indicated that he had no doubt that the film represented an indecent exhibition under Lord Chief Justice Parker's definition ('something that offends the ordinary modesty of the average man'—R. v. Stanley, 1965).

If the number of statutes that can be applied to cinemas is fewer than was once thought (the *Blow Out* verdict implies that the Metropolitan Police Act of 1839 cannot be used against cinemas either), there remains the common law. The 1959 Act tried to supersede and abolish the common law of obscene libel but in this it failed and charges can still be brought. In many cases of alleged obscenity it is possible to frame the prosecution under common law rather than under the Act, thereby denying the defendant the defence of public good, the right to call expert witness, the right to have the article judged as a whole, and the knowledge of the maximum sentence that can be imposed.

In any case the Act only extinguished common law with regard to those cases falling within its terms. As Zellick has noted in an important article, if films are excluded, 'there is nothing to prevent the operation of the common law in all its antique rigour' with all the handicaps for the defence mentioned above and only one advantage : the necessity for the prosecution to prove an ulterior intent. Zellick concluded that 'the exhibitors of films, robbed of the 1959 Act's shelter, may well have preferred the controlled tyranny of the Obscene Publications Acts to the anarchic terrorism of the common law'.[9]

Recent events have done little to clarify the legal situation. In July 1972 a six-minute British cartoon entitled *Sinderella* which had twice been rejected by the B.B.F.C. was seized by police acting on behalf of the Director of Public Prosecutions. The latter ultimately decided not to proceed against the film, but the Bow Street magistrate was of a different opinion and took out a personal summons to be heard in his own court. Not surprisingly the defence, in a two-day hearing in December, were unable to shake the magistrate's conviction that the film was obscene and its exhibition was banned within the jurisdiction of the court—although it could be shown elsewhere with impunity.

Eighteen months later at the Old Bailey a number of people connected with the Exxon club, Islington, were accused of fraudulently evading the import prohibition on indecent articles and of keeping a 'disorderly house' by showing indecent films. One of the films involved was the notorious *Deep Throat*, which when seen by one of the Board's examiners in New York had been described as 'hard-core pornography'. The film had, in fact, already been acquired by a British distributor, Jimmy Vaughan, who had bought it precisely because he believed it to be indecent, hoping to use it to challenge the obscenity laws. Throughout June and July 1974 (coincident with the Old Bailey trial) Vaughan tried to organize a conference on censorship to be held at the National Film Theatre with the intention of showing *Deep Throat* as an example for discussion. His stumbling block was the pornography section of the Customs and Excise department. All films imported into Britain have to go through Customs, whose main function is to measure them in order to calculate the import duty. Occasionally during this procedure, material comes to light that forces the department to consider its other duty—to ensure that no indecent films are allowed into the country. Random checks are also made but the administration of the Customs Act is necessarily haphazard. Assessment of indecency is also unpredictable, although the Board is sometimes consulted in cases of particular difficulty. It is not unknown for films to be let out of bond to be seen by the Board. In Murphy's words, 'even where they have seized a print they are very happy to release it to us and to accept our informal undertaking that we will ensure, in the case of rejection, that the distributor ships the print straight out of the country'.

Vaughan had hoped that *Deep Throat* could be shown to the conference under a similar arrangement, and had gained the support of the chairman of the G.L.C.'s film viewing sub-committee. The Customs had, however, been under some pressure from 'anti-permissive' groups to tighten up their control of imports and they were not inclined to relax their rules. A spokesman explained that the importers had 'told us that it was indecent and that this was why they wished to bring it in, for showing as part of a discussion on indecency. We told them that if they brought in an indecent film we would almost certainly seize it.'[10]

A few days later, however, the Old Bailey jury reported that, after eight hours' discussion, they were unable to agree on the meaning of indecency. Their confusion was understandable in view of the law's inability to provide anything but tautologous definitions and conflicting verdicts. Within the previous three months, for instance, two courts had accepted extraordinarily broad interpretations, ruling that certain widely circulated magazines were not only indecent but even obscene under Section 3 of the 1959 Act. At Bath, in April, 146 out of 238 magazines had been condemned, including *Penthouse*, *Mayfair*, *Forum*[11] and *Intro*—although *Playboy* and *Men Only* were cleared. Two months later, at Shrewsbury, twenty-five of twenty-six magazines were confiscated, including on this occasion *Men Only*.

These were extreme decisions indicating how strictly the test of obscenity can be applied. If this standard were to be accepted generally, the milder term 'indecency' would obviously cover a very wide range indeed. In October 1974 a case was set in motion that promised to throw some light on cinematic indecency. At Great Marlborough Street Magistrates' Court, the manager and owners of the Jacey cinema in London's Charing Cross Road and the distribution company, Fancey Associates, were committed for trial on a summons under common law alleging the exposure of an indecent exhibition. The film involved was *More About the Language of Love*, of which more will be heard in the next chapter. Here it is sufficient to note that it had been rejected by the B.B.F.C. but passed 'X' by the G.L.C. Police, acting on the instructions of the Director of Public Prosecutions, had raided the Jacey where the film had been showing for seven weeks. The *Blow Out* trial had indicated that a G.L.C. certificate was no bar to a successful prosecution; this case threatened to undermine the legal status of the local certificate. It is also significant to note that the film was held by the police during the period between its seizure and the trial thus preventing it from being shown in the interim.

Whatever the verdict, it was bound to have serious repercussions for the censorship system. If the film were found to be indecent the position of the Board of Film Censors would be strengthened to a degree which its officers felt to be embarrassing and undesirable : the industry would be bound to take the view that the Board's certificate amounted to a *de facto* protection against prosecution, and that to exhibit without the certificate would be an invitation to legal action. On the other hand an acquittal would inevitably lead to pressure on the Board and the local authorities to relax their standards at least as far as sex was concerned.

One final peculiarity of the present legal situation must be noted. The Cinematograph Acts which authorize licensing arrangements apply to all exhibitions with two exceptions—shows in private houses and club performances. The Obscene Publications Act specifically provides for private exhibitions—but not for clubs. As Zellick has commented, 'the ludicrous result is to leave some films—namely those shown in cinema clubs—subject neither to pre-censorship nor the Obscene Publications Acts, but instead, and unwittingly to be sure, to the common law; whereas all other films are subject to *both* pre-censorship and the common law'.[12]

The club 'loophole' had long been a matter of concern to governments formed by both major parties. In the Lords debate of 21st April, 1971 it was finally announced that action was to be taken.[13] This was the occasion on which Lord Longford had thrown himself into battle against pornography, concentrating his fire during that debate largely on the cinema and the B.B.F.C. 'We cannot look to any one man, himself the servant of the film industry or part of it, to act in place of the law

of the land. A minimum step . . . is to bring the film firmly
under the Obscene Publications Act, and to review the whole
set-up of the Film Censorship Board.' After Lord Ferrier had
assured the House of a 'definite link between international Com-
munism and the distribution to adolescents of certain pornographic materials', Lord Windlesham had announced the Government's intention to curtail the freedom of cinema clubs since
'under the existing legislation, these exhibitions cannot be effectively controlled, and there seems no doubt that offence is caused'.

Eighteen months later, in a further debate in the Lords,
Viscount Colville let it be known that concrete proposals had
been worked out but that it was thought that they might best
be incorporated into a Private Member's Bill. Colville's remarks
were so unspecific that the Board was forced to ask the Home
Office for clarification, whereupon it was informed that the intention was to close the clubs altogether, whilst not interfering with
genuine art-clubs such as the National Film Theatre and the
I.C.A.

Whether through intention or as a result of faulty drafting, the
Cinematograph and Indecent Displays Bill, the contents of
which were first made known in March 1973, was a much
wider-ranging document. All non-profitmaking clubs and societies
were to be affected if they charged for admission and advertised
their programmes publicly. Leslie Hardcastle, Controller of the
National Film Theatre, immediately declared that 'under these
regulations we would have great difficulty continuing to function'.
In a number of other ways there were strange contradictions
between the Bill and the expressed aims of the Government. In
particular the distinction between obscenity and indecency which
had been painstakingly made by Windlesham in the Lords debate
was now ignored. Windlesham had argued that people should
not be exposed to obscenity, but that with regard to indecency,
which has a 'more transient effect . . . it has not been thought
necessary or right, in a free society, to prohibit a person by law
from knowingly exposing himself to the risk of being infected'.[14]
The new Bill, however, proposed to apply the test of indecency
rather than obscenity. It was also curious that Robert Carr, the
Home Secretary, should argue in defence of the lack of a definition of indecency that this was for the public to decide when
the Bill specifically ruled out trial by jury, thus leaving judgements
to magistrates.

The main effect of the Cinematograph section of the Bill

would have been to give local authorities licensing power over all clubs run for commercial purposes as well as those which charged admission and advertised. The extension of local authority control clearly meant an extention of censorship, while all such establishments would have had to submit their films to censorship by the B.B.F.C. Film was also affected by the Indecent Display section, clause six of which covered film titles. This part of the Bill was even more controversial than the other since its range was startlingly wide. As Geoff Robertson noted in the *Guardian*, it threatened prison sentences for 'chemists who display contraceptives and vibrators, private art galleries which hang Rubens nudes, the management of the National Theatre which permits Diana Rigg to appear naked in *Jumpers*, publishers who advertise books like Terry Southern's *Blue Movie . . .*'.[15]

Ironically, coincident with the introduction of the Bill, a report on *Censorship and the Cinema* appeared, published by PEST, the 'Progressive Tory Pressure Group'.[16] This pamphlet not only concluded that 'providing that no evidence to the contrary emerges, there is no reason why pornography should not be freely available to adult audiences', but specifically attacked the new Bill as 'an illiberal and badly advised move', arguing that the Home Office was 'tackling a loophole in the law with a legislative axe instead of a scalpel'. The report caused some embarrassment since among the vice-presidents of PEST were Robert Carr and Lord Windlesham, while Home Office officials Mark Carlisle and Viscount Colville (and fifteen other members of the Government) were honorary members.

As it happened, no sooner had opposition to the Bill forced the Home Office to start considering modifications, than the announcement of elections and the subsequent defeat of Mr Heath's Government in February 1974 killed it altogether. The incoming Home Secretary, Roy Jenkins, showed no inclination to favour such legislation. A similar Bill was given an unopposed first reading in the Commons in June, but as a Private Member's Bill without Government support its future was bleak.

But in following the convolutions of the laws relating to censorship we have got ahead of our narrative. In the next chapter we return to 1971 and study the events leading to the crisis that quickly faced the new censor.

4

MURPHY'S WAR

TREVELYAN'S YEARS AS Secretary were not marked by many serious censorship controversies.

> Of course there was press comment and criticism since in my day film censorship came to have news value but there was usually a reasonable balance between the critics who considered us to be too restrictive and those who considered us to be too liberal. I had a few complaints from local authorities but usually found that by meeting them personally I could regain their confidence : local authorities work through committees, and committees tend to follow the lead of a few dominant members. I had a few, but only a few, letters from individuals, usually from people of extreme views, and I always made a point of replying to those letters personally. . . . Experience taught me that the wise course was to take notice of comment and criticism but not to be unduly influenced by it, to make what we believed to be the right judgement and decisions at the time, and then to defend them if necessary. My successor seems to be working on the same lines.[1]

The previous chapter has indicated how this policy was becoming increasingly hard to follow as the cinema moved away from the family audience to concentrate on those minorities who retained the cinema-going habit. The introduction of a revised classification system in 1970 was an attempt to come to terms with these trends, but it offered only a partial solution. Distributors immediately began to invest in some of the more restrained foreign product that had hitherto been ignored. In any case, numerous films still fell way beyond the bounds set by the Board. Extreme brutality, sado-masochism, bestiality, etc. continued to be banned, while many European sex films are so visually explicit that they would undoubtedly be prosecuted if shown. The same applies to the recent spate of American sex films following *Deep Throat*, such as *The Devil in Miss Jones*, *Boys in the Sand* and *Behind the Green Door*. The Secretary sees a number of films each month which distributors are considering, and informally offers advice on their chances of being passed. More often than not he discourages the purchase of these productions.

The surprise Conservative victory in the election of June 1970 was an indication of the turn to the Right that was evident at this time. It was an encouraging sign to the anti-permissive groups. In September 1970 the Archbishop of Canterbury called on Christians to protest against obscenity and blasphemy, while pornography was attacked in a report by the Board of Social Responsibility of the Church of England in November. By 25th September, 1971 the recently formed Festival of Light was able to attract 35,000 people to a meeting in Trafalgar Square, while there were other demonstrations up and down the country. This pressure group quickly had a great deal of success in alerting local authorities and making clear both to themselves and to the public their powers over cinema licensing. Until this time the local authorities had operated a policy which was rather more liberal than that of the B.B.F.C. In the two years up to late 1971 local authorities had passed films rejected by the Board on some 150 occasions. Now many began to be alarmed by the Festival of Light campaign. At the same time the eruption of hostilities in Northern Ireland had created a greater awareness of violence as a major problem in society. Continuous news reports of bloodshed and semi-warfare within the United Kingdom made many people wonder what had gone wrong and look for possible causes. Not for the first time the media were held to be partially responsible by many people.

A combination of events, therefore, led to the censorship crisis of the winter of 1971–2, most of which were clearly beyond the control of the Board. There was one way, however, in which the Board was responsible for the situation that developed. Its failure to produce a consistent policy with regard to sex education films between 1968 and 1971 may have seemed unimportant at the time, but the consequences were far from trivial, for, unable to make up its mind about the correct action to take, the Board evaded its duties and sought the guidance of the local authorities. By testing local opinion in this way, the Board not only failed to find a solution (for the councils clearly showed that there was no consensus even among themselves) but they awakened the authorities to their powers. These had largely lain idle for many years but now, encouraged by the Board to enter the fray, many councillors showed themselves eager to flex their rediscovered muscles.

It is very easy to criticize the Board in retrospect, but the sex education films did present a thorny problem. They were much more visually explicit than anything that had previously been passed, but their educational value clearly qualified them for special consideration. Since sex education was now being taught in schools it would have appeared anomalous to have banned this material even for adults in the cinema. Various books had been published without stirring up serious public indignation or attracting obscenity charges, and while the Board had never allowed that what is available in book form should also be acceptable on the screen, it was undeniable that most of those in need of sex education were unlikely to get it from books. There was thus a reasonable argument to be put forward in favour of these films, as many medical and psychiatric experts were prepared to agree.

The crux of the matter was whether the Board was convinced that the films were made with the intention of being educative rather than simply using this to cover a real appeal to more prurient interests. It happened that one of the first such films to be submitted for censorship was very clearly a film made with integrity, and one which the Board had little hesitation in passing. This was a German film called *Helga*, which proved to be the first in a series of such films. *Helga* was in no way sensational and had a very clear educational purpose. Another film presented at this time, however, failed to convince the examiners of its sincerity and it was at first turned down. However, the Board was eventually convinced by the distributor that the producers of the film were well-known and respected figures in the field of sex education in Germany and finally this film—*The Wonder of Love*—was passed, after a panel of doctors and psychiatrists had agreed that it could be helpful to some people and that there was nothing that they felt should be removed before the film could be shown in public. The Board did, however, insist on certain cuts although it would seem that in part this was to cover up what amounted to a complete change of mind.

Neither of these films produced any significant outrage, but a third film that was passed at this time did arouse opposition. The certificating of *Love in Our Time* was bitterly attacked by that organ of righteous indignation, the *News of the World*. The decision was also widely criticized from other quarters, so that when, a year later, further sex education films were submitted, the Board was in a less generous mood.

The success of the German films in British cinemas naturally stimulated British producers to follow suit. Not without reason the Board was inclined to suspect the motives of these films. The makers were aware of this problem and went to great lengths to stress the good intentions behind their films. The first of these British efforts was *Love Variations*, the central idea of which was to demonstrate different sex positions. The press handout prepared by the company announced : 'The film does not seek to entertain—only to inform. The producers wish to point out that although the film is frank, comprehensive and explicit it will almost certainly prove unrewarding to those looking for titillation or sensation and will be of interest only to those motivated by a sincere desire to be informed.' The Board accepted this argument but, in April 1970, rejected the film on the curious grounds that it was not primarily designed as entertainment. However, the letter to local authorities explaining the ban did not attempt to influence them to follow suit, indicating the indecision of the Board.

After some authorities had passed the film, it was resubmitted to the Board in October and, after some deliberation, issued with a certificate. An explanatory note was sent to local authorities which throws some light on the Board's assessment of public opinion :

The film was passed by the G.L.C., and has been shown in a London cinema for several weeks. It has since been passed by quite a number of other licensing authorities, but refused by others. . . . We have been watching the position and trying to assess public opinion. Press comment, including the reviews in the trade press by two experienced women, has been favourable to the film, and such reports as I have had have given me the impression that many people who have seen the film think it helpful; indeed I have had comments from older people that they wish they had seen it when they were young. We have been impressed also by the serious and dignified publicity for the film, which contrasts favourably with much film publicity these days. In the circumstances we have decided that we will now pass the film in the 'X' category.

Twenty-five authorities refused to accept this logic and continued to ban the film. The Board's evidence was certainly thin : only two dozen authorities had actually passed the film whereas a rather greater number had rejected it. Meanwhile a Swedish film *Anatomy of Love* had had a similar history. Originally banned because there was 'a difference of opinion on whether educational films of this kind should or should not be shown in public cinemas, which are essentially places of entertainment', it also was subsequently passed a few months later.

At the same time a second Swedish picture, *Language of Love*, appeared. Although the Secretary thought that it was 'the best of its kind I have seen', it contained some highly explicit scenes, including intercourse, which the Board felt to be unacceptable. Once again the matter was left to individual authorities, and the film was passed by the G.L.C. with a number of cuts.

The film was resubmitted early in 1971 and again in February 1972, but rejected on both occasions. Each time the application coincided with events that inclined the Board to avoid controversy. First there was the Lords debate on pornography and the furore over the sex education efforts of Dr Martin Cole. The second submission was at the time of the *Straw Dogs/The Devils* row.

In addition it was becoming clear to the Board that the local authorities were unhappy with the way in which sex education films were being dealt with. Many were highly critical of the tendency to pass films that had been turned down only a short time before, feeling that this was evidence of a lack of a consistent policy. The Board was also alarmed to realize that the whole problem was alerting councils to their potential power which some were already beginning to use.

But the firm stand taken over *Language of Love* had been taken too late. A serious mistake had been made in the handling of these films which had resulted in dissatisfaction among both the local authorities and the distribution companies involved. For the latter the issue was by no means a minor one. Sex education films represented for a short time the sort of gold-mine for which small distributors are continually searching. Even without a national certificate *Language of Love* (which had been obtained on a 50/50 profit-sharing basis with the Swedish owners without any down payment) made almost £1 million in this country. The Board's vacillations had important financial consequences for the industry as well as causing some loss of confidence.

Although a firm policy was clearly necessary, there was no agreement within the Board on what line should be taken. Lord Harlech and the older examiners were unsympathetic to the genre while Trevelyan, Murphy and the younger examiners were prepared to believe in its sincerity. None felt that such pictures could cause any harm; the problem was solely one of taste. Were these films suitable for presentation in public cinemas? In general the public's answer seems to have been in the affirmative, although some cinemas took the precaution of showing only to audiences segregated by sex. In most places, however, the films played without comment. Despite this, the decision not to accept *Language of Love* meant that a line had been drawn beyond which the Board could not go—for the time being at least. Clearly this line had not been drawn in Sweden, for a series of follow-ups were made, each more explicit than the last. None of these was bought by distributors here, for obvious reasons. However a compilation film was made, including what was felt to be the less 'offensive' sections of these films, called *More About the Language of Love*, which was seen by the censors in November 1972. It clearly went far beyond what the Board was used to passing and there was no question of its being certificated as long as the first of the series remained uncertificated.[2] The film's later history has already been noted.

The Board's dilemma was well illustrated by its attitude to *The Body*, not a sex education film but one which aimed to be an illustrated guide to the human body, and which naturally included consideration of the sexual side. There was no doubt of the sincerity of the film and the integrity of its makers, and the film was largely thought suitable for teenagers. Nevertheless the Board was unwilling to set a precedent by allowing copulation in an 'AA' film, and therefore, with much misgiving, gave it an 'X' certificate. Trevelyan, however, felt strongly that older teenagers should be able to see the film, which he believed to be of great educational value, and was prepared to encourage education officers to arrange special screenings of the film for older school children.[3] Thus, within four months of their introduction, the new categories were found to be inadequate, leading Trevelyan to recommend for teenagers a film from which he had excluded them.

Although the commercial appear of sex education films was predictably short-lived, the damage had been done. By appealing to the local authorities for guidance, the Board had sown seeds of doubt about its ability to be the sole arbiter of public taste in the cinema, a small but important step towards the undermining of the Board's authority. Much larger strides were to be made during the months that followed the appointment of the new Secretary in July 1971.

Stephen Murphy, once a teacher at Manchester Grammar School, had been working in the mass media for twenty years, the first Secretary to come from such a background. After ten years at the B.B.C. he had had a similar spell with I.T.V., first in a creative role, latterly as senior programme officer for the Independent Television Authority, as it was then called. This post involves censorship in all but name, although the standards required by a family medium like television are rather different from those to be applied in the context of the cinema.

Unfortunately for Murphy the build-up of pressures erupted almost at once. Trevelyan has remarked that it takes many months to feel oneself into the role of censor. Murphy had no opportunity for a gentle introduction, for a number of films appeared that immediately drew the fire of the Festival of Light and its supporters.[4]

The first of these had in fact been passed by Trevelyan but its opening had been delayed by the non-availability of a cinema. *The Devils*, directed by Ken Russell, was based on *The Devils of Loudun* by Aldous Huxley, a semi-documentary account of religious mania and persecution in seventeenth-century France. It was hardly designed to appeal to the evangelical groups now attempting to reassert Christian values. Nor did it impress the Board's examiners when first seen by them in Soho Square in February 1971. They felt that it was 'a nauseating piece of film' that will 'appeal chiefly to the prurient'; that 'it plumbs really filthy depths' and 'sensationalises the subject out of all measure'. The examiners concluded that 'we would all be very glad if the picture could be left to the local authorities since we cannot see much possibility of it being toned down sufficiently for us to feel at all happy about it, or for the Board's general standards in regard to sex and brutality not to be at risk in consequence of passing the film'.

This was hardly a satisfactory solution in view of the Board's experience with sex education films and, in any case, Trevelyan and Harlech did not share this opinion. Both had seen the film in January and were keen admirers. Inevitably the examiners had to give way and a long list of cuts was prepared and submitted to Russell. The director accordingly re-edited and sent the film back early in April. At the same time he wrote a letter explaining his point of view. The film has been so extensively vilified that it is worth reading Russell's defence, for, contrary to popular interpretation, he argued :

> What I set out to do was to make a deeply felt religious state-ment—and I believe that despite the fact that I have butchered the film at your bidding far and away beyond anything I dreamed of . . . what remains still just about retains my intention, albeit in a watered-down version. After all, I did not set out to make a cosy religious drama that would please everyone but a true film about the horror and blasphemy perpetrated against human beings by their fellow men in the name of Jesus Christ. This is an eternal theme and a true one as a glance at the horror in Northern Ireland will remind you.

Russell also pointed out the factual basis of his film, arguing that he had only departed from what actually happened by bowdleriz-ing certain parts of the story, and questioned who or what was being offered protection by the pretence that such things did not occur—'Certainly not the Catholics, of whom I am one. We've been persecuted in England on and off for 500 years and need no one's solicitude—we can look after ourselves.' He concluded by emphasizing that 'the film has two themes—religious corrup-tion and redemption—the sinner who becomes a saint. I think (and I believe practising Christians will agree) that I have made a deeply religious film.'

The revised version still divided the Board but there was a majority feeling that the film could be accepted. One examiner felt that 'although it remains a film of considerable impact bordering on the sensational, I consider that the film has been greatly improved and is now acceptable, subject to additional cuts'. Other examiners remained unconvinced, but Trevelyan was determined to pass the film and Lord Harlech was 'im-pressed by the obvious sincerity' of Russell's letter and by the extent to which Russell had 'co-operated with us by modifying the film in accordance with our suggestions'. A few further cuts were requested and made, and an 'X' certificate was given in May.

When the film opened that summer it immediately encountered

great opposition. Its subject matter naturally attracted the attention of the Festival of Light who, seeing it as a useful issue on which to concentrate in order to attract support and publicity for their cause, organized a vigorous campaign against the film. The movement's chief spokesman, Peter Thompson, public relations officer for Aims of Industry, wrote to the G.L.C. complaining that *The Devils* was 'offensive, repugnant, and likely to injure the moral standards of society'. Dr Mark Patterson, chairman of the council's film viewing sub-committee, however, reported that it was not 'within the purview of his committee to ban the film, the policy being to accept films passed by the B.B.F.C.' He argued that if his committee were to take action against individual films in this way 'we would end up by having total chaos'.[5]

Other authorities, however, did not take this point of view. Surrey, for instance, announced that members of their committee were 'unanimously agreed that the film was objectionable and should not have been released for public showing. They felt that it went beyond the bounds of good taste in its blasphemy and unnecessary scenes of indecency, cruelty and torture.' More important still, the council took this opportunity to generalize beyond this one case and to announce what amounted to a major change of policy : 'They feel experience has shown that there is a need to call in for inspection certain films that have already been granted an "X" certificate by the B.B.F.C., but which because of their specially controversial content might be considered to offend against public feeling and decency or be likely to encourage crime or violence.'[6] This loss of confidence in the Board was detectable elsewhere. Tunbridge Wells, for example, in banning *The Devils*, commented that they also had 'serious misgivings about the standard which the Board seems to be adopting'.[7] Altogether fourteen local authorities overturned the Board's decision and rejected the film. Moreover, censorship was now a matter of public debate and the Festival of Light, encouraged by this early success, found no difficulty in arousing concern over other films. The next major controversy, however, did not stem primarily from the action of such pressure groups.

It was the film critics who pounced on two of Murphy's earliest judgements. *Trash*, a film by Paul Morrissey and Andy Warhol, had in fact originally been held up by Trevelyan. It represents a day in the life of a New York couple, one of whom is a male transvestite, the other a hustler whose drug use has rendered him impotent. The Board has always been very careful about films involving drugs, and although this film could hardly be said to have glorified drugs in any way, the Board had felt unable to pass a film that dealt so largely with this subject. Murphy, who on appointment had proclaimed his intention to continue his predecessor's policies, felt disinclined to overturn one of his judgements so quickly, especially on such a touchy issue. The fact that neither Murphy nor his examiners had high opinions of products of Warhol's 'factory' was also a factor in this decision. Nevertheless the Secretary was loath to reject the film out of hand, as the previous Warhol production *Flesh* had been passed in 1970 and shown without undue comment. He suggested to the distributors, Vaughan Films, that they should wait and see how the critics responded at the forthcoming London Film Festival. This plan did not appeal to the distributors, so Murphy resorted to the other method of opinion-testing and asked the G.L.C. to see the film. As it happened, the G.L.C. unanimously rejected the film without even feeling the need for discussion, and Murphy was able to argue that, given this reaction by the traditionally liberal G.L.C. viewing committee, he could not conceivably pass the film. He explained to Vaughan that 'we are very unhappy about giving the impression that drugs are an ordinary part of the scene'.

Straw Dogs was a more obviously commercial film made by Sam Peckinpah, a director with a reputation for making realistic, and therefore violent, Westerns. This particular film was made and set in twentieth-century Cornwall, a fact which probably accentuated the distaste felt for it by so many commentators in this country. Murphy had first seen the film at its rough-cut stage, and expressed the opinion that it could not be accepted as it stood. As a result of his comments parts of the film had been re-edited before it was officially submitted. A long rape scene had been shortened and broken up by cuts to another scene, while the violent battle at the climax of the film had also been reduced. Murphy and all four examiners who saw it were agreed that the film, although undeniably savage and shocking, was of outstanding quality. This unanimity meant that there was no need to consult the President, and an 'X' certificate was given. Clearly neither the Board nor the distributors were prepared for the controversy that was to follow. The examiners, who had so disliked *The Devils* a few months before, were agreed on the 'massive impact' but described it as 'compulsive viewing' and 'an outstanding picture'. Murphy had now seen the film three times and some sections several times more. He found it 'shattering' but 'honest' and was determined that censorship should not stop people seeing 'urgent and important things—even if it hurts'. The distributors were dissatisfied with the Board's deliberations and expressed themselves 'disappointed that you cannot grant the film an "AA" certificate', noting that in America it had been given a certificate that allowed the admission of children.

Straw Dogs opened in London on 25th November to hostile reviews. Nearly all the critics found it unnecessarily brutal and its attitude to violence repugnant. Alexander Walker wrote in the *Evening Standard* that 'it appears to cater for those possessed of the instinctual frenzy of a glutton's appetite'. Margaret Hinxman in the *Sunday Telegraph* found the violence 'unnecessary and obscene' and there were few who disagreed with her. On 17th December a letter appeared in *The Times* signed by thirteen critics,[8] in which they challenged the Board's decision.

Sir, A great deal of criticism, some of it well founded, some of it the product of prejudice and apprehension, is currently being directed at violence on the cinema screen, especially violence accompanied by extreme sexual aggressiveness. We acknowledge that it is probably not possible to establish a Quota System for either sex or violence—or, indeed, desirable to do so, since in each case it is not the quantity, but the filmmaker's intention behind the display of these elements and the effects they have in the finished work which ultimately provide the standard of judgement.

However, we wish to underline what many of us have already indicated and condemned in our separate reviews of the film *Straw Dogs*; that in our view the use to which this film employs its scenes of double rape and multiple killings by a variety of hideous methods is dubious in its intention, excessive in its effect and likely to contribute to the concern expressed from time to time by many critics over films which exploit the very violence which they make a show of condemning.

Furthermore, we wish to draw attention to the now serious and growing inconsistencies of film censorship which passes for public exhibition such a violent film as *Straw Dogs*, yet so far has withheld any certificate at all from the film *Trash*.

The film censor has been quoted as saying that it is his Board's desire not to have drugs made to seem a natural or acceptable part of the contemporary scene which has made it deny *Trash* a certificate.

We would welcome a statement from the Secretary of the British Board of Film Censors, or from his President, Lord Harlech, who has so far remained silent on the issue, even when the continued existence of his Board was being called into question by several of the signatories to this letter, as to how the film censorship system can reconcile its attitude on *Trash* with its attitude on *Straw Dogs*. Is violence a more acceptable part of the scene, in the censor's eyes, than drugs?

This concerted attack by so many leading critics was obviously a serious challenge to the position of the Board at a time when it was already being attacked from within the industry as well as from outside it. However, the consensus amongst the critics was, to some extent, more apparent than real, for there was considerable divergence of opinion among the signatories of the letter about the qualities of both films.[9] Not all had been quite so antipathetic towards *Straw Dogs* in their original reviews. Cashin in the *Sun* had gone no further than to say that it was 'a powerful and sensational film that will scare the apple sauce out of you', while Malcolm of the *Guardian* seemed to be very much in two minds. He wrote on the one hand that 'the film does not know where to stop. It out-Hammers Hammer when it simply doesn't need to,' but on the other that 'I won't see anything gratuitous about it at all'. Moreover many of the signatories explained elsewhere that there had never been any intention of implying that the film should have been banned. Melly later wrote that 'we made it clear that none of us was in favour of banning *Straw Dogs*'.[10] The letter is, however, slightly ambiguous in this respect.

Murphy, amongst others, felt that the real objection was to the rejection of *Trash* and that *Straw Dogs* had merely been drawn in as a useful contrast. But when the reviews of *Trash* appeared a year later it was clear that there was no unanimity over this film. Although the majority praised it, one or two wrote violent attacks. Cashin was one who seemed to have no doubts about what he called 'the most obscene film I've ever seen', while Walker argued that '*Trash* breeds in the viewer something worse than voyeurism. It breeds indifference.' He concluded: 'It hardly matters whether such a film is obscene or not. There are worse things than shocking the bourgeoisie or outraging conventional morality and one of them is callousing our sensibilities and compassion. . . .'

Murphy was unrepentant in the face of criticism of these decisions, defending *Straw Dogs* as a serious attempt to say something about violence. His position was not unsupported. When Granada TV arranged a discussion programme on censorship with the participation of an audience selected as representative of the population as a whole, their views were 'less hostile to *Straw Dogs* than the critics'.[11] Murphy also argued that the many meetings he addressed up and down the country, with very different audiences, suggested that the film was acceptable to the overwhelming majority of cinema-goers. In addition neither *Straw Dogs* nor *The Devils* had encountered similar trouble in other countries. *The Devils* had been banned only in Greece, Spain, Portugal and Ireland. Even in Italy, the home of Catholicism, there had only been private protests in two towns, neither of which led to the withdrawal of the film. *Straw Dogs* was considered suitable for fifteen-year-olds in Sweden, a country with a traditionally tough approach to film violence, and was 'R' rated in America, allowing the admission of accompanied children. Even the South African censor demanded only minor cuts.

Within a month of the opening of *Straw Dogs*, the Board was presented with another problem. This was Stanley Kubrick's *A Clockwork Orange*, the basic theme of which was the concept of choice, and which therefore had a great deal to say about censorship. Its philosophical content was however to be largely ignored in the debate that followed, for although it was a film that would, in more normal times, have aroused little controversy for its violence, it came at a point in time when it was likely to arouse notice. 'Having missed the boat where the indiscriminate violence in *Straw Dogs* was concerned, all kinds of pressure groups, newspaper "campaigns" and the all-purpose commentators who thrive in the media now latched on to *A Clockwork Orange* as the current whipping boy for the industry's "irresponsibility".'[12]

The situation was aggravated by some ill-advised advertising which emphasized the sensational aspects of the film. Nor was some of the promotional material helpful towards the public image of the picture. One interview in particular, appearing as it did two days after *The Times'* letter, increased the burden on Murphy's shoulders. Adrienne Corri, who appeared in the film, confided to the *Sunday Mirror* that she was 'scared to see herself' since 'this was violence beyond anything I ever imagined would appear on the screen.' Such comments were no doubt designed to increase public interest in the film, in which they succeeded admirably. But they also led the *Mirror*, and no doubt others, to ask : 'How much more violence, sadism, and rape is British film censor Stephen Murphy going to let movie-makers get away with?'

The film critics, however, were as favourable towards this film as they had been critical of *Straw Dogs*, although this attitude was rarely shared by feature and editorial writers. This occasionally led to curious situations where contradictory appraisals of *A Clockwork Orange* could be found in the same newspaper. One issue of the *Sunday Telegraph*, for instance, found deputy editor Worsthorne describing it as 'muck in the name of art' while his film reviewer was calling it a 'masterpiece'. Even those associated with the Festival of Light seemed at first to be in two minds. Lord Longford called it 'tremendous' and, while expressing doubt about its effects on the public, denied that it could be described as pornographic. Peter Thompson's reported opinions varied widely. In a letter to Warner Brothers who were handling the film, he apparently announced that 'to someone who has committed violent acts and who has been mentally ill, this film seems to have an awful lot to say to society. . . . My honest opinion is that this is the best film I have ever seen'.[13] On the other hand, in a letter to the G.L.C. he described scenes as 'corrupting, degrading and likely to lead to crimes against persons and society', and argued that 'in its present state it is unfit for viewing by the general public'.

Murphy himself was in no doubt about the quality of the film and his opinion was shared by the examiners. In a letter to local authorities defending his passing of the film he was to write :

This is one of the most brilliant pieces of cinema, not simply of this year, but possibly of the decade. It is likely (although the Board did not know this at the time when the film was submitted) to win major international awards. In the countries in which it has so far been released it has received virtually universal approval, and, to the best of my knowledge and belief, it is only in Britain that even the faintest disapproving whisper has been heard. . . . It is a valuable contribution to the whole debate about violence.

Murphy was not the only public figure under pressure at this time. The situation in Northern Ireland had gone from bad to worse, forcing the problem of violence into the public conscience and on to the front pages. A hard-pressed Home Secretary, the ill-fated Reginald Maudling, forced in an interview to make his position clear, gave the opinion that there was probably a connection between the rising crime rate and increasing cinema violence. He revealed that because of his 'personal concern' he was planning to see *A Clockwork Orange*. This announcement, which was greeted with widespread support in the press, naturally implied that the Home Office was gravely dissatisfied with the performance of the B.B.F.C., and was bound to undermine its general credibility. It was an unusual and ill-conceived move for a number of reasons, pointed out in a forceful leader in the *Evening Standard* :

> Although his intentions are good, Mr Maudling's decision to pay an official visit to the controversial film *A Clockwork Orange* is thoroughly bad in principle and in practice. . . . If the Home Secretary's wish was to acquaint himself with the growth of violence on the screen, he has all the opportunities any private person has of visiting the films currently on show in London. But to single out for mention a specific film before it has opened publicly is certain to suggest to some people, among them the more illiberal forces of opinion, that the film merits the scrutiny of the Minister responsible for curbing the abuses of law and order. That Mr Maudling should visit the premises of B.B.F.C. to see *A Clockwork Orange* is itself unprecedented; and whatever the courtesy extended him by the film censor it smacks of the bank inspector come to vet the books.[14]

In fact the film was actually seen at the Admiralty and whatever Maudling's feelings (and no press statement was issued) no further action was taken. It is possible that Maudling had never actually intended to intervene but had felt it necessary to show his concern to appease certain pressure groups, or it may have been that other problems prevented him from implementing whatever plans he had formulated. Either way he had greatly increased Murphy's difficulties.

Meanwhile another knife was being sharpened. The G.L.C.'s film viewing sub-committee had decided to see *A Clockwork Orange* for 'information purposes only'. The committee's chairman, Mark Patterson, stressed that 'there is no question at the moment of our taking a vote whether to ban it. . . . We are not looking at *A Clockwork Orange* to check on Stephen Murphy, but to see what Stanley Kubrick is up to'. If true, this indicated a new policy for the G.L.C. A more likely explanation perhaps can be found in other statements by Patterson at this time. In an interview with Alexander Walker on 28th February he 'indicated his committee's concern with more than matters of taste and obscenity in films; he left Walker with the impression that the violence then occurring dramatically in Ulster, at Aldershot or in the miners' picket-lines was causing some members of his committee to be anxious about films reflecting social and political unrest without offering acceptable solutions. He also spoke of the desirability of seeing more of the films which the censor certified so as to keep members informed.'[15] Walker pointed out that such a move was calculated to cause extreme disquiet in the industry, which was already very nervous about the number of authorities banning films. Undaunted Patterson announced in a press release on 1st March that the G.L.C. intended to 'keep a closer watch on controversial films, particularly those passed by the censor for public viewing'. He also reiterated his highly controversial political opinions, arguing that 'in the context of violent times they had to consider the wide, general political and social implications of films, particularly those which reflected anarchy and did not provide answers'. Such statements seem to be a long way from the G.L.C.'s 1965 decision that they would ban only films that offended against the law. Of lesser implication, but of more immediate concern to the B.B.F.C., was Patterson's call for scrutiny of the censorship situation at a national level, and his suggestion that the Government set up a royal commission.

Although the G.L.C. in fact continued to support the Board, this sign of unease on the part of so influential a body was the final straw for many in the film industry. Without ever admitting that the nature of the films being made was a major factor in the crisis, a number immediately turned on Murphy. As far as some sections of the industry are concerned the Board's main functions are to shield them from criticism and to ensure that

films are accepted by the local authorities. Until this point the
industry had remained silent, neither lending support to the
censor, nor openly attacking him. It might have been thought
that the committee which had unanimously appointed Murphy
only a year before might have argued in his defence, but in
fact it was a member of this committee who was to lead the
attack. In a speech in Glasgow early in March, Kenneth Rive,
then president of the Cinematograph Exhibitors' Association but
also an executive member of the British Film Producers' Association and on the council of the Kinematograph Renters' Society,
explicitly challenged Murphy, calling him 'the wrong man for
the job', and arguing that his decisions were too liberal and that
he was too loath to cut.[16] He added that as 'the film industry
appoints the censor, so it is up to us to put our house in order by
getting rid of him. He has got completely out of touch with
public opinion.' Although this was a statement of his personal
view, Rive maintained that most of his C.E.A. members were
in agreement. The trade paper *CinemaTV Today* reported this
speech under the headline 'Murphy Must Go',[17] and the national
newspapers quickly picked up the controversy, many taking the
opportunity to attack the Board.

Murphy was not altogether without supporters. At a meeting
called by Jimmy Vaughan (of Vaughan Films) a discussion was
held on 'the crisis of censorship in the light of recent statements
of the G.L.C., other local authorities and certain so-called spokes-
men of the film industry' and a motion declared those members
of the industry present to be opposed to 'multiplicity of film
censorship [as operated by local councils] which is qualitatively
inferior to the Board, whose task is solely that of judging films'.
John Trevelyan also publicly defended his successor, while many
of those on the creative side of the industry were more concerned
to see the abolition of censorship rather than its extension.

However, until this moment, Murphy had lacked the support
that he needed most, for the Board's President, Lord Harlech,
had been out of the country for two months with the Pearce
Commission in Rhodesia. His influence and experience were
sorely needed for even severe critics like Rive evidently placed
great faith in Harlech's opinion. On his return to Britain on
10th March he at once affirmed his faith in the Secretary, in
whom he expressed 'complete confidence'. He pointed out that
the industry itself had more than a little responsibility for the
films produced and emphasized that the Board had been faced in

recent months with 'a greatly increased number of films exploiting sex, violence and sadism', as a result of which more films had been banned and cut during Murphy's six months of tenure than during the last six months of Trevelyan's term of office. He 'categorically' denied that there had been any change of policy and stated that 'to the extent that it is humanly possible we have tried to be consistent'. Finally he pointed out that only a very small number of authorities had over-ruled the Board's decisions and expressed the intention of retaining the confidence of the authorities.

Harlech also called a private meeting with representatives of all sections of the industry at which it was agreed, according to *CinemaTV Today*:

1. that Lord Harlech . . . should meet the heads of the film industry to discuss the whole issue of censorship.
2. that in future Lord Harlech himself will deal with local authorities when they query certificates of films, and that Harlech will 'be more directly involved' whenever censorship is under attack. Stephen Murphy will remain silent in public: Harlech will be the 'front man'.
3. Murphy's position as censor will be reviewed at the end of his first year to see whether or not his contract should be renewed.[18]

This statement would seem to re-interpret yet again the relationship between the two offices but in fact it was never really operationalized. Harlech had neither the time, the expertise nor the inclination to take up a more dominant role, and the purpose of this announcement seems to have been primarily conciliatory. It did, nonetheless, obviously put Murphy in an unenviable position, his bargaining power weakened by his position as a Secretary 'on trial'. His embarrassment was eased, however, by the industry's decision that expediency demanded support for the B.B.F.C. Criticisms such as those expressed by the President of the C.E.A. were to cease, and Rive was taken to task by Michael Relph, chairman of the F.P.A., who pronounced that it was wrong for any section of the industry to try to dictate to the Board. *CinemaTV Today* also called for support for the censor arguing that there was no viable alternative to the present set-up.

Meanwhile Stanley Kubrick had become very concerned that the climate of opinion might lead to further attacks on his film if it were shown in the provinces. He therefore persuaded the distributors to delay its general release so that for a year *A Clockwork Orange* could be seen only in one cinema in London's West End, where it played to large audiences. For in spite of Fergus Cashin's demand in the *Sun* that 'if Stephen Murphy must continue as censor, let him be strong enough to go on the studio floor and warn the film-makers, face to face, that the public will not tolerate mindless pornographic violence', the films that had precipitated the controversy all proved to be highly popular. *The Devils* had played to large audiences wherever the local authorities had passed it, causing its distributor to comment on its general release that 'every situation without exception is doing excellent business'. *Straw Dogs* had a similar history, playing for two or three weeks in many places and being held over for six or eight weeks in large centres. *A Clockwork Orange*, during the year when it was confined to the West End,[19] was seen by well over half a million people, who paid more than £430,000 for the privilege. In the lists of the biggest box-office successes of 1972, *The Devils* lay fourth, *Straw Dogs* fourteenth and *A Clockwork Orange*, despite its limited exhibition, eleventh. *Straw Dogs* was Rank's third biggest grosser, and *The Devils* was fourth for E.M.I.[20] The cinema-going public was apparently in no doubt about its opinion of such films, and it is clear that the publicity had done them no harm at all. As Lord Eccles, the Minister responsible for the Arts, had said, 'the only censor is the audience, which will decide whether it wants (violence) or how soon it gets fed up with seeing it'. If the B.B.F.C.'s job is to assess public opinion, its decisions to pass these films would seem to have been vindicated.

In the wake of *A Clockwork Orange* a number of other films appeared which seemed, in theory, likely to arouse controversy, but by this time the press had lost interest in the topic. In journalistic terms any subject has only a certain amount of news-value. Just as each succeeding moon-shot had brought ever-decreasing press and public interest, so censorship in its turn fell out of favour. In any case it is not always easy to predict what will have the special ingredients necessary for newspaper coverage. On a number of occasions the Board braced itself for criticism that never materialized.

Shortly after the rejection of *Trash*, for instance, a film had been submitted that had all the makings of another headache. This was *W.R.—Mysteries of the Organism*, a film by the Yugoslav, Dusan Makavejev, whose earlier *The Switchboard Operator* had been an embarrassment to Trevelyan. The new film was concerned with the sexual and political theories of Wilhelm Reich, and included some very explicit sexual scenes. It had been the sensation of the Cannes Festival of 1971 where a correspondent had written that 'it could almost be described as the prototype of a film designed specifically to offend censors of every country of whatever political or moral leaning'.[21] Surprisingly the Board decided that it could be passed, but asked for cuts. The Yugoslav film-makers responded that they would not and, in some cases, could not, make the extensive cuts asked for, and would apply for a local certificate from the G.L.C. In an internal memorandum to his examiners, Murphy explained why he had considered it necessary to concede on all points. His remarks also cast light on the wide range of considerations which influence a judgement.

'I don't mind the G.L.C. certificating dirty little films we turn down,' he wrote, 'but I *do* mind the G.L.C. certificating an important, interesting, and, as we are all agreed, not salacious film which has attracted a good deal of attention. Secondly, of the two Cannes films (*The Go-Between* apart) which filled the press, we are holding up *Trash*. Thirdly, *W.R.* is politically fascinating and ought to be seen; it will never go further than a tiny few art-houses.' He concluded by pointing out that a lot of films had been (justifiably) rejected in recent months and that he felt it important to 'go out on a limb on one liberal judgement'.

In public Murphy was more reticent, saying, 'I thought it was a good and important film. It makes you think. If someone has the courage to make a film like this in a country where he's liable to be put in prison, it would be ridiculous to ban it in the home of freedom.'[22] Contrary to his fears, the film raised little controversy, even though it eventually received quite wide exhibition.

Other films which worried the Board included *The Nightcomers* and *Innocent Bystanders*. The former was directed by Michael Winner, and represented a speculation on what might have led up to the situation which opens Henry James's *The Turn of the Screw*. The Board was very worried about a series of sado-masochistic encounters between Marlon Brando and Stephanie Beacham, whereas Winner argued that his picture was no more violent than others that had been certificated. Nor was the director inclined to co-operate with the censor, for the film was a labour of love which he had waited many years to make and for which he had received no payment. Lengthy bargaining finally led to a compromise that fully satisfied neither party and which the Board felt could become a target for complaints. However, although there was some comment, the film was not a success, receiving only a limited release that diminished its potential as a source of controversy.

Innocent Bystanders was a British spy thriller which was rejected in its original version in July 1972, despite its producers' belief that it merited an 'AA' certificate. Eventually a cut version was passed 'X', although Murphy suspected that he might have been unnecessarily lenient. Once again the anticipated criticism never came, and censorship remained a dead issue throughout that summer. Helped by a marked decline in the number of really violent films, the Board found its decisions largely unchallenged. It was to be a case which had its origins in another medium that brought the subject back to the front pages.

The stage show *Oh! Calcutta!* had opened in New York in June 1969 and in London a year later. It had been devised by Kenneth Tynan, then literary advisor of the National Theatre, ostensibly to fill the gap between burlesque and the night club: 'it occurred to me that there was no place for a civilised man to take a civilised woman to spend an evening of civilised erotic stimulation'. The critics did not take kindly to civilization and dismissed the show as a weak cocktail of feeble sketches, schoolboy humour and poor taste, laced with too much nudity and not enough wit and imagination. Some commentators were more severe. Senator Keating, writing in the Obscenity Commission Report, called it 'pure pornography, a two hour orgy' and complained that 'never in Rome, Greece, or the most debauched nation in history has such utter filth been projected to all parts of a nation. If there is or ever was any such thing as public decency these actions offend it.'[23]

There were those in this country who agreed with the Senator. Sir Gerald Nabarro tabled a Commons motion calling for Government action and the V.A.L.A. and Festival of Light campaigned to have the show stopped. A complaint was referred to the Director of Public Prosecutions, but after the script had been studied and the theatre visited by members of Scotland Yard's Obscene Publications squad, he declined to take action. The Attorney-General refused to allow a private prosecution, and the show triumphantly transferred from the Round House to the

Royalty Theatre. Not surprisingly, *Oh! Calcutta!* became a re-sounding financial success, and arrangements were soon being made in America to immortalize the show on celluloid so that civilized stimulation might be offered to a wider, and more profitable, audience. The resulting film was no more nor less than a video-recording of the New York version of the revue. As such it was calculated to cause considerable embarrassment to authorities in this country. By the time the film arrived here the play had been running unmolested and without any apparent undue consequence for over two years. Yet the film version presented more nudity and stronger language than anything that had at this time been certificated. If passed, it would create precedents with far-reaching ramifications. As Murphy commented at the time: 'If we accept the material contained in *Oh! Calcutta!*, then we must revise a considerable number of judgements over the past two or three years, both in respect of films we have rejected and of cuts we have made.'

The Board, in fact, were in no difficulty over the film. They had no doubt that most local authorities would reject it on the grounds of taste, and, so long as the play was confined to London, their position was impregnable. Nor indeed had Tigon, the distributing company, expected a Board certificate: their target was the G.L.C. whose defences were obviously less secure. Before a film can be submitted to local authorities, however, it is the practice that it is first seen by the Board, and *Oh! Calcutta!* was accordingly viewed, and unhesitatingly rejected by the Board in October 1972. One examiner estimated that of the twelve sketches which constitute the film, two were acceptable, two were borderline cases and the remaining eight were beyond what could be permitted. The distributors immediately applied to the G.L.C. for a local certificate. Councillor Illtydd Harrington summed up one view of the awkward position in which the council found itself: 'If we are supposed to ban on film scenes you can see live on the West End stage, the G.L.C. committee is in a ridiculous position.'

The film viewing sub-committee saw the film on 9th December and a 7–6 vote reflected the opinion that, while the picture was unacceptable as it stood, a cut version might be passed. Early the following month a revised version was submitted and accepted by a majority of 6–4 on the grounds that it was 'sufficiently in-offensive to merit a showing'. Mark Patterson, the committee chairman, defending the decision, declared that 'far too many critics of our sub-committee's decisions base their opinions on hearsay and gossip'. Fittingly, a member of the council who had not seen the film but who was stirred by the 'weight of public opinion' (apparently represented by twelve letters), invoked a standing order under which a sub-committee decision must be reconsidered by the 'appointing body' if eight council members so wish.

Accordingly the film was referred to the full council and an instant and vigorous campaign was launched by the Viewers and Listeners Association and the Festival of Light in an attempt to influence the verdict. This effort was led by G.L.C. councillor Frank Smith who argued that 'we must protect people from the evils' represented by this 'debased series of filthy sketches', adding that the council had received protests from 'ordinary church people everywhere'. Pressure was also being brought by Raymond Blackburn, ex-barrister and former M.P., who threatened to prosecute Patterson for aiding and abetting a common law crime, and to bring proceedings against the G.L.C. restraining them from 'authorising or purporting to authorise the commission of an illegal public nuisance'.

Reviewing the G.L.C. meeting that decided the fate of the film, the *Guardian* reported that 'it was clear that councillors had been subjected to an unprecedented letter-writing and lobbying campaign. Interventions from the public gallery became so pronounced that the chairman threatened to bar the public from the meeting.' In the event the sub-committee's verdict was reversed by a substantial majority (62–30), and *Oh! Calcutta!* remained unseen until the G.L.C. reversed its decision in 1974.[24]

This rejection of the sub-committee's decision clearly undermined its autonomy and forced the chairman to describe his position as 'fairly uncomfortable'. It seemed certain that the committee would be forced to revise its traditionally liberal policies which had always been based on the assumption that London constituted a particularly sophisticated audience. As a result it had been common practice in the past for the B.B.F.C. to use the G.L.C. as a sort of court of appeal. Borderline films would be seen by the viewing committee and, if passed, reactions to the film in London could be used as guidance by the Board. If the full council continued to have its way this function could no longer be fulfilled and the Board would become the final arbiter. This increase in responsibility was by no means welcome in Soho Square, particularly as the Government was announcing proposals to do away with cinema clubs at this time.

Thus the Board's two lines of defence were simultaneously threatened, with the result that its burden seemed certain to be increased at a time when its reputation and morale had barely recovered from the battering of the previous twelve months. Murphy's period of 'probation' was now officially ended, but his position was by no means secure.

Despite this, in November Murphy took the bold step of finally passing *Trash*, subject to cuts totalling three-and-a-half minutes. Jimmy Vaughan, the film distributor, was delighted at this 'victory' in his 'two year battle with the censor', but he promptly made further cuts in the film, supposedly designed to eradicate 'longueurs'. These cuts did, however, include the removal of close shots of heroin injecting, the loss of which undoubtedly diluted the anti-drug message of the film.[25] Unfortunately, by this time, interest in Warhol, which had been stimulated by the showing of *Flesh* two years before, had evaporated—as Murphy had assumed. Vaughan's victory looked as though it might not be measurable in cash, until a fortuitous series of events suddenly turned the cult figure of Andy Warhol into a household name. An injunction preventing the showing on television of David Bailey's documentary on Warhol attracted wide attention, so that Warhol's own work, which had never been popular with a mass audience, became the focus of widespread fascination. *Trash* was the obvious beneficiary. Despite attempts by Councillor Smith to persuade the G.L.C. to ban the film it opened to large audiences on 8th February. As it happened this success was short-lived, for the film could not match its publicity, while the broadcasting on 27th March of Bailey's programme, which was judged to be more boring than sensational, rapidly killed off the interest which its banning had done so much to create.

Meanwhile the media had been carefully incubating a new scandal. Bernardo Bertolucci's *Last Tango in Paris* had provoked wide comment abroad. Pauline Kael, reviewing its New York première, had called it 'a landmark in movie history' : in Paris it had opened simultaneously in seven cinemas. The popular press in Britain avidly seized on the film as the next sensational censorship issue. From mid-December 1972 until the opening of the film in London on 15th March, 1973, an extraordinary amount of space was devoted to this 'deeply corrupting film'.[26]

The *Sunday Mirror* had seen the potential of the story long before there was even a copy of the film in this country. Their correspondent had summarized the plot as follows: 'Brando, hung up over wife's suicide, meets sex-hungry colonel's daughter. Their minds click. He seduces her in five minutes flat. Then follows a series of blistering sequences calculated to knock the bottom out of the backstreet porno film market.'[27] Besides betraying a touching ignorance of the content of real 'blue' films, this account hardly represents a fair indication of what the film contains. Nevertheless, the majority of the correspondents who carried on the story adopted a similar tone. Around this time press fascination with the media as news reached an amazing level, well exemplified by the issues of 6th February when the three main stories in the tabloids were the court verdict in the Warhol case, the union blacking of I.T.V. in response to the I.B.A.'s banning of a documentary about architect John Poulson, and further trivia about *Last Tango*.

Coverage continued in a generally lurid vein, reaching a new peak in the week when the censor's decision was finally made. Speculation about this decision was as frequent as it was ill-informed. The general impression conveyed throughout was of a Board desperately seeking a solution to an unusually difficult problem. In fact the film did not present a particularly intractable case. Murphy had seen the film first in December and had considered that it could be submitted complete. It was seen officially by the Board in the presence of Lord Harlech a week later, when only two scenes were singled out as being to any great extent difficult. The first was essentially a case of strong language married to a visual in which 'perversion' was implied but not shown. Since this scene represented the heart of the picture and could not be removed without severely damaging its meaning, no cut was called for. Less acceptable was the more visually explicit sodomy episode. Exception was taken to a shot in which Brando uses butter to lubricate his partner, and the Board recommended that this scene be considerably reduced. The film's distributors were quite prepared to take out the thirty feet demanded by the censors, but Alberto Grimaldi and Bertolucci, the producer and the director, were not happy with this decision. Eventually, after long negotiations between the censors and the film-makers, a compromise was reached. Murphy was prepared to admit that the requested cuts did damage the dialogue to a serious extent, and the success of the film in America and France, together with the collapse of attempts to prosecute it in Italy, suggested that the British censors were being unduly tough in comparison with authorities elsewhere. On the other hand, it was not an appropriate moment for Murphy to relent completely. *Oh! Calcutta!* had just been banned by the G.L.C. and *A Clockwork Orange* on its first release in the provinces had already been turned down by Hastings. In the end the cut was limited to half the original demand and the film was duly passed with an 'X' certificate.

The saturation press coverage had created the climate in which the film was to be judged. It was now generally thought of as a 'problem' picture, and this definition coloured all reactions to it. The anti-permissive lobby did not hesitate to take advantage of this situation, setting out their views in no uncertain terms as soon as the censors' decision had been announced. Mrs Whitehouse called for the resignation of Murphy and his whole Board on the grounds that they had been overcome by a bout of 'collective madness'; Raymond Blackburn threatened, and later initiated, legal proceedings (which he eventually withdrew); and the Festival of Light unveiled its plans to put pressure on the local authorities. This latter policy was guaranteed a measure of success. Councils were already aware of the film through press coverage, and a number needed little encouragement to demand that it be vetted before local exhibition could be allowed. Many announced immediately that they would not rely on the Board's decision, and some of these later rejected the film. Festival of Light pressure was a major factor in the banning of both *Last Tango* and *A Clockwork Orange* in places up and down the country. The reactions of the local authorities will be considered in more detail in a later chapter, but the important point is that the increasing number who were challenging B.B.F.C. certificates represented an equivalent diminution in the Board's authority. This further deterioration in the relationship between the censors and the local authorities seriously weakened the whole system which depends on agreement between these bodies.

Meanwhile the press at once started the search for the next sensation. Some tried to build up Pasolini's *Canterbury Tales* into an orgy of sex, although it in fact contained only three scenes which represented any censorship problem. Others suggested that the American film *Deep Throat* might be brought to this country. *Deep Throat* had become something of a cult in the States, where its production cost of £10,000 had been recouped more than a hundred times by the end of 1972. However, to imagine that this film bore any relationship to the sort of picture that had been causing problems in this country was patently absurd, for *Deep Throat* was unashamedly pornographic by almost any definition of that term, including numerous shots of detailed sexual acts. As Murphy commented cryptically, 'this is not the type of film likely to be submitted to the Board'.

Needless to say there *were* films that could have been built up in the same way as *Last Tango*, but which, for one reason or another, never generated this sort of publicity. *Portnoy's Complaint*, a faithful version of Philip Roth's celebrated novel, is an obvious example. In America its release caused a scandal. Here it passed almost unnoticed, despite the fact that its language was quite as forthright as that used in *Last Tango*. Yet it was the language as much as anything else that had been objected to in Bertolucci's picture. There is a clear conclusion to be drawn from from the fact that *Portnoy* made no money at all and disappeared without even a full release, while *Last Tango* received wide showing all over Britain and ran in London for many months. The difference in quality between the films was by no means the only factor. In addition, of course, London cinemas in particular were full of sex films of minimal quality which raised few objections, although many of them displayed more flesh and fewer morals than *Last Tango*.

The next serious challenge to the Board was to involve a very different sort of film. The comedy *No Sex Please, We're British* had presented the Board with a classification problem. The examiners generally favoured an 'A' certificate, but both Murphy and Lord Harlech were concerned about the subject matter (which revolved around pornographic books and films and included a scene in which two prostitutes play central parts) and insisted that an 'AA' was more appropriate. The distributors promptly applied to the G.L.C. pleading for an 'A'. When the film-viewing sub-committee saw it they astonished everyone by deciding on a 'U'.

The distributors were naturally alarmed at the confusion (and expense) arising from the need to advertise the film under different categories in different areas, and approached the Board for a reconsideration. Having heard that other authorities were intending to follow London's example, Murphy decided to compromise by changing the certificate to 'A' which the distributors were happy to accept.

This change of mind forced the Board to rethink a number of other concurrent decisions which in the light of the 'A' for *No Sex Please* now seemed anomalous. *Paper Moon* had been another film to divide the Board. Although passed for children throughout the world there were those who felt that the language was stronger than was traditionally allowed in junior certificates in this country. In fact there had been attacks on the film on these grounds in America, and the Board had eventually decided to adhere to its strict policy over films for children and insist on an 'AA'. Now this certificate seemed ridiculously severe and the decision was reversed after the removal of one or two of the swear-words (notably 'shit' which had also been taken out of *Live and Let Die*). *The Lovers, Don't Just Lie There*, and *Jeremy* were other pictures which benefited from this general review.

Murphy was determined that these concessions should not be seen as a change of policy, but as a necessity arising from a unique set of circumstances. While determined to retain the innocence of the 'A' and 'U' categories he felt that his hand was being forced by television which was now showing 'AA' material at all hours. In particular the popular 'Kung Fu' series was now showing on I.T.V. on Sunday afternoons (although it was later switched to an evening slot). The Board had, in fact, seen the pilot for this series as well as a number of other television shows before reaching these decisions. Despite this the examiners gave only reluctant support for the category changes, doubting the Board's ability, having given way once, to stand firm in the future. Their fears were amply justified.

Michael Winner, an outspoken critic of the Board, had now completed his film *Scorpio*. Essentially an unexceptionable spy thriller it included one scene which gave the Board grave concern. Burt Lancaster, in order to gain information, douses a potential informer with petrol and threatens him with a match. It was a vital episode that could not be cut in any way, but which the Board felt to be potentially dangerous. The fact that a similar case had just been reported in the press, and that this was the time of several large-scale fires (Summerland, Butlin's) and of the incendiary devices in London stores, ensured that this particular hazard was very much in the public mind.

Murphy felt that the film would have to be 'X' rated even though the rest of the story was not in this category. Winner promptly applied to the G.L.C. for reclassification, accusing the

Board of going into a 'panicky and tragic retreat' and of being 'grossly over-influenced by the vociferous minority who make it almost a profession to attack films'.[28] The G.L.C. clearly agreed for they gave *Scorpio* an 'A' certificate, a lead that was quickly followed by Brighton and Hertfordshire. Other authorities, however, rated it 'X' or 'AA' and the G.L.C.'s decision was attacked by film critic Alexander Walker :

> I am afraid Scorpio proves that our well-intentioned local authority has boobed badly in the matter of censorship ratings. I am all in favour of elected councillors giving the widest possible freedom to films that they have the legal power to censor. As wide, certainly, as books and plays that they have no legal power to censor. But the job of censorship is not a part-time one—still less one for amateurs. Even the professional censor has run into difficulties which the G.L.C.'s recent decision over *Scorpio* can only compound.

He concluded by deprecating such 'conflicts of authority that expose film censorship to ridicule and possibly children to risk'.[29]

Once again the Board was forced to rethink and to change its certificate (to 'AA', although the film continued to be shown as an 'A' in London). Giving way to pressures of this sort is undoubtedly the right course of action in theory. The Board should be open to persuasion that it has misjudged public opinion and should be prepared to admit its mistakes. Unfortunately in practice this is usually interpreted as weakness and lack of conviction, and probably leads to more criticism than the original wrong decision. Not that this is a new problem. As with all aspects of censorship the same ground had been trodden before, as the following passage, written in 1921, suggests. 'A recent case in which a film, after having been granted an "A" certificate, was, on the strength of newspaper clamour, "recalled" by the Board for "closer inspection" has certainly not enhanced the "dignity" or added to the sense of "detachment" with which the censor carries out his duties.'[30]

When this storm had abated, a period of relative calm followed. The various court cases described earlier not only consumed most of the energies of the anti-permissive lobby, but also worried the industry to the extent that it felt less inclined to attack the censor at a time when the courts seemed to be taking an even more restrictive line. The prosecution of *Last Tango in*

Paris, which continued through most of 1974, put a muzzle on most potential critics of the Board from the 'liberal' point of view. The very real possibility that a film passed by the censor might be found to contravene the Obscene Publications Act certainly stilled criticism of this sort from the industry, which still held that the Board's main duty was to protect them from legal action.

Nevertheless, two films were released in the latter half of the year that might have been expected to cause a stir. In fact both opened to exceptional business without any great public outcry. *Emmanuelle*, after being held up for political reasons in France, took over £2 million in its first six months when it did open there. Here, Penelope Houston noted that '*Emmanuelle*, at the 630-seater Prince Charles, racked up a bigger take in its first three weeks than *That's Entertainment*, showing simultaneously at the 1,645-seater Dominion and backed by star power, sympathetic reviews, and some old-fashioned drum-beating for big studio pretensions'.[31] *The Night Porter* had been unable to find a distributor until it was shown privately to six critics, five of whom were enthusiastic. It was then advertised as 'the most controversial film of our time' and became a commercial success, taking £100,000 in its first twelve weeks in the West End.

Murphy was thus able to contemplate retirement as 1974 drew to a close in the belief that 'after the terrible problems of 1970 and 1971 we have not come out too badly'. Yet two films submitted at around this time indicated how he had been forced to compromise the liberal hopes with which he had approached the job four years earlier. *Immoral Tales*, directed by Walerian Borowczyk, was rejected on the grounds that two of the episodes (involving fellatio and flagellation) were unacceptable, while *Life Size*, starring Michel Piccoli as a dentist with a fetish for life-sized dolls, was turned down although the examiners had agreed on cuts. It must at least be hypothesized that peace had been achieved through some measure of concession.

THE BRITISH BOARD OF
FILM CENSORS

T H E O F F I C E S O F the British Board of Film Censors occupy the second floor of No. 3 Soho Square, convenient premises within a few minutes of Wardour Street, the home of the film industry—but extremely modest when compared with the spacious block occupied by the equivalent American body. In fact the whole operation is carried out in two large offices, two small offices, a projection theatre, a projection room and a waiting room. The staff also is smaller than the imposing title might lead one to believe, consisting of the President, Secretary, four examiners, an accountant, two projectionists and two secretaries—a small enough body to maintain a high level of camaraderie.

As we have seen, the Board was originally created on the instigation of the trade associations. This fact has led to the frequent accusation that it is a body whose primary allegiance is to the industry, which can therefore exert considerable pressure which the Board is in no position to resist. In fact the Board has been independent from the start. We have already seen from the various warnings and advice offered by the Board to film-makers that even in its earliest days the Board took a far from humble view of its role. Indeed, it could with some justice be criticized for taking an excessively patronizing and holier-than-thou attitude towards what early Presidents clearly considered to be a somewhat vulgar trade.

The main tie was, and continues to be, a financial one, but a close inspection of the arrangement reveals this to be very much less suspect than might be imagined. A letter signed jointly by the Secretaries of the manufacturer's and exhibitors' associations explained how the final system of financing the Board was arrived at :

As formulated by the Manufacturers' Association, [the scheme] was submitted to the Renters'[1] and Exhibitors' Associations. The Renters' Association came to the conclusion that censorship was purely a matter which interested the manufacturers, and that body left it to be dealt with by the manufacturers as they thought best in the general interests of the trade. . . . A committee of three manufacturers, who will retire respectively at one, two and three years, will control the financial side of the organization, and this committee will be strengthened and supported by an equal number of representatives from the Exhibitors' Association.'[2]

In fact the exhibitors play no part, and financial responsibility has always rested solely with the Kinematograph Manufacturers' Association (K.M.A., later the I.A.K.M.). Originally this body, contrary to its title, included most of the important production companies but these soon left to join their own association so that the I.A.K.M. became purely a group concerned with the manufacture of cinema technology—with no direct interest in the business of censorship at all. Its importance has declined considerably since 1912, until now the overseeing of the Board's accounts is its only major duty. The Board's first Secretary, Brooke Wilkinson, was Secretary of the I.A.K.M. and subsequent Secretaries have also combined the roles.

The Board is non-profitmaking and relies for its income solely on sums charged for viewing films. Every film officially seen by the Board incurs a fee, so that the Board is financed by numerous small payments from a large number of different companies. There is, therefore, no direct pressure resulting from the economic structure, such as might arise if the Board received grants from any source. Sufficient income is generated to cover the running costs of the Board, by charging each film a fee related to its length. Present charges (introduced in January 1974) are a minimum fee of £4.40 for the first three minutes, 88p per minute for the following fifteen minutes and £13.20 for each subsequent period of fifteen minutes or less.[3] Thus a 100-minute feature is charged £103.80 (plus 8 per cent VAT and £7 to cover the cost of the actual certificate made up by National Screen Services). This process raises an annual sum in the region of £50,000 which is sufficient to cover salaries, rent, maintenance and replacement of projection and office equipment and other administrative expenses.

The I.A.K.M. has one other important function, for it is the body which formally appoints the President. At first no regular system for filling the post was adopted, but the two most recent Presidents have been appointed in roughly the same way, so it appears that a satisfactory method has been arrived at. Lord Morrison's name was proposed after discussions between the Secretary of the Board and the Chairman of the I.A.K.M. The latter recommended him to the I.A.K.M. council and after 'informal private consultation' with the Home Secretary and the associations of local authorities, to a joint committee of the film industry. Lord Harlech became President after a similar process, although the Secretary seems to have played a larger part. In this case at least it seems that former roles have been reversed and that the President was selected in great part on the initiative of the Secretary.

Trevelyan, it will be remembered, had been the first Secretary not to have been the personal appointee of the President. He had been appointed by a committee representing the I.A.K.M. and the other trade associations, after six applicants had been interviewed. This system seems to have been modified when a successor to Trevelyan was sought, for only one candidate was seen by this appointing committee who were therefore merely ratifying a decision already reached by the President, the retiring Secretary and the chairman of the I.A.K.M. In theory any appointment could be nullified by the Home Office, but the controversy that such an action would create makes this unlikely.

Trevelyan has described the problems of finding a suitable Secretary. It is a job that requires an assortment of talents, for not only must the Secretary have a wide knowledge of films combined with appreciation of the technical aspects of cutting and editing, but he must also have administrative abilities and the necessary public relations skill to handle the many different people and organizations interested in his work. Any person with the necessary experience in these fields would be asked to take a considerable cut in salary for accepting a job with very little security of tenure and no possibility of promotion. Similar difficulties are encountered in the selection of examiners. Vacancies have not been advertised on the grounds that it would result only in a large number of unsuitable applications. When a post *was* advertised in 1972 this assumption was justified, for the job was finally filled by the far from satisfactory use of personal contacts. A file of persons who have expressed interest in the Board is also kept, which is referred to when a position falls vacant. This informal system is possibly necessary, for the post of examiner is an unusual one.

In the first place the Board cannot offer a career as there is little possibility of promotion—only Trevelyan has been promoted from examiner to Secretary, while the Presidency seems to be a political appointment. Secondly, the conditions of employment are peculiar, for examiners work only three days a week (although they must be prepared to be called in on other days also), and are not highly paid. As a result it is a job which appeals most obviously to the semi-retired or the relatively young who may use it as a brief stepping-stone in a different career. Neither of these groups is entirely satisfactory for the Board's purposes, and a Board composed entirely of such people would certainly be unbalanced.

Nor are there any specific qualifications that are thought desirable. Indeed the official leaflet emphatically states that 'the Board does not seek to employ as examiners people with specialist qualifications, or people who represent organizations or professions'. They look for people who have a good educational background—normally a University degree—a sense of humour, an ability to work well with other people, and a love of films. It is an advantage if an examiner has had experience of working with children and young people, or a knowledge of one or more European languages and has travelled extensively.' Trevelyan adds that an examiner should have 'definite views but also the ability to compromise so that there could be a reconciliation between divergent views'.[4] Naturally this means that no examiner can hold an extreme opinion. No one in favour of complete abolition of censorship or supporting policies put forward by the Festival of Light could fit happily into this system. There is therefore a wide range only of moderate views. Furthermore, as we will see, the 'ability to compromise' means that examiners must not only be prepared to accept the decision of the majority, but also the decision of the minority if that minority includes the President or Secretary. As there is also a rule that examiners make few public statements and then only after having gained permission from above, it is clear that the role is neither powerful nor glamorous.

There seems to be only one definite prohibition with regard to appointments—that 'applicants who have had previous employment in the film industry are not normally accepted'. This may seem to be a very haphazard system but it is not easy to see a more satisfactory solution, although the Board's avoidance of people with specialist knowledge seems illogical. In Norway, for instance, it is a requirement that examiners not only display a deep knowledge of the cinema but also that they are versed in the social sciences.

Redford appointed four examiners in 1912 but this number has not remained constant. At one time there were as many as seven, while for some years there was a practice of employing part-time examiners who worked only one day a week, and in Trevelyan's time there were generally three full-time and two part-time examiners. It is now felt that the part-timer does not see enough films to be able to maintain a standard of judgement consistent with the rest of the Board, so there are, once again, four full-time examiners.

Every morning two examiners report for duty. They immediately retire to the Board's projection theatre where, throughout the morning and early afternoon, they watch the day's films, often in the company of the Secretary. A typical day's viewing would include two or three full-length feature films, one of which might already have been seen by the other examiners who wanted a second opinion on the picture, various reels of material re-submitted to check that the right cuts have been made, and a number of advertisements, shorts and trailers. A large part of each day's work is being seen for the second or third time, demanding close inspection of celluloid ranging from a few feet in length to whole films. This chore, together with the high percentage of poor quality exploitation films, makes the job considerably less appealing than might be imagined. Enthusiasm for the cinema is hard to maintain under these circumstances: on many days the films seen are no more entertaining or less repetitive than the average material inspected by any quality control department. A full day of confrontation with a series of German sex 'comedies', for instance, is not a happy experience. There is also a good deal of paperwork to be done after the day's viewing is over.

All films to be exhibited in public cinemas in Britain must be examined by the Board, with the exception of the fast-disappearing newsreel. To cope with this, between four and six hours of film is looked at every day. The great bulk of this is seen on the premises, a system which has the great advantage of convenience and speed, but also some drawbacks. The size of the screen is an obvious problem, for it measures only 8ft 6in by

4ft 6in, smaller even than those in the proliferating mini-cinemas. The examiners are well aware that much of the power of certain scenes may be lost when they are projected in such circumstances. On the one hand, it may make it difficult to evaluate the qualities of a film that is designed specifically for a large screen; on the other, reduced size fails to convey the extremes of violence now sometimes to be seen, so that examiners are taken aback to discover that a film that had seemed mild in the theatre, appears much stronger when blown up several times. The lack of audience reaction in the very unnatural atmosphere of the viewing theatre is another handicap, while the high sound volume customary in many cinemas can appear to intensify violence.

Occasionally films are seen elsewhere. The Board's projection equipment cannot deal with all types of film, so that some (e.g. 70mm prints) have to be examined where there is the necessary hardware. Sometimes distributors refuse to let a print out of their hands or claim to be able to project it better, and on rare occasions the only opportunity to see a film is at a press show, although this hardly provides conditions suited to the needs of the examiners.

While watching each film, the examiners make copious detailed notes, summarizing the plot reel by reel and documenting all passages that might present 'difficulties' with particular thoroughness. As early as possible a decision is made about which category seems most appropriate—although this decision may have to be revised if the film changes its character later on. The theory is that nearly all films have a 'natural' category into which they fall, presumably corresponding with the audience which the film-makers had in mind during production. At present there are four such categories :

'U'—Passed for General Exhibition.
'A'—Passed for General Exhibition but parents/guardians are advised that the film contains material they might prefer children under fourteen years not to see.
'AA'—Passed as suitable only for exhibition to persons of fourteen years and over. When a programme includes an 'AA' film, no person under fourteen years can be admitted.
'X'—Passed as suitable for exhibition to adults. When a programme includes an 'X' film no person under eighteen years can be admitted.

If a film is acceptable for one of these classes, a form is completed which notes the name and length of the film, the name of the distributing company,[5] the initials of the examiners concerned and the proposed certificate. This form is filed and the details transferred to a monthly sheet which lists all films passed by the Board and which is circulated to all interested bodies. A second form is sent to the distributor who checks that all details are correct and returns it with the fee, whereupon a certificate is issued.

Very often it is thought that the feeling and nature of a film make it suitable for one category but that one or two scenes require trimming before it can be accepted. The Board clearly prefers to cut a film to fit the 'right' category, rather than simply to award it a more restrictive certificate in its complete form. Nor, unlike their American equivalents, are the censors eager to cut films for a junior certificate if an 'X' or an 'AA' seems more apt. In the end, however, this sort of decision finally rests with the distributor who can reject cuts and opt for a senior category or ask the Board to cut for a junior one.

Occasionally a film is submitted that presents particular difficulties. Sometimes the two examiners cannot agree on the 'right' category for a picture, or on the extent of cuts necessary to make a film acceptable. As soon as such a situation arises, or if the film raises more profound questions, it is seen by the other examiners and by the Secretary. It is then discussed in detail, and usually a general agreement is reached. If not, or if the film raises questions of policy, the President is called in. His decision carries very great weight, and is usually, but not necessarily, final. In certain circumstances, experts may be asked for guidance on certain points, particularly with regard to medical and psychiatric problems.

If cuts are required, detailed specifications are sent to the distributors on an 'exception slip', for, contrary to popular belief, the Board does not cut film itself. Cutting is, in fact, a highly skilled operation, and achieving a cut that will not be noticed by the public is no easy task. The job is always done either by print managers employed by the distributors or by the filmmakers themselves, for there are often complex technical problems to be overcome. For instance the visual and sound tracks do not coincide on celluloid : one runs several frames ahead of the other because they are 'read' at different places in the projector. Consequently one cannot cut straight across the film without chaotic results. If there is a musical accompaniment the problems are increased for any cuts will cause havoc with the soundtrack, while a visual cut may mean the loss of an essential piece of dialogue and vice versa. In theory these are not problems that should concern the Board, but in practice they cannot be ignored. It is distressing enough when cuts destroy the rhythm of a sequence, but considerably worse if they render the plot incomprehensible or result in characters apparently 'jumping' from one spot to another. The Board does its best to take account of these factors, and it is by no means rare for cuts to be waived simply because they present insuperable technical problems.

The exception slip itemizes every change required by the censors, and is an important document in all subsequent negotiations for there is a gentleman's agreement that the Board will not ask for further cuts, unless the slip specifically states that it is referring only to 'minimum' cuts, implying that others may be requested. The following fictitious exception slip was actually prepared for the information of the Hong Kong Government Office, and gives a fair indication of the form and content of a typical slip :

Film : The Heat and the Hate
Stupendous Productions Inc.   16th March, 1973
Reel 1. The scene in which Jonathan is making love to Angela must stop before any suggestion of fellatio.
Reel 3. There is no need for the repeated knife-blows : cut out all but the establishing shot.
Reel 4. The fight between Jonathan and Timothy must be substantially reduced : in particular removing all kicks to the crotch and close shots of injuries inflicted by broken bottle.
Reel 5. All shots of Timothy using a whip on Samantha to be removed.

When cuts have been made, the revised version must be sent to the Board to ensure that all that was required has been done. Films are usually checked by at least one of the original examiners, and if, as often happens, it is felt that less has been taken out than was demanded, the process is repeated. At any stage the distributor or film-maker may object to the Board's requests, whereupon a dialogue with the Secretary ensues. This may consist of no more than a brief telephone call, or it may be a series of meetings over a period of weeks or even months. A very large part of the Secretary's time is occupied by negotiations of this sort, and in most cases a solution is found. Given that there are no hard and fast rules governing the operation of censorship, there is naturally much room for manoeuvre in these arrangements. The Board operates a system of case-law based on the many thousands of decisions made over the years. Since this case-law is not open to study by outsiders, it is clear that the advantage lies largely with the censor. Distributors and producers may argue on the basis of those few recent cases of which they are aware, but such a hand holds few aces. Occasionally the Board is prepared to accept a compromise, but more often the distributor has to step down and either accept the Board's decision or take his film to the local authorities or the club circuits. Total deadlock, however, is rare.

Often distributors and film-makers disagree with the certificate that has been awarded and attempt to induce the Board to change their view. This the Board is generally unwilling to do, unless it was in two minds over the decision in the first place. Occasionally a film is made which does not seem to fall happily into any one category. *The Life and Times of Judge Roy Bean* was one such. The Board was inclined to feel that it was 'AA' material, but director John Huston, producer John Foreman and the Cinerama distributing company were determined to seek an 'A'. Accordingly, after lengthy bargaining, a reduced version was passed. *Our Miss Fred*, a vehicle for Danny La Rue, was another which presented a problem of this sort. The Board wanted to cut slightly for an 'A', but the distributors refused and accepted an 'AA'. On release this version was a commercial failure and the cuts were eventually acceded to. *No Sex Please, We're British* was another example with, as we have seen, unhappy consequences for the Board.

Any film rejected by the Board may be submitted for local certification and it is the usual practice for authorities thus approached to consult the Board, which is always prepared to explain its decision and provide any other relevant information. Any film may be resubmitted to the Board after a suitable lapse in time and this is particularly likely to happen if a number of authorities have given favourable verdicts, for the Board takes local decisions into account as an important reflection of public opinion. In general, however, the Board does not wish to give the impression that it has no standards of its own, and is rarely keen to reverse a decision unless some time has passed. Thus *The Wild Angels*, turned down in 1966, was not certificated until 1972, and then only in a cut version.

The Secretary also communicates with local authorities in other ways. As often as possible he meets councillors to explain the Board's work and hear about local grievances. He also spends a lot of his time talking to other people involved in censorship, from film-makers, producers and distributors on the one hand, to censors from abroad and members of pressure groups on the other. In this way he hears a broad cross-section of viewpoints and is often able to deal with potential problems before they have become serious. It is partly because such a large part of the Board's work is done through informal discussions of this sort that the Secretary necessarily occupies an all-powerful position in the running of the office. The examiners and even the President have much less contact with this side of censorship.

One task that is shared by Secretary and examiners is that of script-reading, but unlike the P.C.A. in America this is no longer an important aspect. In the past over a hundred scripts a year were read and commented on by the Board, but this number is now much reduced, although some companies still find it helpful to have projects vetted at script stage. A major problem that possibly accounts for the decline in script-reading arises from the great speed with which public attitudes, and consequently, censorship decisions, have changed in recent times. It is often a number of years from first script stage to the finished picture, so that advice given early on can be meaningless by the time of final submission. As an example, it might be noted that an early script of *A Clockwork Orange*, written by Terry Southern, arrived on Trevelyan's desk in 1967, when he described it as 'most unlikely to be shown in this country'. Many other projects that would have been discouraged at that time, would now cause no trouble at all.

In any case advice given at script stage is never offered as more than guidance. The right is reserved to take a different line if necessary with the finished film, and it is on the basis of the film alone that final decisions are taken. Script approval is no guarantee of eventual certification. Nor does the Board offer detailed written hints to film-makers about what to avoid. This is partly because contemporary standards are too fluid to be captured in any list of 'Dos and Don'ts', partly because the Board does not seek to apply a rigidly consistent set of standards.

The Board actually makes very few public statements about its work. Its policies can only be discovered by a study of decisions and how they are reached. A rare account of its official policy was made recently in the form of an 'aide-memoire' to the Longford Committee. This is worth quoting for the light it sheds on the Board's view of its own role.

The story of the origins of the British Board of Film Censors is a complicated one. Its current function—as compared with its strictly legal situation—is clear. The power of censorship is in the hands of local authorities. The B.B.F.C. exists to act as an intermediary between local authorities and the film industry. Its success or failure can be measured simply in terms of the acceptability of its judgements to the majority of local authorities in Britain. If it moves too far in advance of public taste—as reflected in the local authorities—they will cease to accept its judgements. If it lags behind, it will lose its influence over the film industry : no production or distribution company is going to amend a film at the Board's request if it knows that, simply by showing the film to individual local authorities or to groups of local authorities, it can have it exhibited in its original form. . . .

As the cinema seeks to readjust to its changed social position, following the spread of television, more and more films present problems to the Board. Nevertheless, it must be reiterated that the Board's decisions seem, by and large, acceptable to local authorities on the one hand and to the industry on the other. It is this general acceptance which has enabled it, during the last four or five years, occasionally to certificate a film of merit which falls beyond the limits it would accept in films of lesser calibre. In this way, without losing the confidence of most local authorities, or the film industry, the Board can test reactions of the cinema-going public (which tends to be much younger and possibly more tolerant than the public at large. It has been estimated that more than 60 per cent of the cinema-going public is between the ages of sixteen and twenty-five). It seems likely that the current polarization of public attitudes will increase, rather than diminish, the number of 'controversial' decisions to be made by the Board, though so far only one film, *The Devils*, has aroused any detectable measure of protest, in the form of complaints to the Board, complaints to local authorities, or complaints to cinema-managers. Most protest, whether in favour of a film denied a certificate, or against a film granted one, seems to be generated by the press.

These 'controversies' have led some critics to suggest that film censorship is no longer desirable : it has led others to suggest stricter censorship. It is the Board's view that film censorship at its present level should continue, and that the controversy over, say, half a dozen films a year, amounting normally to no more than 1 per cent of the films viewed, certificated, cut or 'banned' would not justify the abolition, or even the modification of a system which seems to gain broad general acceptance. The Board would never claim to be infallible in judgements. It does claim to perform a useful social service conscientiously.

This brief outline raises a number of points. In the first place, there is the ambiguity surrounding the Board's position as 'intermediary' between the industry and the public. Originally there was no problem : the Board was unashamedly a creation of the industry, designed to prevent the spread of local intervention. Almost at once, however, the 'monster' had assumed a mind of its own, refusing to be a mere tool of its creators. In fact the Board rapidly developed an air of superiority, regarding the industry as a highly suspect body of entrepreneurs whose chief interest was in making money, an assessment that was not wholly in error. At the same time there was no question of attending to public opinion which was regarded with some contempt.

It is only comparatively recently that the Board has modified standards which have traditionally been stricter than the local authorities have demanded. Some commentators have compared the undogmatic pragmatism of the British system with the rigidity of the American. Actually, there has been little difference between them. The Production Code Administration was always prepared to bend its own rules to the extent that the Code was probably more flexible than the unwritten rules of the Board. In any case O'Connor's forty-three rules were recorded permanently enough in black and white to give lie to the claim never to have had a code.

At the same time there has been a consistent effort to play down the role of protector of the industry, emphasizing instead the desire to reduce activity to the minimum demanded by the public. Even Watkins used to argue that an examiner should

have 'a healthy dislike of censorship'. The main problem now
therefore is how to estimate what the public wants. This task is
increasingly difficult as it becomes clearer that there is little
agreement on this. Murphy has commented that 'in Britain, as in
many other countries, there was—until a few years ago—a public
consensus of what is, and what is not, acceptable. That consensus is no longer as strong as it was'. Such a point of view
probably overestimates the extent of agreement in the past: it
seems likely that it is more realistic to argue that a wider range
of opinions has always existed and is now becoming more evident.
In addition Murphy is confident there has not been as comprehensive a breakdown of accepted values as study of the press
and other commentators might lead one to believe. He is sure that,
despite the loud voices of vocal minorities, a strong measure of
consensus still remains.

A major difficulty is the inadequacy of the Board's ability to
judge this consensus. Even the most controversial issue elicits
only a handful of correspondence, all of it of an extreme nature.
Board members attend and address public meetings up and down
the country and see films in public cinemas as often as possible,
but this hardly leads to a deep understanding of the reactions of
a cross-section of the public. As a rule, the Board can only
assume that because 99 per cent of the population does not object
to 99 per cent of its decisions, that it is taking the right road, but
this is not necessarily a correct deduction. In any case, it is not
really the public who judge the Board's work, but the local
authorities and there is no reason for believing that they are any
better informed of public feelings about film censorship than the
film censors themselves.

The Board, therefore, faces a dilemma. It must retain the
confidence of an industry which is being forced by circumstances
to produce increasingly 'difficult' material. At the same time it
must ensure that their products are acceptable to local authorities a number of whom are growing more militant and demanding more censorship (although the G.L.C. calls for less). While
the cinema-going public, which consists largely of young people
escaping from the family-oriented material presented on television, reacts favourably to 'permissive' films, pressure groups
campaign energetically to ban these very pictures. All the while
the press lies in wait for any controversial or inconsistent decision, demanding stricter control one day, less censorship the next.

What considerations then are in the censors' minds as they

strive to walk this precarious tightrope? Essentially the Board attempts to do three things. Firstly it must operationalize the local authorities' statutory duty to protect children. Secondly, it keeps watch for anything that might 'deprave or corrupt' or have any undesirable influence or effect upon audiences. Thirdly, it tries to judge public taste and to protect audiences from material that would be greatly and gratuitously offensive to a large number of people. Its certification policy acts as a public information service, giving people some idea of what to expect in any given category. In the next chapter we will consider how this policy is put into practice.

THE BOARD AT WORK

THE B.B.F.C. HAS always been very much a reflection of its officers. In recent years the Secretary has been the major influence, particularly during the years of Trevelyan's relatively enlightened dictatorship. Yet there are also very powerful constraints on the Board's ability to shape its own policy. The pressures applied by the local authorities, the law and the public necessarily limit the extent to which the Board is autonomous. This lack of freedom has never been more evident than in the first years of Stephen Murphy's term.

His television background inclined him to seek to implement three major beliefs about how a body such as the Board should be run. In the first place he was determined to continue the liberal approach of Trevelyan's latter years. Unlike his predecessor he had had personal experience of working creatively within the media, and his career as a producer naturally gave him understanding of and sympathy for film-makers. Even as a television censor he had been employed by the I.T.A. which was inevitably more liable to see the producers' point of view than those of critics from outside the industry. An early interview indicates that he foresaw his role partly in terms of protecting film-makers from those who desired repression. 'The paradox about this job is that if the much-publicized Puritan backlash continues to gather force and strength our responsibility here could become to fight for more freedom for creative people rather than to act in a restrictive capacity.'[1]

Circumstances have not enabled him to carry on this fight as extensively as he would have liked. The Board must always take its cues from other situations and events rather than be a leader of opinion as envisaged in Murphy's comment. Unlike the B.B.C., for instance, the Board's status and position does not allow it to move ahead of public opinion, for the film industry has little inclination, let alone duty, to educate. It continues to see itself, and is seen as, primarily, an entertainment medium which must respond to the demands of its audience.

Murphy's liberal policy was also inhibited by the failure of the second part of his approach. In his own account he came to the post 'with a kind of Wilsonian concept that, in the twentieth century, censorship could only be justified if it was openly conducted and our decisions publicly defended'. As we have seen his attempts to break down the secrecy which surrounded the Board's work quickly ran into trouble. In part this was due to his own inexperience. In television he had never been exposed to public view and criticism and he underestimated the difficulties of handling this aspect of his new job. Allied with his misfortune in being plunged straight into controversy, this naivety proved disastrous. His efforts to inform the public debate about his decisions proved counter-productive. Instead of generating wider understanding of the Board's predicament his public performances and statements merely added fuel to the fire and escalated his problems. His belief that he could use the press to put across his view of how film censorship should be handled was dashed, as his remarks were used simply to stimulate sensation. His television appearances demonstrated that he was no match for the more experienced practitioners whom he faced. As he ruefully commented later, he learned 'long and bitterly that we can operate more flexibly, and that more justice can be done, without the press around one's neck the whole time'.

His stumbling was thrown into sharp relief by comparison with his predecessor's brilliance in this respect. Trevelyan, while never seeking publicity, had always obtained it when it was necessary and had handled it with statesmanlike aplomb. His wealth of experience in public life and his years as an examiner, when he had been able to study the problems of running such an office, enabled him to establish a happy relationship with the press, a foundation upon which he was then able to build, so that when controversy arose he was master of the situation. Murphy lacked this rare ability, while his policy deliberately exposed him to the sort of attack which he was ill-equipped to face: 'I made the early mistake of seeking publicity to justify our decisions and attitudes. It has since been my experience that, while I continue to cultivate personal relationships with the press, and while I continue to give background information to those journalists whom I trust, I say as little as I can for publication and quotation. By and large, my experience has been that press hysteria wears itself out, and that stories, however inaccurate, tend to die if they are not kept alive by denial and counter-denial.'

The third element in Murphy's approach was the belief in a more democratic structuring of the Board than Trevelyan had favoured. Here again experience soon demonstrated that this was easy to advocate in theory, harder to put into practice. The industry has grown accustomed to the Secretary dominating the Board and is, not unreasonably, suspicious of too much power accruing to examiners whose names and qualities remain secret. In any case the whole operation of the Board is geared to a system in which the Secretary makes the major day-to-day decisions and carries the can in the event of criticism. Unless the whole way in which the Board functions is fundamentally altered it is impossible effectively to transfer power away from the Secretary. Whether he likes it or not, he is the boss. Murphy has tried to draw his examiners more into the process of decision-making, but the success of such a policy is severely limited in a situation when it is the Secretary who has to defend all decisions in public and to become the sole butt of all criticism. Given this state of affairs it is hardly surprising if the Secretary is loath to give way on any major point.

As a result Murphy's efforts to change the Board have achieved little. It remains an essentially autocratic institution in which authority resides almost entirely with its two officers. Nor has Murphy's more intellectual leaning enabled him to introduce any more logic into censorship than already existed. An element of the irrational is endemic in any procedure which involves a good deal of decision making 'according to the seat of my pants' as Murphy admits is the case. The problem is exacerbated by the need to consider a wide variety of other pants, from those of the law and the local authorities to those of the man in the street. All this 'evidence' must be weighed up in an area in which so many terms (such as obscenity, pornography, eroticism, violence, etc.) are ill-defined.

The basic tenet that underlies all policy is that the Board 'makes no claim to set itself up as a guardian of public morality. It seeks, rather, to reflect intelligent, contemporary public attitudes.' Every effort is made to find out what the public thinks. Research and opinion polls are studied, public meetings are attended, comparisons with other media are made, but in the end it is largely a matter of the Board making personal judgements backed up by its knowledge of hundreds of previous decisions.

Table 1 below shows the results of the Board's deliberations in recent years. The changing nature of the cinema is clearly reflected, for, despite increased liberalization, an ever-growing proportion of films falls into the more restrictive categories.

TABLE 1   FILMS SUBMITTED: 1954–74

Year	Certificate				Rejected	Footage (in millions of feet)
	U	A	AA (Introd. 1970)	X (Introd. 1951)		
1954	347	154		28	8	5.1
1958	261	197		71	12	4.9
1962	171	168		102	15	3.9
1966	132	114		111	13	3.7
1967	130	133		112	14	3.7
1968	99	124		169	11	4.0
1969	91	114		219	18	4.2
1970	104	84	77	212	23	4.4
1971	98	76	77	228	22	4.4
1972	78	81	77	221	27	3.9
1973	62	84	82	249	29	4.2
1974	72	82	94	266	22	4.4

In fact these statistics overestimate the number of 'U' films, for each episode of serials (however short) is counted as an individual feature. The apparently regular increase in films rejected is also misleading. For one thing there had also been a high incidence of rejections in the twenties and thirties, but this statistic is, in any case, virtually meaningless unless one can also consider the number of films not submitted at all. The majority of rejections still fall into the sex-exploitation category in which the number turned down is simply a reflection of the number submitted. The major distributors rarely purchase a film that cannot be passed in some form.

The extent to which the Board influences imports can be judged by the fact that the Australian censors are said to have seen 500 martial arts films. The Board's severity on oriental violence has meant that only a small proportion of these ever reached this country. In a similar way British production is controlled. The Board's reaction to what it feared to be the beginning of a spate of cheaply made sex films discouraged the realization of many embryo productions.

These examples illustrate how the Board is as often concerned with trends as with individual judgements. Disagreements with local authorities quite often arise when the latter view one example of a currently fashionable genre and see no reason for the censors' harshness. The explanation may well be that the Board has become concerned on an overall level. It felt, for instance, that the flood of martial arts pictures was introducing an unacceptable volume of violence : each film was rated according to the general context of the cinema at that particular moment. Thus the Board sees itself as conducting 'a continuous control operation, giving a general idea of what we will accept'.

Table 1 has shown the extent to which the cinema has become an adult medium, but it cannot indicate how many films were passed in their original form. This is the function of Table 2. The relatively small amount of cutting in the junior certificates indicates that most films fall into one or other of these categories without much trouble. Contrary to the intentions of the Board when it revised the categories in 1970, it is the 'X' certificate film that is still subject to heavy cutting. Half the films passed in this category have had something removed at the insistence of the B.B.F.C.

TABLE 2   FEATURE FILMS CUT: 1970–4

Year	Total films passed	Total films cut	'X' films passed	'X' films cut
1970	477	167	212	98
1971	479	165	228	111
1972	457	179	221	126
1973	477	201	249	148
1974	514	218	266	169

It is less easy to give statistics on the types of cut that are made, but Table 3 is a tentative attempt based on the Board's records for 1973. Cuts may vary in length from a few frames to whole scenes and a small number of films contribute a large proportion of the cuts demanded. In 1973, for instance, a number of 'martial arts' films were subjected to heavy cutting of violence. The table does at least illustrate how 'sex' and 'violence' or a combination of the two, remain the Board's chief preoccupations even when the 'X' certificate is being considered. These will be discussed a little later but let us turn our attention to the first of the three main considerations mentioned at the end of the previous chapter—the duty to protect children.

TABLE 3   CUTS MADE BY THE BOARD IN X-RATED FILMS
DURING 1973

Number of cuts made on average each month	Reason for cut	Number of films involved
22.4	Sex	6.1
29.4	Violence	7.2
5.8	Sex and violence	2.9
2.1	Offensive dialogue	1.2
1.9	Bad taste	1.1
0.4	Drug use	0.4

This is probably the least controversial of the Board's activities, and the one with which it is least equipped to deal. Even the majority of those who oppose censorship for adults favour some form of protection for children, for there is little doubt that some films can be frightening or worrying and possibly even harmful to young people. The vast majority of parents undoubtedly welcome the classification system. It is sometimes argued that no body should have the right to take parental decisions and that this is a private matter between parent and child, but such an argument takes no account of the fact that few parents have the time or inclination to discover which films might be suitable for their offspring.

The 'U' certificate is issued to films to which no parent could possibly object and to which anyone over the age of five may be admitted (except in London where the minimum age is seven). Control over this category has tightened since the reorganization of the classification system in 1970. Before that date the 'A' certificate excluded all unaccompanied children. Now that it has reverted to an advisory status, many films that might have been accepted as 'U' are rated 'A' instead. The 'U' certificate is thus reserved for entirely unexceptionable films, sometimes to an almost absurd degree. A shot of a poster advising about V.D. in a documentary sponsored by the Coal Board was removed recently, although similar advertisements can be seen on the underground and elsewhere.

If there is any doubt at all, an 'A' is given, warning parents that the film contains something that *might* worry them. Sex and violence are kept to an absolute minimum and will only be allowed if essential to the plot. Bad language is also severely restricted. 'A' films are usually permitted only the most commonly used terms (bloody, etc.) and then not in profusion, although in rare cases some allowance is made for films which depend on realism, and which therefore cannot avoid some swearing. This is an area in which the Board has found it hard to maintain its standard. The increasing use of bad language, even in films made for children, has forced some concessions to be made.

Murphy is openly puritanical over the 'junior' certificates, and a small part of the decline in the number of films in these categories may be assigned to his determination that children's films will be beyond reproach. A particular concern is that young people might be inclined to imitate behaviour on the screen. There have been cases of children seriously injuring themselves copying Batman and other heroes, and there is little that can be done about this, but the Board endeavours to remove anything that might encourage dangerous imitation. Names of poisons are kept out of films appealing to children, and the details of crimes committed by minors are kept obscure whenever possible. The Board disapproves of scenes that include behaviour like shoplifting made to seem easy and natural, and any use of easily available weapons by children is discouraged. Sequences in which children are violently threatened by adults are also frowned upon, while any films that deal with problems of mental health are not considered suitable for young audiences at all. The grounds for this inflexible ban are not clear, but there is a historical explanation in terms of the Board's traditional anxiety about mental disturbance. For many years the subject was denied even to adults.

Two problems arise over this strict classification policy. Firstly it is possible to argue that children are being overprotected; that in ensuring that children are defended from material that *might* disturb them, the Board is also denying them access to ideas.

Is it true that children cannot handle anything more demanding than the sort of bland entertainment that makes up the bulk of the 'U' and 'A' categories? In America there has been a conscious effort to restrict children to films that do not stimulate the mind in an unconventional way. The recently retired head of the Rating Administration there made his attitude very clear. The 'C' category (equivalent to our 'U') should, in his opinion, only include films in which 'there is a clear, both implicit and explicit, definition of right and wrong. In this regard, the broadly practised social mores are not challenged.' In addition, violence must only be represented 'as a force in the service of law and order' and sex must be presented only 'within the context of a loving relationship'. Yet, despite this attitude the American certificates are much less restrictive than ours. Films like *Bonnie and Clyde* and *The Go-Between* were passed as suitable for children.

It is debatable whether it is desirable that children should be presented with an unreal version of the world. It can be argued with some reason that it may be more 'harmful' to present an anodysed picture of the results of violence, leaving the impression that it is a trifling matter. This leads to the second problem associated with censorship for children—the difficulty of assessing what might upset or disturb them. The tendency is to assume that children are worried by the same sorts of things as adults, only to a greater degree, but there is some evidence that this is not so. Not only may they need less protection than is sometimes imagined, but they may need a different sort of protection. The facility with which children digest the grisliest fairy stories is one indication that the tenderness of the young may in many cases be more imagined than real. On the other hand they may be disturbed by things that seem totally innocuous to the adult.

The age range covered by the junior certificates is unhelpfully large. At one end, five- to eight-year-olds are generally incapable of following a story told on film, being unable to see the relationship of scenes separated by a cut. At the other, many young teenagers are positively contemptuous of 'children' from whom they are desperate to disassociate themselves. The problem is aggravated by the fact that chronological age is not necessarily closely correlated with emotional development.

Unfortunately the Board has no particular expertise in handling this dilemma. As Hunnings noted ten years ago, 'perhaps the most serious defect of the British Board is that although it is admirably constructed for censorship under a liberal system such as the present one, it is extremely ill-adapted for the next and final stage of film censorship—the protection of children'.[2] It is not surprising that the Board has had more complaints in recent years about a 'U' film (*Lost in the Desert*) than it has had about almost any other film.

The 'AA' category was introduced in 1970 to reduce the wide gap between the 'A' and the 'X', and to allow the age restriction on the latter to be raised from sixteen to eighteen. The industry has never been very happy with it—it cuts out the family audience without attracting those seeking 'adult' entertainment. Few 'AA' films have been great commercial successes, and many companies prefer to accept cuts for an 'A' rather than to appeal to the teenage audience which, in any case, finds it all too easy to gain admittance to 'X' films in many places. Despite this reservation the 'AA' provides a useful bridge : the old system with restriction only at age sixteen was clearly unsatisfactory. Some countries even divide the audience into four age ranges but this places a further burden on cinema-managers trying to estimate the ages of potential customers.

Adult censorship can be dealt with under two headings. First there is the problem of material that might be personally or socially harmful. Violence is naturally the principle component, and imitation is again one of the worries. Trevelyan has recorded how 'we removed from films shots of easily manufactured weapons, such as wire nooses, and where possible, shots of knuckle-dusters and chains used as weapons. We were also careful to remove as far as possible the more dangerous karate blows and rabbit punches which could cause serious injury or death.'[3] Benedek's *The Wild Ones* was rejected in 1954 purely because it was feared that the film might encourage the growth of motorcycle gangs in this country : it is still banned in certain areas despite the fact that it has been shown on television. *Incident* (1967) was turned down not because of its violence but because its central theme—two hoodlums terrorizing passengers on an underground train—was thought to be too easy to copy.

The recent spate of martial arts films from Hong Kong and Singapore has presented new problems of this sort, although the tongue-in-cheek approach has reduced the impact. Nevertheless, in all these films one popular weapon, the chain-stick (three hollow metal rods linked by a chain) has been removed from all scenes. In some films whole sequences have been cut to eliminate the use of this weapon which the Board felt to be too easily copied and too dangerous. Although publicity posters frequently feature chain-sticks (e.g. *Enter the Dragon*) they are never seen in action in the films themselves. Unfortunately, this policy leads the Board into all sorts of inconsistency since many highly accessible instruments of aggression (such as knives) cannot be banned.

There is plenty of evidence that Murphy is more restrictive than his predecessor on this sort of issue. He always removes the recipe for Molotov cocktails which Trevelyan had not worried about, and is particularly concerned that films should play no part in the escalation of violence in Northern Ireland. He feels that the public as a whole is becoming more abhorrent of violence and that he has wide support for his efforts to clamp down on screen manifestations. 'We are cutting back on violence with great ferocity, so much so that there is no relationship between our certification and that of the M.P.A.A. I think we can safely assume that we are, in terms of violence, amongst the toughest censorship boards anywhere.'

The rationale, of course, is that exposure to violent material may have a corrupting effect on audiences. Murphy is well aware that research evidence is inconclusive, but argues correctly that long-term effects are not known. 'If one goes on implying time and time again that violence is an acceptable way of solving problems, do we not in the end make it more likely that our children will accept violence as inevitable?' On this basis, he concludes that no risks should be taken and eliminates the large proportion of screen violence that is unnecessary or gratuitous, by which is meant anything that does not contribute towards plot or characterization but emphasizes sadistic pleasure and glorifies the use of force. This aim of reducing violence to that which is essential for plot or character development explains one apparent 'oddity' about the Board's attitude—the dislike of 'over-kill', the repeated shooting or knifing of dead or dying bodies. This is regarded as sadistic and unnecessary, in contradistinction to the initial killing which is obviously essential. In Murphy's words 'it's the quantity of violence not the intensity of violence which gives us most concern. The reiteration of violence, where it is replayed again and again for gratuitous effect, is what we are trying to eliminate.'

Peckinpah's *The Wild Bunch* was the first major film in recent years to be accused of glorifying violence. Its endlessly repeated slow-motion deaths gave the film a balletic poetry that conveyed the true horror of bloodshed as unconvincingly as television replays match the real rigours of the penalty-area. Peckinpah's technique was adopted *ad nauseam* by numerous directors who capitalized on the easy effect that could be achieved. *The Wild Bunch* was cut, but not heavily.

The passing of *The Devils* in 1971 convinced the industry that the Board was now 'soft' on violence and a whole series of extremely brutal films were imported in the hope that they could now be shown. The Board responded by indulging in some of the most brutal cuttings and banning in its history. The point that 'excessive' violence was not going to be tolerated was soon taken by distributors. Yet the attempts to stem the flow of blood in films is increasingly anachronistic in a world where few countries seem to share our concern on this score. Elsewhere directors are being encouraged to go to great lengths to convey the most horrifying forms of violence imaginable. Detailed shots of decapitations, sexual torture, tearing out of tongues, etc. are included to a degree almost unimaginable to those accustomed to the standards of the B.B.F.C. Modern techniques and equipment can attach an all too convincing realism to this sort of material. The problem is exacerbated by the fact that these techniques are now being used, not only for films whose appeal is purely to the sensation seeker, but also in genres that have always been devoid of real violence. The Western, in particular, has changed its character since Leone and Peckinpah introduced 'real' blood and death into the hitherto fairy-tale world of Tom Mix and Roy Rogers. A bloodless Western is now almost unimaginable.

Yet there is undeniably a case for arguing that the Board, in reacting to this sort of material and to the considerable criticism it has received, has inclined too far the other way. Many people in the film industry certainly feel that this is the case, although they are obviously not impartial observers. Michael Winner is one who has repeated this point vehemently (and often abusively) in recent years. Writing at the end of 1972, for instance, he stated : 'Film censorship in Britain is now tighter than in most other comparable countries. *The Godfather*, for example, which plays here as an 'X' for eighteen and over, and cut at that, is on view in America for seventeen year olds unaccompanied, and for any age with a parent or guardian. My previous film, *Chato's Land* went out as an 'X' here with scenes cut which were passed for exhibition to children of any age in America. I could cite hundreds more examples.'[4]

Even some members of the Board itself were not sure that they had not become too restrictive. Coincident with Winner's outburst one examiner expressed some worry that 'while cutting back on the trashy films which include gratuitous violence, we are also cutting back on the reputable majors, and refusing what would have been acceptable only a year or so ago. If *The Wild Bunch*, *Bonnie and Clyde* and *Straw Dogs* were to come in today I doubt whether we would pass them without asking for reductions. . . . I can't help feeling that the warning bells sometimes ring too soon and for too long.'

Unconsciously the Board had been influenced by the steady flow of adverse comment in the press which resulted from the strenuous activities of the pressure groups. On a conscious level the reappearance of local authority censorship on a wider level than for many years was a factor that could not be ignored. By early 1974 Murphy himself had become convinced that repression of violence had been taken too far. In particular he felt that the Board's demands were tending to take the horror out of the horror film. The supremacy of the British industry in this genre in recent years has led to a tradition, not shared in Scandinavia, that allows these films more scope than might be expected. Even trailers had always been permitted to give a good indication of the contents of these films. Now it was apparent that the Board was removing the whole point of the films by insisting that the horror be diluted. To test that this was so, a special showing of trailers of Hammer horrors was arranged. It was instantly clear that there had been a very considerable change of policy since the trailers had been passed only four or five years previously. One examiner was so amazed that he refused at first to believe that they had indeed been accepted in the form shown. Some reconsideration of approach was undoubtedly indicated.

The problem of drugs also comes under the heading of 'effects'. The Board has always had a policy of discouraging the treatment of this subject, but in recent years the matter has had to be faced. A number of drug films have been banned, notably Corman's *The Trip*, rejected in 1967 after three psychiatrists had condemned it as 'meretricious, inaccurate in its representation and therefore dangerous'. The film remains unseen by general audiences here, although drugs have featured prominently in many films since the heroes of *Easy Rider* financed their trip with a drugs deal.

The more liberal approach now adopted (at least towards soft drugs) is evident in an article written by an examiner in September 1973. He noted that 'one has to draw distinctions between the relative strengths of the drug theme in individual films. *The Man with the Golden Arm* and *Trash* were specifically about addicts, while American youth-films sometimes have scenes in which youngsters pass around a joint. In these latter cases this is precisely the sort of reflection of cultural norms which one looks for if films are to have a realistic social setting.' Unfortunately it is just this sort of treatment of drug-taking as a normal part of every-day existence which is most often attacked by those who demand that all references to drugs be expunged from the cinema.

Question marks also hang over other aspects of the handling of drugs. It might be questioned whether it is necessarily logical to restrict drug films entirely to adults, for example. One American commentator has noted that 'many people feel that unglamorous films about addiction . . . should be rated "GP" instead of "R" so that teenagers could have easy access to these movies. Several exhibitors showing *The Panic in Needle Park* announced that they were disregarding the "R" rating and allowing anyone over ten or twelve to see the film unaccompanied.'[5]

More fundamentally, the whole issue of the 'dangers' of drug use is far from straightforward. There is some evidence that soft drugs are harmless, while the influence of the cinema in conditioning people to accept drug-taking as 'normal' has not been established. The assumptions on which the Board bases its policy are probably no more vague and unsupported than those held by other bodies, but there is a great deal of supposition at all levels.

The second aspect of adult censorship involves the assessment of public taste and the main category falling under this heading is, of course, sex. The growing freedom of the cinema to deal with sex has been charted in various publications, and there is no doubt that the modern public is more tolerant than in former decades. Yet there are obviously wide variations of opinion on the subject with different age-groups and classes regarding different things as unacceptable. Inevitably the Board has a middle-aged, middle-class bias. Equally inevitably most of the reference groups to whom it looks for guidance have the same bias. On the other hand examiners are exposed to a startling range of sexual material every week leading to the claim that they become inured to cinematic frolics and incapable of imagining the reaction of the ordinary public. Perhaps it is for this reason that the Board has a relatively rigid set of criteria to apply to sex on the screen.

One of the difficulties facing the Board is that it is dealing with two different kinds of film. In the first place there is the blatant sex film, exhibition of which is unlikely to go far beyond the Charing Cross Road. Such films have only a tenuous story and consist almost entirely of a variety of sexual adventures. Secondly, there is the general release 'X' film that may include sexual episodes but which is intended as more than an excuse for studies of nude bodies.

The two types present rather different problems. The sex film appeals to a self-selecting audience which knows what to expect and is not going to be shocked or offended, whereas general release films may be shown all over the country to audiences who react very differently to the explicit treatment of sex. The matter has been complicated by the tendency for the clear distinction between the two types to break down in the last year or two. The redevelopment of large cinemas into complexes of two or more much smaller ones showing more specialized material has led to the appearance of sex films on general release. The A.B.C. circuit in particular has been encouraged to adopt this policy by the great financial success of *I Am a Nymphomaniac* on release in 1972. It is now less easy to predict how wide a film's exhibition may be.

The Board has never really made up its mind whether the two types merit different treatment. On the one hand it can be argued that the sex film is harmless enough and that there is no strong argument for not giving the 'macintosh trade' what it pays for. On the other there are always the vague but ever-present legal requirements and a general unwillingness to apply two sets of standards. Recently a sharp difference of opinion has arisen. One examiner feels strongly that cutting sex films is pointless and dishonest.

In the face of the argument that we ought to be discouraging sexploitation films I can only say that we have to be convinced that we are stopping a social harm by doing so and that while hard pornography is still taboo, sex without sadistic overtones is what the self selected audience which goes to the sex film ought to be permitted to see. It may be argued that we have in this country the virtue of a twin system which allows the cinema clubs to show sex films and that sex material ought to be distributed through this channel. This would make sense if we rejected all sexploitation material as not meriting Board certification and had a neat distinction between commercial cinema which we classified and censored for classification, and the sex trade which was left to the club cinemas and the law. We operate a half-way house, however, and do certificate material which has no other purpose than to titillate the audience, irrespective of the minimal plots on which the sex is hung. Basically I am arguing that if we are going to allow sex films then let us do just that, drawing the line at pornography, but eliminating the hypocrisy and teasing which characterizes sexploitation in this country and cheats the paying audience.

However, this remains a minority view and the Board continues to cut these films quite savagely, so that the majority of foreign-made sex films are never even brought into this country. One result is that distributors are finding it increasingly hard to find material that can be imported. It is common for buyers abroad to see a dozen films, none of which are suitable. Those that are bought are usually heavily cut by the distributor prior to submission to the Board on the grounds that the complete film might well be rejected entirely. The certificated version of such films is sometimes little more than half the length of the original, though this owes as much to the need to reduce footage to provide a shortish double-bill as to censorship requirements.

Despite assurances that the censors are more concerned about violence than sex, the cutting of sex films still constitutes a major item in the Board's job. A large number of these films are submitted and it is frequently a long and arduous struggle to whittle them down to an 'acceptable' level. The Board has a number of rules which it applies with some determination. 'Perversions' tend to be frowned upon, and in particular, anything that hints at sado-masochism even in a humorous way. One such epic, entitled *Dagmar's Hot Pants*, included a sequence in which the heroine tried to enlist the help of friends to make up a four-some. A series of shots showed the friends explaining on the phone why they could not get away at that moment. One girl being half-heartedly whipped exclaimed that 'I'm just too beat' while another, heavily

roped, apologized that she was 'all tied up'. Both the beating and
the bondage were cut although the sequence represented the
height of wit by sex film standards.

The aim behind this sort of decision is to ensure that sexual
violence is kept to a minimum, and that sex and violence do not
become linked. A great many films are now being made which
exploit this sort of thing to a very extreme degree, and it is the
Board's belief that such films constitute the most potentially
harmful of all. Whether this concern is necessarily justified except
with regard to a tiny number of unfortunate individuals is uncertain, and, in any case, the most common form of sexual
violence—rape—can rarely be entirely cut as it usually makes an
essential plot point. The *Straw Dogs* case indicates that the Board
is prepared, in certain circumstances, to countenance quite long
and detailed rape scenes.

Other regulations seem uncommonly arbitrary. Suggestions of
oral sex are sometimes permitted, but no 'split beavers' (shots
between the legs). Sex play is accepted as long as it doesn't take
too long, while over-indulgent orgasms are also cut. Pleasure must
evidently be kept within bounds. Most curious of all, certain
positions in intercourse are allowed whereas others are not. Shots
of women astride their partners are invariably removed—a prohibition which one examiner has described as 'comic and baffling'
and which nobody seems able to explain—while entry from the
rear is also not approved. Such rules no doubt encourage consistency of decision, but any logical explanation for their retention is not forthcoming.

The average general release picture is scrutinized even more
closely in order not to outrage too large a section of the public,
although the growing sophistication and tolerance of the majority
has meant that even these films are now given considerable scope.
A major breakthrough was the certification of full-frontal nudity
in 1968. Prior to this the Board had adhered to Vonnegut's
maxim that 'the difference between art and pornography is
bodily hair'. The series of events that resulted in the collapse of
this thesis give some indication of how the Board's mind works
on these matters, and of the various factors involved.

The film that finally precipitated the change was the Swedish
Hugs and Kisses, which contained a fifteen-second shot of the
heroine studying her naked reflection in a full-length mirror. The
Board asked for the scene to be cut, but its motives are obscured
by Trevelyan's two conflicting accounts. In one interview he

stressed that the Board was worried about legal difficulties, noting
that the fear of court action continued to inhibit magazines like
Playboy and *Penthouse* from showing pubic hair. 'If I allowed
the scene to remain, film-makers might say "pubic hair is in"
and that would exacerbate the problem. If a successful prosecution were brought . . . the distributor would be entitled to say:
"Your Board should have protected us from this".'[6]

Elsewhere he implied that quite different motives lay behind
his strategy: 'When my Board asked for cuts in the nude scene . . .
we were really testing public opinion. There was no massive
outcry one way or the other, and some local authorities even
passed the film with the pubic hair left in.'[7] In reality, both
versions no doubt tell a part of the truth, but if the case was
really being used as a test of public opinion it underlines once
more the inadequacy of the Board's censors. Public outcry could
hardly be expected when probably only a relatively small number of people were even aware of the film or its cuts. The Board
was evidently much impressed by the fact that 'there was an
extensive press, and with hardly any exceptions it supported the
view that the human body was not obscene'.[8] When the provincial press reacted in the same way, the film was passed without the cut. In the meantime *If . . .* had been accepted with a
similarly unerotic nude scene.

Whether this was a satisfactory form of opinion testing seems
doubtful, but there was little subsequent objection to the new
policy. The comparison with standards in other media is obviously
important although direct parallels are never drawn. In his letter
to local authorities explaining the cut in *Hugs and Kisses* Trevelyan had commented that 'the showing of pubic hair on the
screen might be considered by the courts to be obscene if proceedings were taken. The legal position is by no means clear, but
I understand that this is a commonly accepted view since publications on sale which feature naked girls do not show the pubic
hair.' This sort of comparative process is not a very satisfactory
method of assessing the legal situation at any one time, for all the
media tend to watch each other, hoping that someone else will
have the courage to cross the next threshold. Hugh Hefner, editor
of *Playboy*, for instance, has indicated that he in turn looks at
films to judge what will be permissible in his magazine.

Murphy, true to his background, has shown himself more
likely to use television as the medium of comparison, noting that
'the quite astonishing liberalization of television' in the seventies

confirms his belief that the Board has not moved ahead of public opinion. He is quick to point out that many of the strongest scenes from 'X' films have been screened on television without complaint, while on one occasion a scene that had been cut from a film was inadvertently shown without a single protest.

Sexual explicitness is not of course the only subject that raises the problem of taste. Increasingly in recent years films have set out with the precise intention of challenging traditional values. The whole raison d'être of a number of films has been the attack of accepted bourgeois ideas of 'good taste'. The surrealist tradition (and few films are more 'shocking' in this sense than *Le Chien Andalou* which was made in 1928) is still vigorously alive and a wide range of other perspectives underlie the numerous voices that offer criticisms of society that some might construe to be 'tasteless'. No political, social or religious institution is immune from this attack.

The Cannes Festival of 1973 provided many examples of films of this sort, many of which provoked wide discussion and attracted considerable acclaim. Writing in *Films and Filming*, Ken Wlaschin noted: 'The message this year was loud and clear: "good taste" is under attack and "bad taste" is in. The era of hard-core political films appears to be ending and is being replaced by a new movement of extreme and often outrageous satire. The target is bourgeois-establishment taste and at Cannes there were films featuring every kind of activity that could scandalize, *épater* or simply bait the bourgeoisie.'[9]

The winner of the Critics' Prize at Cannes that year was Ferreri's *La Grande Bouffe* which did indeed fall foul of the Board's evaluation of public taste when, retitled *Blow-Out*, it appeared at Soho Square in June 1973. The plot centred on four middle-aged Frenchmen who retreat to a large house owned by one and proceed to eat themselves to death. There was no violence and no particularly explicit sex but the Board found it offensive largely due to its detailing of the men's inevitable problems in digesting vast quantities of food. The death of one in a resounding crescendo of noise as his stomach rebels at its treatment was one scene to which objection was taken.

Sensitivity over such bodily functions is an especially British phenomenon, but it may be doubted whether it is shared by all sections of the population. Taste is a notoriously difficult concept to define and one that is bound to be linked with sectional interests. Any censorship on these grounds is very susceptible to

attack for it involves what the Board has expressed itself anxious
to avoid—the suppression of ideas. The accusation of bad taste
can all too easily be used as an excuse for stifling criticisms of
society such as Ferreri's allegory on the evils of consumerism.

Thus far the Board's policies are consistent if challengeable—
and consistency is a virtue highly regarded by the industry. However, in the last ten years a completely new approach to censorship has been gradually incorporated into the Board's deliberations. Before the sixties the quality of the films being reviewed
had never been considered to be a relevant factor, but by 1964
even the usually conservative Lord Morrison was arguing that
'the element of the artistic should be taken into account'. Since
then the judgement of quality has become an increasingly important part of the Board's work. Films of merit are treated with
more respect than straightforward commercial ventures on the
grounds that artistic or social value represents a 'redeeming
feature'.

A brief review of some recent decisions shows how certain films
have gained from this new interpretation of censorship. Some
cases—*A Clockwork Orange*, *W.R.—Mysteries of the Organism*,
Last Tango have already been met. *Don't Look Now* was another
film that impressed the censors enough for them to allow a
highly erotic love scene between Julie Christie and Donald
Sutherland. *Fritz the Cat* and Forman's *Taking Off* were also
highly thought of by the Board, who passed them uncut, only
for certain local authorities to reverse the decisions.

More controversial was Alexandro Jodorowski's *El Topo*
which was submitted in June 1973, three years after it had been
made. Informed commentators had predicted that it would never
be shown in Britain, but the Board was generally impressed even
though some examiners felt it to be more suited to presentation
at regional film theatres or the I.C.A. Harlech however was
convinced that the quality of the film and its allegorical nature
made it passable despite the continuous bloodshed and violence :
despite also the fact that no one at the Board claimed to have
much idea of what the film was about.

In fact the director himself came to London to discuss changes
that might be necessary for certification. Eager to ensure wide
exhibition of his picture he co-operated willingly with Murphy.
He gave his own account of the negotiations to Derek Malcolm
of the *Guardian*, registering his pleasure at encountering such
'a charming and rational man. When I went to see him about

El Topo, I told him I knew of his difficulties and that I hoped he would appreciate mine. I wanted to show the film in London and could he please tell me what his problems were? He told me, and I happily acceded. He is not a butcher and though he took cuts, he did not harm the film. He laughed when I told him that the Venus de Milo has no arms but it is still a masterpiece.' In the end about three minutes were removed.

A lengthy list of such cases could be compiled—Bergman's *Cries and Whispers*, Scorsese's *Mean Streets*, Cavani's *The Night Porter*. Similar reasoning explained the 'AA' for *Blazing Saddles* when a less accomplished film would probably have been rated 'X'.[10] Such examples show the value of the policy, but it does also introduce a number of problems.

Firstly, it cuts right across the need for consistency which has often been regarded as the most important aspect of decision-making. Inconsistency has always been the main criticism of the Board during times of trouble, for many producers and distributors would like to be told exactly what is and is not permissible at any one time. Now inconsistency is inevitable.

Consideration of quality also makes the Board's decisions less predictable for distributors who often are genuinely unaware of the reception their films will receive at Soho Square. Small companies in particular often have little idea of the Board's standards and seem not to learn a great deal from their experiences, while, a little cynicism notwithstanding, most of the people connected with most films believe in their product. Total involvement over a long period can result in a below average effort coming to be considered a masterpiece.

More serious, however, is the whole issue of how quality is to be evaluated. No one at the Board has any special qualifications in this respect, although the enormous collective experience on hand is a great asset. Nevertheless judgement of quality is invariably subjective and affected by the dictates of fashion and arbitrary changes of taste. Decisions must be made quickly on the basis of personal reactions, tempered by the known 'form' of the film-makers, a process that is bound to favour the established director and distributor. A name like Truffaut or Fellini in the credits naturally evokes certain predispositions, although the point has not been reached that exists in Sweden where Bergman's films are never cut. Indeed, a conscious effort is made to be fair to unknown directors while a famous name is by no means a guarantee of trouble-free certification. Pasolini's recent films, for instance, have been poorly received at the Board, and fairly severely dealt with as a result.

Nor are the opinions of critics necessarily given any weight. It is, in any case, rare that critical opinion is available when decisions are made, but even when these verdicts have been given the Board is prepared to ignore them. *Blow-Out*, for example, had had a very favourable critical reception, but was not highly thought of by the Board who insisted on cuts that the French producers were not prepared to make. Murphy expresses the belief that the Board has been 'right' more often than the professional critics—a view which he is aware can never be proved wrong.

Despite this, a lengthy list of cases of films which were cut or banned but which eventually acquired high reputations can be drawn up. The career of Vilgot Sjoman throws up three examples of films which would seem to have deserved a better fate. *491*, made in 1966, was a more brutal and realistic view of adolescent delinquents than Truffaut's more sentimental *400 Blows* and was rejected even though Trevelyan found the director to be 'a man of honesty and integrity and a film-maker of quality'. It has remained banned ever since. *I Am Curious— Yellow* (1967) was described as 'profoundly moral' by the Swedish censors and acclaimed by many critics. The Board refused to pass it for some time and only agreed to reverse the decision after eleven minutes had been removed. *Troll* (1973), a comedy, was turned down for its sexual content, but later passed under the unprepossessing title *Till Sex Us Do Part*.

As noted, horror films have generally been accorded lenient treatment, so it is ironic that two of the rare attempts to elevate the genre were the subjects of severe cutting. Carlos Clarens has written of *Peeping Tom* that 'in spite of its theme, the movie was far less gory than the most dignified of the Hammers. Critics and censors, united for once, seemed to find the display of terror more deplorable than actual blood-spilling.'[11] Yet the Board only felt unable to ban the film because the project had been passed at script stage. Michael Reeves's *Witchfinder General* has had a mixed reputation, but some critics at least hold it in high regard: one has suggested that it could be 'transferred into a pivotal position in the history of English cinema'.[12] Trevelyan felt that the film failed in its aim of showing the horror and degradation of violence and appeared to glorify sadism, so he insisted on very heavy cutting.

Robbe-Grillet's *Trans-Europe Express* remains banned to this day despite the credentials of the director. A recent writer has analysed it as a comedy in which 'the sadistic sex passages which caused it to be banned in the U.K. are not of long duration, and are so placed as to hint at a kinky joke in the course of a deliberately souped-up melodrama'.[13] When evaluation of a film can change so rapidly that an unconsidered supporting film of last year can become the masterpiece of next, it is inevitable that those censorship decisions that reflect opinion at the time of original release can appear incomprehensible a short time later. In the meantime films may have been irreparably damaged by the censor's demands.

Of course it is also possible for the Board to be impressed by a film that is otherwise unrated. The Dutch film *Turkish Delight* was highly thought of when submitted early 1974 and cutting was reduced to a minimum even though, on purely objective grounds, the film could well have been banned. The Board's judgement was, to some extent, vindicated when *Turkish Delight* was nominated for an Oscar in America, but in this country it was resoundingly panned by the critics as pretentious pornography and the commercial successes it had achieved abroad were not repeated here.

In general, however, it is perhaps surprising how rarely the Board is seriously in error. Certainly very few films of high status attract comment as a result of action by the censor. This may in part be a result of the fact that few people are aware of what has been cut from films. It is rarely in the interests of either the industry or the Board to let it be known that cuts have been made. Indeed, there is a gentleman's agreement that the Board does not make such decisions public for fear of harming the box-office. But some credit must attach to the Board which has trodden a reasonably sure path through the quicksands of aesthetic appreciation. In few cases has it compromised over films of undoubted quality.

On those occasions when worthy films have seemed to suffer it has often been the case that circumstances have dictated action. As one examiner has commented : 'the truth of the matter, never explicitly acknowledged, is that film censorship consists mainly of political (small "p") decisions'. At all times the Board is forced to take into consideration not only the content of films but also the atmosphere of the moment. Circumstances quite unconnected with the films being considered may demand a particular

approach, so that a picture submitted at one point in time might
receive quite different treatment if it had appeared a few months
earlier or later. Though the Board tries to be fair to every film,
political expedience time and again leads to concessions. This is
not a problem that is unique to the Board: as Farber has indicated the same pressures are just as hard to resist in America.[14] A
film censor can, perhaps, be likened to a referee attempting to
control a potentially explosive football match. While he knows
that he has rules to apply which allow him only a limited degree
of freedom of interpretation, external criteria such as the mood
of the crowd and players or the state of the game often force
themselves into consideration. Such factors may well influence
him to book or severely lecture a player whom, under other
circumstances, he might have been tempted to send off the field.
Discretion on such occasions is often wise and necessary. Reactions to the 'R' rating in America of *Panic in Needle Park* have
already been noted, yet the Board felt unable to give it even an
'X' when it was first submitted in 1971 because the *Trash* controversy had made drug films too hot to handle. As an admirer
of the film, Murphy advised the distributors to re-apply in six
months. As it happened, because of internal company problems,
the film did not reappear until 1974 when it was passed uncut.

The overall problem of balancing consistency of decisions
against the consideration of quality is one that has not yet been
fully resolved. Fierce disagreement exists within the Board over
which is the most important criterion. On the one hand it is
argued that it is vital that serious film-makers should not be
unduly hampered by the demands of censorship and that there is
no requirement to apply the same standards to all films; on the
other that the Board has a duty to give the industry some idea
of what is permissible at any one time and that standards of
taste are not subject to aesthetic considerations. It seems certain
that upholders of this latter point of view are fighting a rear-
guard action that is doomed to defeat. Harlech and Murphy
seem determined that, whatever certain sections of the industry
may feel, the quality factor is of paramount importance.

There remains, however, the serious problem of constructing a
logical defence of this policy. The impossibility of reaching agreement on what constitutes a 'good' film is one insuperable obstacle.
Another is the lack of any theoretical reason for treating films of
different qualities in different ways. There is, of course, no evidence at all that 'good' films are less 'damaging' to viewers than

'bad' ones. If anything the opposite is probably true. The more convincing a picture, the more it enthralls and involves its audience, the greater its impact is likely to be. The propaganda films of Leni Riefenstahl, such as *Triumph of the Will* and *The Olympic Games* are generally considered so effective because they are so expertly made. So much so that a number of commentators roundly criticized the B.B.C. for transmitting *Triumph of the Will* on television in 1973, fearing its potency almost forty years after its production. To take a more recent example, the sheer power and brilliance of Kubrick's *A Clockwork Orange* undoubtedly contributed to the outrage at that film. The images of horror were so effective that many viewers were led to believe that the film was more explicitly violent than it was.

Barrister and writer John Mortimer has raised a rather different point, arguing with reference to books: 'I would like to form a society for the Defence of Bad Literature. Every writer has, it seems to me, the inalienable right to fail, and I think it's highly inequitable that the talented should be permitted access to erotic fields denied to the clumsy, talentless majority. We should not only be able to defend to the death other people's right to say things with which we disagree: we must also allow them to do it in abominable prose.'[15] Presumably a similar argument may be made for the cinema. It does seem illogical that a man is allowed to show certain things, to put over certain messages, only if he has the expertise to do it well.

Nor can it be argued that the policy has wide-spread support for there is, of course, no necessary correlation between quality and popularity. A large proportion of the population would doubtless vote *The Sound of Music* as the greatest film of recent years, a defensible judgement in terms of pure entertainment. Furthermore many of the controversies which have undermined the authority of the Board have centred around films which have been accepted on the grounds of their perceived quality. Many local authorities either do not appreciate the new policy or do not share the Board's evaluations.

But it is not only feature films themselves which cause problems. The advertising of films has also played a large part in fuelling and igniting censorship rows. Trailers have always caused headaches for the Board. As early as the twenties the showing of trailers for adult films during programmes for children was the subject of angry debate. In 1959 there was trouble when trailers for *Callgirl* and *The Trollenberg Terror* were screened after a showing of *Tom Thumb*. More recently, as we have seen, the showing of a trailer during a Disney programme was a major factor in sparking off the crisis of 1971.

The main problem is that, while there are four different categories into which films are placed, there are only two for trailers —'U' and 'X', and the vast majority are 'U'. Given the pattern of exhibition in this country, whereby public cinemas often show very different programmes in successive weeks it is essential that all films to be shown on general exhibition have a 'U' trailer. It is only for films made or bought specifically for the small number of cinemas that show exclusively 'X' films that an 'X' certificate trailer is acceptable. The introduction of 'A' and 'AA' trailers would introduce enormous administrative problems resulting from the necessity to ensure that 'AA' trailers were not shown with an 'A' film and so on. Moreover the Board argues that it is impossible to make such fine distinctions in viewing a trailer lasting only 60–180 seconds.

As a result the makers of trailers—who may be the distributors or producers or a specialist firm, have the problem of producing a 'U' trailer for all films, that will give some impression of what the picture is like. The difficulties of 'selling' an 'X' film with a 'U' trailer may be imagined. Most trailers are, in fact, made by two firms, National Screen Services and General Screen Enterprises, who have vast experience of dealing with such situations. They also have a shrewd idea of what is likely to be acceptable to the censors.

As both violence and sex become more explicit, the problems grow. The Board is anxious that trailers should bear some sort of relationship to the film itself. Not only must every scene in a trailer appear in the complete film, but the trailer must also be fairly representative of the complete work. Whether the Trades Descriptions Act actually covers films is uncertain, but the Board feels that its spirit should be adhered to and does not allow trailers to include every instance of sex and violence that appears in a feature. The industry is unhappy with this policy and claims that trailers no longer attract audiences—an interesting reflection on what the distributors feel to be the selling points of their pictures. One group has given up trailers altogether.

It seems likely that the point is rapidly being reached at which it becomes impossible to make a 'U' trailer for a film that gives any reasonably accurate guide to its content. Since the introduction of the new categories in 1970, the 'U' certificate has been rather more restrictive than in the past. Yet, the number of 'U' films is, of course, falling: only about one film in six is now placed in this category.

In certain cases even the titles themselves are thought hardly suitable for the 'U' certificate, but the Board has little control in this respect. In fact there are two opposing points of view over titles, each with some validity. On the one hand it is argued that titles which make clear the nature of the films being shown are a good protection for the Board, as there are unlikely to be many complaints from people entering cinemas under a misapprehension. On the other, the tendency to over-emphasize the sexual content of films not only gives a false impression of the Board's work, but misleads the public by promising more than is delivered. This is often the case with foreign films that are imported and exhibited under a totally misleading and irrelevant title. Often the film is seen by the Board under its original title or with a direct translation, and only after it has acquired its certificate is the new title substituted. The duller the picture the harder a distributor will search for a really provocative title.

Unfortunately the Board is impotent to stop this practice. Although all title changes have to be approved by the censors, there are provisions laid down by the Board of Trade for the renaming of films which give an official seal of approval to the process. The B.B.F.C. did make one attempt to control title-changing, but the result only demonstrated the futility of such efforts. The film in question had been originally certificated under one title, but renamed and unsuccessfully exhibited under a second. The distributor's response was to try with a third title. His choice, *The Importance of Being Sexy*, was not approved by the Board—although it seems innocent enough. Presumably the decision to fight this case was a result of frustration and annoyance at the process in general: although there must also be doubts about the fairness to the public of a film being shown under two entirely different titles.

The distributor promptly applied to the G.L.C., pointing out the existence of the Board of Trade's machinery for registering such changes and challenging them to say that a film which had their tacit approval under one title was so changed in its nature that it became offensive under another. Not surprisingly, the film was passed and the Board was forced to accept that it has little power in this respect.[16]

However, there is a body that technically can control titles, although only as a side-effect of its powers over advertising. The Advertisement Viewing Committee, under the chairmanship of the Kinematograph Renters' Society, deals with publicity in relation to the cinemas of the West End of London. All front-of-house displays, newspaper advertisements, posters and stills for 'X' rated films must be passed by the committee which consists of representatives of the K.R.S., Cinematograph Exhibitors' Association, the British Poster Advertising Association, the *Evening Standard*, the *Evening News*, the Association of Independent Cinemas, London Transport Advertising and British Transport Advertising.

The committee was formed in the early sixties after some years of concern at the ways in which film advertising was developing. As early as 1953 Arthur Watkins was expressing his worries in one of the trade periodicals, presumably hoping to influence the people concerned: 'The British Board of Film Censors is not concerned *with* film publicity, that is it does not censor posters and advertising. But the Board is very concerned *about* film publicity. . . . Publicity of this kind has two undesirable effects. It can alienate the average decent member of the public from the film . . . it leads local authorities to become uneasy about the films to be shown in their area.'[17] Watkins matched action to words by calling a meeting with the trade, at which the Board was assured of co-operation. Watkins warned that if necessary, the Board would not hesitate to embark on the censorship of advertising, though on what basis this was to be done is not clear. Watkins no doubt assumed that the industry would be unaware just how empty this threat actually was.

Evidently there was insufficient improvement, for the K.R.S. committee was eventually formed to deal with publicity, the immediate stimulus being the horror films of the period. Although it had some effect it never imposed as strict a standard as the B.B.F.C. would have liked. It is the G.L.C., however, which has the power to exert pressure on the committee and in 1972, as documented in a later chapter, they demanded tougher measures, especially with regard to front-of-house displays. There have been signs of a stricter attitude on the part of the K.R.S. committee recently, as evidenced by its rejection in September 1974 of the title *Tango of Perversion* to which not even the Board had objected. The G.L.C. has also take action over titles, being concerned to ensure that they give some idea of the content of films : thus *The Girl Traders* became *The White Slavers*, although whether this is any less ambiguous is debatable.

London Transport also seems to have decided to impose stricter control and has banned a number of posters, including two, *Sex Farm* and *On The Game* purely on the grounds of unacceptable titles. In June 1974 London Transport Advertising announced that because of 'a mounting number of complaints' posters might be turned down 'however innocuous' they might be—the trouble apparently being 'a recurrent problem—graffiti'. A recent revision of the L.T.A. conditions governing advertisements has included a note that 'advertisements depicting murder, scenes of terror, horror or acts of violence will come under close scrutiny'.[18]

This sign of dissent apart, the K.R.S. committee continues to set the tone, and not only for London. Publicity is expensive and the campaign used for the capital is always adopted for the rest of the country as well. There is therefore effective censorship everywhere. What does seem curious is that only 'X' films are under any form of control. 'AA' films which may be quite explicit sexually suffer no such restriction. A curious case arose over the film *It's a 2 Foot 6 Inches Above the Ground World* (later renamed *The Love Ban*) for which a poster was devised showing a pair of naked male legs with briefs at ankle height. The distributors, British Lion, agreed to raise the pants to full mast on the same day that they were advised by the B.B.F.C. that the film had been reclassified as 'AA'.

Until this point one aspect of the B.B.F.C.'s work has been completely ignored, for the reason that it is quite different from its other tasks. This has to do with the treatment of animals in films, for which the Board has a particular responsibility. Concern about the use of animals had been growing throughout the thirties. In America horses in particular were being subjected to barbaric methods to achieve dramatic effects, notably during the making of Darryl Zanuck's *Jesse James* (1939) when a horse had been thrown from a cliff to drown in the stream below, and Michael Curtiz' *The Charge of the Light Brigade* (1936) which had killed scores of horses and a number of men. The outcry that arose led to the incorporation into the Production Code of a clause demanding the compulsory consultation of the American Humane Association in all productions involving animals. A representative of that body now has to be present on all such films, with the result that the training of animals has become an important offshoot of the movie industry. Producers of films made in America have to go to very great lengths to ensure that animals are protected, and a trained beast is now so valuable that this care is an economic necessity. In August 1973 the *National Humane Review* reported that, in the previous year, 48 films had required 299 days of supervision and that 4,388 animals had been involved, including 1,616 horses, 685 cattle and 416 dogs, not to mention a sloth, a skunk, a hippopotamus and a cockatoo.

Not surprisingly, the British had been alerted to this problem even earlier. In May 1934 the Board had called a conference attended by representatives of such bodies as the R.S.P.C.A., the National Canine Defence League, the Natural History Museum, the Public Morality Council and others, to discuss the matter. The chairman, Edward Shortt, then President of the B.B.F.C., had outlined the principles upon which decisions were based at that time :

(1) Nothing should be allowed on the screen which portrayed cruelty, or, even if there were no actual cruelty, appeared to portray it.

(2) We could not allow any incident if it could reasonably be supposed from the film that means had been adopted which necessitated cruelty, or restraint of the animals which amounted to cruelty.

(3) We could only be held responsible for what was depicted on the screen.

This last point referred to the problem of whether, in the case of a film the making of which had clearly involved cruelty, it was sufficient to remove only the offending scenes and to pass the rest. Legal advice had been sought and 'counsel advised us that if a producer whose film we had rejected in those circumstances brought an action in the courts for us to show cause why we had rejected the film we should lose, and that we are, as censors, only responsible for what appears on the screen'.

During the preceding months the Board had been subjected to much criticism for allowing the exhibition of certain films in which animals appeared. The National Council for Animal Welfare had been particularly severe, to the extent that the Board considered taking legal action on the grounds of libel. Since the situation was clearly unsatisfactory, the Board called upon the conference to 'appoint a small committee to inquire into these matters' and to offer the censors some guidelines. The result was

the Cinematograph Films (Animals) Act of 1937 prohibiting 'the
exhibition or distribution of cinematograph films in connection
with the production of which suffering may have been caused
to animals'. The Act specified that no certificate was to be given
'if in connection with the production of the film any scene represented in the film was organized or directed in such a way as
to involve the cruel infliction of pain or terror on any animal or
the cruel goading of any animal to fury'. British films generally
have a consultant from the R.S.C.P.A. on location to ensure that
no cruelty is indulged in, and the Board check up with the
R.S.P.C.A. if there is any concern.

There can, of course, be problems with films made outside the
U.S.A. and Britain, and a great number of American-financed
films are now made in countries such as Spain, Mexico and Italy
where production costs are much lower, but where there are also
no restrictions on the treatment of animals. Peckinpah's *Pat
Garrett and Billy the Kid* encountered trouble on these lines.
Particular difficulty was found in the case of *Outback* (1971), a
film shot in Australia and designed, in part, to criticize the barbaric 'sport' of kangaroo shoots. The film showed in detail the
killing of a number of animals, and the Board was concerned
that, whatever its point of view, the film might transgress the
law if the hunt had been specially staged. This fear was allayed
by the producer who wrote that 'as I had insisted . . . that I would
only make it on the condition that no animals were killed for the
sake of making the film, we decided to send the camera unit out
with professional kangeroo hunters, who are licensed to shoot
the animals, and who kill every night thousands of kangeroos
for commercial gain, and for the camera to record this'. He added
that scenes of a fight between a man and a kangaroo were done
under the supervision of the local animal welfare representative.
The Secretary was not entirely happy and showed part of the
film to the R.S.P.C.A. in London, who were quite satisfied that it
should be shown, but who suggested that a statement about the
film's production should be added, and such a note was
eventually included at the end of the film.

Slightly different problems were met with a film version of
Jack London's *Call of the Wild*, about huskies in nineteenth-
century America. Made by the British director, Ken Annakin, in
Norway in 1972, it showed fights to the death between dogs and
also a scene of human brutality when a dog was brutally beaten
with a large wooden stick. This film presented two levels of

decision. First, had it been made in such a way as to satisfy the 1937 Act? Secondly, as it was made with a young audience in mind, was the simulated violence too powerful? The second question was a straightforward censorship issue, though it raised the interesting point of whether children would be more alarmed at human violence to animals or at animal violence to other animals. It was eventually decided that the former is more objectionable, the latter being a natural phenomenon that children will more readily accept. The beating scene was therefore reduced and the dog-fights were left to be dealt with in the light of reports from the company on the use of animals in the film.

It turned out that the Norwegians had been even more concerned with this aspect than the British. Not only had they insisted on having a veterinary surgeon, a police inspector and the dogs' owners on the set, but they had refused to allow the use of drugs in order to simulate death. The strictness of the authorities had, in fact, made it very difficult for the director to make the fight scenes convincing, and had left him with an acute shortage of footage. As a result of this report, no further cuts were requested by the Board.

Waterloo, made in Russia, was another film that caused concern. The R.S.P.C.A. were convinced that, on occasions in the film, it was possible to see that the horses used were terrified. More often it is extremely difficult to be sure if cruelty or clever editing is involved. Techniques are now so expert that it is easy to mislead the viewer into thinking that cruelty has taken place. There was some public indignation at a scene in *Patton* in which a mule is apparently shot, for clever shooting and editing had made the scene almost too realistic. In fact the mule had been put to death painlessly and the producer did have trouble with the A.H.A. on this score.

A more serious difficulty arose over *Ulzana's Raid*, a film made by Universal in Arizona, starring Burt Lancaster. The story concerned the conflict between the U.S. Army and the local Indians, but the basis of the plot was the importance of horses to both sides in the desert terrain. Consequently there was a great deal of 'shooting' of horses. Traditionally this effect is given by stunt riders bringing down their mounts, but in these days of ultra-realism this is not a perfectly satisfactory device. In addition it was necessary for riderless horses to be 'shot'. The producers therefore fell back on the trip-wire and the concealed pit. These devices ensure spectacular crashes to earth, but also considerable suffering. The American Humane Association representative naturally objected to these methods and eventually left the film altogether. The Association called for the deletion of all objectionable footage, but this request was ignored by the company. The *National Humane Review* commented that 'for the first time in more than three decades an American film company has deliberately misused animals in the production of a motion picture shot on location in the United States'.[19]

As a result of this history, when the film was seen by the Board the distributors were invited to send their cutter to the viewing to see exactly what cutting was required and to advise on the technical possibilities. In the end a superb cutting operation meant that the deletions could barely be detected.

In 1974 the American film *Cockfighter* was shown at the Edinburgh festival. It contained scenes—documentary footage, according to Roger Corman—that could never be accepted by the Board. In fact it was a very different version, the result of extensive re-editing for American television, that was eventually submitted. There does usually seem to be a way around these problems, although it must be doubted whether simple cutting or re-editing really fulfils the spirit or even the letter of the law. There would seem to be a strong case for arguing that any film which involves cruelty to animals should be rejected *in toto*. Certainly only this sort of action would discourage such productions, which was clearly the aim behind the Act.

POLITICAL CENSORSHIP

THE GRAVEST CHARGE made against censorship is that it is liable to have political implications. Although the B.B.F.C. has never been Government controlled, we have seen that it has frequently been open to influence. Indeed, in its early days, its very independence made it an easy target for pressure. As Ivor Montagu noted in 1929, 'at any time the Government may, by legislative revision, replace the Board. From time to time Public Morality and other bodies clamour for its replacement. How inevitable, therefore, that consciously or unconsciously it must strive to anticipate the Government's wishes. How satisfactory to the Government to see its wishes anticipated and yet to be able to reply to any inquiry with a Pilate-like washing of the hands.'[1]

There is no doubt that from its inception the Board was highly amenable to instructions from Whitehall. Sir Sidney Harris has recorded how, in its very first year of operation, the Board was unashamedly throwing away its apparent independence.

> Mr Wilkinson kept in touch with the Home Office, and was able to help in dealing with complaints made to it. For instance, in July 1913 representations were made by the South African Government that misleading impressions were being given by certain films being shown in England of disturbances in Johannesburg. The films were seen and modifications were made to remove the objection. Similarly in November 1913 a film was exhibited picturing the escape of prisoners from Portland prison in which there were discreditable features including alleged and unfounded bribery of prison warders. Amendment of the film was secured by the Board.[2]

This policy of yielding to influence from official quarters was continued during the inter-war years, although the Board was steadily consolidating its position and moving towards one of greater strength. O'Connor, who was President from 1916–29 outlined his attitude in a statement to the Commission of 1917 : 'I thought it was necessary to keep, not only in touch with, but in the friendliest relations with the Home Office, and that I think that I have succeeded in doing.'[3] He also told the Commission of the forty-three rules which he had drawn up to guide his examiners. Many of these explain why his relations with the Home Office were so amicable, for among items that were not to be allowed were : references to controversial politics, scenes tending to disparage public characters and institutions, incidents having a tendency to disparage our Allies, scenes holding up the King's uniforms to contempt and ridicule, and 'Relations of Capital and Labour', by which is meant anything that suggested conflict between workers and employers.

Under these rules 'laid down by the Board' many films were banned, most prominent being the early Russian output of Eisenstein and Pudovkin. Thus *Battleship Potemkin* was refused certification on the grounds that it dealt with recent controversial events,[4] while exception was taken to *Mother* because its scene was Russia, its actions concerned a strike and it showed the forces of order firing on a mob. *Storm over Asia* was unacceptable because it was anti-British, showed the British trying to set up a puppet government in Mongolia and showed the locals sweeping the British out. These and other films were banned because of their 'controversial tenor. The content expressed was in disagreement with Government policy.' All were thought by the Board to be 'dangerous to the peace', while Knowles reports an admission by O'Connor speaking of *Mother* that it was 'his duty to consider the Government's wishes rather than his own personal views'.[5]

Eisenstein made clear his opinions of such activity in the June 1933 issue of *Close Up* where he referred to the twin evils of censorship of production and exhibition. At that time he was in difficulties over his attempt to film *An American Tragedy* for Paramount, who declared it to be 'a monstrous challenge to American society'. They demanded the removal of all the themes of social concern, leaving 'a strong, simple detective story' and 'a love affair'. Part of their fear lay in the worry that the American censors would reject a film which made criticisms of American civilization. Ironically, when the film was finally made (by von Sternberg) to Paramount's specifications, it was turned down by the B.B.F.C.

G. W. Pabst was another whose experiences in Britain and

France led him to condemn a structure that made it impossible
for him to realize his projects in capitalist countries. Almost all
his films were severely cut in this country.[6] But it was not only
socialist film makers who ran into obstacles in the form of
censorship. None other than D. W. Griffith had a film (*America*)
banned 'on the wish of a high authority' because its account of
the war of independence was considered to be offensive to
Britain.

Rachel Low has commented that 'the most important and
most distasteful censorship cases of the decade were those of
Mother, Potemkin and Herbert Wilcox's *Dawn*'.[7] The latter
was a British film telling the story of Nurse Edith Cavell (played
by Sybil Thorndike). The German ambassador exerted pressure
on the Foreign Secretary, Austen Chamberlain, arguing that the
film might re-awaken bitterness and enmity. Accordingly the film
was banned, although it had been seen by neither Chamberlain
nor the B.B.F.C. The former was nevertheless able to express 'a
great repugnance' for it, while the Board opined that 'the theme
of this film renders its exhibition in this country inexpedient in
the present circumstances'.[8] Controversy in the press over this
decision led to a debate in the Commons when Chamberlain,
'speaking as an English gentleman', described it as an 'outrage on
a noble woman's memory to turn for purposes of commercial
profit so heroic a story'—a very curious point of view. The
film was later passed 'A' by the L.C.C., and other councils, subject to certain conditions.

Edward Short and Lord Tyrrell continued the policy of
O'Connor. The latter in particular, made his position very clear. In
1935 he announced that 'nothing could be more calculated to
arouse the passions of the British public than the introduction on
the screen of subjects dealing with religious or political controversy', while the following year he declared that 'the cinema
needs continued repression of controversy in order to stave off
disaster'.[9] He was able to remark with satisfaction that this country had so far had no film dealing with 'current burning political
questions' and promised to put a check on what he regarded as
the 'thin end of the wedge'.[10] Thus, one among many projects to
fall foul of the Board's rules was a proposal to make a film based
on the exploits of the notorious Judge Jeffreys. An opinion
offered at script stage ordered that 'no reflection on the administration of British justice at any period could be permitted, that
no phrase as lurid as "The Bloody Assize" could be used and

that various incidents in Jeffreys' career would have to be omitted'.[11]

As we have seen, the coming of war put the Ministry of Information in overall charge of censorship, when, for the first time, newsreels also were looked at. It is interesting to note that there were many complaints from both exhibitors and the public at the inclusion in newsreels of scenes of fighting. Such sequences were thought to be highly offensive and gruesome.

Peace brought a return to the old system, but it has already been seen how censorship policies underwent radical changes in the post-war period. In particular, the close ties between the B.B.F.C. and the Government were quickly eroded when the Board dropped its explicitly paternalistic approach. Instances of Governmental interference in censorship issues have been very much rarer in recent years. On a number of occasions neverthe-less, there is evidence of overt political censorship. A brief account of the most important incidents indicates the various ways in which the Board can come to make political decisions.

The Snake Pit was an American film made in 1948 about a journalist who, by feigning insanity, was able to investigate the conditions inside a U.S. mental hospital. The subject matter of this film touched on an area which has consistently worried the British censors who have 'always exercised the greatest reserve about allowing in films any scenes connected with mental institu-tions'.[12] The Board felt that this film could be passed only if 'all scenes where inmates of the mental institution are shown are removed'. The distributors naturally felt that this would damage the film irreparably, and the Board sought outside opinion to clarify the dilemma. The censors of Belgium and Sweden were consulted. In Belgium it appeared that the film was passed for adults only (i.e. those over sixteen), a solution which had never before been attempted here. The Swedish censor replied that no harmful reactions had been reported in that country (where a cut version was open to all over fifteen), and that 'as a doctor of medicine and a psychiatrist I want to say that I found the film very informative and well worth seeing'.

On re-seeing the film the Board concluded that, with cuts, the film could be passed, but only with an 'H' certificate. They reasoned that 'if these cuts were made there would be no firm grounds for rejecting the film, having regard to its already un-contested exhibition in other countries and the fact that it is a

sincere film of outstanding quality'. The film's producer, however, was not keen to accept an 'H' certificate, which he felt gave
a false impression of the film's qualities.

At this point, the Board ducked out of its responsibilities and
referred the matter to the Ministry of Health. The film was now
seen by the Minister and by experts from the Board of Control.
The latter expressed the view that the film would have harmful
consequences since it did not show conditions that were representative of those in British hospitals, it did not show the better
aspects of such institutions, and it would deter the enrolment of
voluntary patients and the recruitment of nurses. The Minister
was impressed by these points, and the producer was duly informed that the film could not be passed. He was naturally
upset and concerned that the Board should be influenced by a
'small body of professional experts'.

Feeling himself on shaky ground, the Secretary of the Board
sought another meeting with the Minister who was prepared to
give his support to the extent of accepting responsibility for the
advice that had changed the Board's decision. Disturbingly it
was 'also agreed that the Ministry would, if necessary, take unofficial steps to mobilize responsible opinion in support of the
Board's decision'. A press release was drawn up, regretting that a
certificate could not be issued : 'it has always been the policy of
the Board not to allow scenes in mental institutions.

For some reason this statement was never made public, and in
fact within two weeks of its composition, discussions with the
producers were renewed. Whether it was concern expressed by
the Kinematograph Renters' Society over the part played by a
Government Department in the affair, or the letters from doctors
and psychiatrists which the producers offered in support of the
film that led to this change of mind is not clear. The latter seems
less likely, as medical opinion seems to have been divided and
statements for and against were received from many authorities.

In the end an unprecedented ' "A"', but no children to be
admitted' certificate was given, subject to cuts of about 1,000 ft
and the addition of a long prologue affirming that 'in this country those who are obliged to seek mental treatment are assured
of every aid to recovery which science can offer them and the
maximum amount of sympathy and understanding from doctors
and nurses alike'. The Board announced, rather unctuously in
the light of what had gone on, in a press release of 13th April,
1949, that 'the film, which deals with a matter of social import-

ance, appeared to the Board to be a sincere and moving picture. With the removal of certain scenes and incidents which seemed likely to cause apprehension or distress, the Board have decided to pass the film for exhibition to adult audiences only.'

Later that same year another film caused problems of a very different nature. *Sword in the Desert* was an account of fighting in Palestine during the Second World War. The *Motion Picture Herald* described it as 'eminently fair in presenting both sides of a touchy question'. In those days, however, events were too recent for a 'fair' account to be acceptable. Without seriously challenging the 'facts' presented in the film, sections of the British press attacked their presentation. 'It will be surprising to British audiences at least, to see the unwonted harshness with which troops in the film treat Jewish civilians . . . certainly distasteful to watch British soldiers being killed by Jews in Palestine in the way depicted on the screen.'[13] The *Evening Standard* called it 'A Film Not for the Eyes of Britons',[14] while the *Express* noted that 'the tolerant British will possibly laugh uproariously, but abroad it may be taken as sober fact'.[15]

The Board, 'after careful consideration', concluded that there was no valid ground for intervention on their part, and left the verdict to the 'discretion and common sense of the cinema public'. Consequently, the film opened at the New Gallery Cinema on 2nd February, 1950. Its première was marked by the distribution of 'Union Movement' pamphlets, and demonstrations and disturbances inside and outside the cinema. The activities of the 'fascist elements' as they were described by the chairman of the L.C.C. Public Control Committee, led to discussions between the L.C.C. and the Home Office. On the latter's advice, the L.C.C. prohibited further showings of the film, not, it was explained, on account of its content, but in order to prevent further scenes of rowdyism. In an extraordinary statement the chairman of the L.C.C. committee, in defending the decision, announced that 'this council will never permit hooliganism, from whatever quarter it may come, to take the place of its censorship in obtaining the withdrawal of films or any other form of entertainment from establishments which the council licenses'.[16] As *Kine Weekly* commented : 'brave words, but it is a pity that neither the Council nor the Home Office is able or willing to implement them'.[17]

More direct Governmental participation in censorship was displayed in the case of *The Fall of Berlin*, a Russian film of the capture of the city that minimized the part played by the Allies. Once again the Board was guilty of seeking advice from those in political power. On this occasion the Prime Minister himself was consulted, Churchill expressing the opinion that in a free country there could be no objection to the showing of the film. Representatives of the Home and Foreign Offices, however, felt that one cut was desirable 'from the political point of view' and one caption was deleted in consequence. Given the green light by the Prime Minister and the Foreign Secretary a certificate was finally issued, but not before the foreword that had already been added stressing the propaganda nature of the film, had been altered slightly.

Once again it is evident that, on crucial issues, the independence of the Board was more theoretical than practical. A serious lack of confidence in its own powers and abilities, allied with a marked tendency to accede to, and even to encourage, political intervention, meant that accusations that the Board was a creature of the establishment could not convincingly be denied. As Ivor Montagu wrote at the time : 'For all the ritual denials of political censorship, however, the ultimate political powers remain crouched in reserve; first as the film life of Nurse Cavell could be banned by the "independent" B.B. of F.C. at a moment when Neville Chamberlain was making up to Hitler, so the Board at the present day could invent reasons for forbidding film revelations of the Nazi past of West German functionaries when Macmillan was making up to Bonn.'[18] Montagu was referring here to two films in the series *The Archives Testify* which consisted largely of captured Nazi film, designed to expose 'war criminals and prominent Nazis who are at present holding positions of power and authority'. The first of these, titled *Holiday in Sylt*, attacked a former S.S. general who had become mayor of the holiday island of Sylt. It was scheduled to be broadcast by Associated-Rediffusion on I.T.V. on 9th May, 1958. Twenty-four hours before the programme was to be transmitted, the film was withdrawn after talks between television executives and the Foreign Office. It was also denied a certificate by the B.B.F.C.

Part 2 in the series was *Operation Teutonic Sword*. According to one account the film 'makes a reasoned argument—fully and copiously documented—why the commander of N.A.T.O. land forces in Middle Europe, General Hans Speidel, is no fit person to handle modern atomic weapons; he was involved, says the film, in a double political murder in 1934 and later, amongst other misdeeds, worked out the orders by which occupied France was governed'.[19]

The film was rejected on two grounds. First, exception was taken to the fact that the film 'made serious allegations against a living person in a prominent position and provided no opportunity for an alternative interpretation of the evidence produced'. This objection if taken to its logical limits would, of course, put all the mass media in a very tight strait-jacket: any form of investigative journalism would immediately become unacceptable. Apart from this major point it is far from true that someone who is the subject of 'serious allegations', especially if he is in a 'prominent' position has no recourse. The media are, in general, only too keen to follow up a story of this nature. Even more importantly, if the film were libellous as the censor's objections implied, redress could always be had through the courts.

The second 'subsidiary' reason for rejecting the film was that it was 'critical of a government with which this country has friendly diplomatic relations without providing an opportunity for its charges to be refuted'. As usual, of course, the reasons for the film's rejection were not made public. There was, nonetheless, some public outcry (led by the National Council for Civil Liberties) that political censorship was taking place. The L.C.C., in fact, finally passed the film, overturning the decision of its Public Control Committee by a vote of 59–58.

The Board's embarrassment was increased when Speidel did refute one charge made in the film and brought a libel action on this basis in Germany. As a result the British distributors cut out all references to this particular episode and re-submitted the film. The Board's main objection was now unfounded, but while they continued to deny that political censorship was taking place, a certificate was again refused. This decision led to the tabling of a motion in the Commons 'that this House, without desiring to make comment on the merits or otherwise of the film *Operation Teutonic Sword*, is of the opinion that the British Board of Film Censors is wrong in refusing to grant a certificate for the public showing of this film, and calls upon the Board to reverse this decision, thereby enabling the British public the opportunity of seeing the film and forming an opinion as to its merits'. The Home Secretary, however, declined to take any action, pointing out that the function of the Board is, in any case, purely advisory. Defending this episode some years later John Trevelyan commented: 'We refused [*Operation Teutonic Sword* and *Holiday on Sylt*], but not on political grounds. We did not think that cinema entertainment was the right place for putting over defamatory material about living persons.'[20]

For some reason Trevelyan did not seek legal advice about the Board's position until some time later, when the 'fuss' had died down. When he did so he was advised that the Board's policy was 'not justified since it was not the job of such an organization to do the work of the Courts, and furthermore that it was most unlikely that the Board would be involved in any libel proceedings since it was not an accessory in the publication of a libel'.[21] Trevelyan comments that 'on receiving this opinion we immediately abandoned our former policy'.

The following year (1960) more Nazi propaganda material was submitted to the Board. This was *The Warsaw Ghetto*, a film made during the war with the intention of stirring up anti-semitism. The censors demanded cuts totalling five minutes which the distributors refused to accept and therefore withdrew from negotiations. The film was thus not actually banned. The Board commented that 'we reached the conclusion that there were certain scenes in films of this kind which might well be regarded by many people as too unpleasant for public exhibition'. Strangely, according to Judith Todd,[22] the very same scenes were passed in the Swedish film *Mein Kampf*. Todd also refers to a further example of political decision-making at this time, alleging that the Boulting brothers' comedy *Carleton-Browne of the F.O.* was denied exhibition in Russia following Foreign Office intervention, presumably on the grounds that its light-hearted look at ministerial fumbling might be taken seriously. Todd concluded that 'in general, the censorship seems anxious to preserve the outward decorum of British public life . . . widespread lid-lifting is discouraged, and it is impossible at present to imagine distribution being obtained for a British film attacking, for example, the administration of justice or corruption in local government : in the unlikely event of a backer being obtained the censor would at the most grant it an "X" certificate'.[23]

Since those words were written, of course, much has changed. Censorship is considerably less restrictive over subject matter, and the 'X' certificate is no longer box-office poison : quite the reverse. In the sixties there were relatively few occasions when the charge of political censorship was levelled. The only recent case involving a British film occurred in 1963 when Nicholas Luard, owner of The Establishment club, announced his intention to make a film based on the Christine Keeler-Stephen Ward scandal that had dominated headlines during the previous winter. At this stage the involvement of a Cabinet Minister had not yet come to light and John Trevelyan, approached by Luard and his American partner, indicated that, in principle, the Board had no objection to the project. Trevelyan had felt some concern on two counts. First, he was doubtful whether the Board should accept a film about real people that might become the subject of legal proceedings. Secondly, the producers had mentioned their intention of using Miss Keeler herself in the main role, and Trevelyan was worried lest the film might be seen as an encouragement to young girls to try to get into films by the same route. Consultation with Lord Morrison, however, had satisfied him that neither was a legitimate ground for intervention.

After this initial reassurance, the producers were naturally surprised to receive a letter from the Board suggesting that the picture 'would not be in the public interest'. This change of view had apparently been brought about by Lord Goodman, the Board's solicitor, who, knowing the full facts of the case, had advised Trevelyan that he would be 'fully justified in discouraging the producer from making the film'.[24] A further setback to the project was the refusal of Equity, the actors union, to admit Miss Keeler as a member. Undaunted the producers moved location from London to Copenhagen where the film, *The Christine Keeler Story*, was made with a professional actress in the main part.

During production the producers claimed that the Government had made direct attempts to prevent the film being completed but no evidence was furnished to substantiate this claim. At the same time Fleet Street rumours suggested that the Board's action to discourage the project had been taken as a result of instructions from the Government. This was strenuously denied by Trevelyan, although the precise role of Lord Goodman remains far from clear.

When the film was finally submitted for censorship it was rejected on the grounds that it presented a 'continuous picture of sordid vice, including sexual perversion' and that it was 'morally objectionable'. Some suspected other motives and a writer in *Tribune* asserted that 'when I asked our censor the reason (for the ban) he readily admitted that it was a political one'.[25] This statement was refuted by Trevelyan a fortnight later, but the writer refused to retract, arguing that the censor 'agreed that the *political* inexpedience of allowing the film's exhibition at that time—so close to the General Election—was taken into account and weighed conclusively in the Board's decision.'[26] This seems an unlikely admission by the ever shrewd Trevelyan, and the whole disagreement probably reflects no more than the dangers of interview by telephone.

However, the story was not yet over. In 1969 the distribution rights to *The Christine Keeler Story* were acquired by another company, who resubmitted the film, arguing that it could no longer be rejected for its sexual content. This the Board readily admitted, but the previous decision was upheld on two quite different grounds. First, 'we cannot ignore the social issues which are involved'; secondly, 'the Board ought not to encourage the exhibition of films about recent notorious court cases'. The first objection is too vague to be helpful, while the distinction between 'social' and 'political' in this context seems hard to make. The second objection sounds very similar to the argument that had been rejected in 1963.

When the film was shown to the G.L.C., Essex and Berkshire it suffered a similar fate. Although the decisions were explained in terms of tendency to deprave and corrupt, one G.L.C. member at least was unimpressed by the explanation, commenting that 'if they had mentioned Profumo that would have been the right reason'.

On the other hand, an application to Classic Cinemas for showing in their Tatler clubs was turned down because the picture contained 'too little overt sex to be of real interest to our members'. Not until February 1971 did the film have a showing in this country—at Derek Hill's New Cinema Club. Newspaper comments expressed unanimous disbelief that the film could have been turned down for the reasons given. The *Guardian* noted that 'Derek Hill . . . feels this to be political censorship and it is certainly difficult to imagine what other motives lay behind the ban on public showings'. The *Observer* denied that there was 'a single obscene image in it' and *The Times* concluded that 'reluctantly . . . we must suspect that Robert Spafford's sad little film is the victim of political censorship'.[27]

Two other films to be rejected in unusual circumstances at this time were by the American director, Samuel Fuller. The first concerned that old censors' bugbear—mental illness. *Shock Corridor* was rejected in 1963 on the grounds that the picture it gave of mental hospital life was far removed from that of hospitals in this country; that it could cause concern to people with relatives in hospital; that it was irresponsible to suggest that someone sane could secure admission to a hospital by putting on an act or that residence in a mental hospital could cause insanity; and that it might have 'bad, possibly dangerous, effects' on viewers with any degree of mental disturbance. The film was turned down again in 1968, although passed 'X' by the G.L.C. *The Naked Kiss* had been submitted in 1964 when the Board had decided that 'the employment of the girl in a home for spastic children was not an adequate compensation for the rest of the material in this film', a comment which sounds more typical of American censors with their old rules of balance between good and evil, with the latter always to be punished. Strangely enough, in *What the Censor Saw*, Trevelyan attacks the P.C.A. for giving a Code Seal to this film and dropping their usual demand for compensatory factors.[28]

It goes without saying, of course, that in the post-war period this country has never suffered the sort of censorship that overtook America during the McCarthy era, when the P.C.A. submitted silently to the sort of pressures that critics of censorship have always warned against. They became, apparently without a struggle, a tool of the Un-American activities campaigners and used their position of power to stifle any project that could have been attacked by the 'Red' hunters. In their defence they naturally argued later that they were trying to protect the industry. One instance may be quoted as an illustration of what can happen to censorship in a situation of that kind. Dore Schary, the respected head of production at M.G.M., had submitted a script to the P.C.A. who quickly detected 'glaring streaks of party-line propaganda'. A letter was sent to Schary warning him : 'It is my belief that you will hear that you are sponsoring a script that is filled with party-line propaganda. I don't know if it *is* party-line propaganda. But it is what will be *said* to be party-line propaganda. It is what is popularly *thought* to be the current party line. Therefore, you are playing with flaming contemporary prejudices, and you are liable to get crucified for it.'[29] Schary ('he was probably nothing more than a Stevensonian liberal. But at that moment, it seemed like a lot more') withdrew the script and the project was dropped.

As pointed out earlier, script-reading is a relatively small part of the British censor's job, and such an incident is less likely here, but there is one notorious case of a film foundering because

of objections lodged by the censor. In 1960 a script was submitted based on Michael Croft's book *Spare the Rod*, a novel
about teaching in a tough, demoralized secondary modern school,
with a strong anti-corporal punishment message. The Board's
opinion was that even after certain scenes had been omitted, only
an 'X' certificate could be hoped for. On this basis no film company could be found to sponsor the production and the project
was shelved. Apparently the censor 'did not believe such schools
as we had shown existed and he was apprehensive that such a
distasteful picture of British life might be seen abroad in countries
such as Russia'.[30] Trevelyan denies that these were his reasons.

So far in this discussion the term 'political censorship' has
been defined in a fairly narrow way. More properly it refers
to any interference with or banning of ideas, and as such almost
becomes synonymous with censorship itself. As Victor Perkins has
said : 'When he deletes a shot from a movie, the censor vetoes
one viewpoint and states another'. This position is of course a
little extreme : the cutting of most films does not significantly
alter the ideas in those films—and in any case, the vast majority
of films are hardly concerned with ideas at all. However, it is
incontestable that certain ideas have been and are banned by the
censors.

Racialist films were beginning to reappear in 1972, and one
film in particular caused great problems for the Board. This was
Uncle Tom by the Italian film-makers, Jacopetti and Prosperi.
In the form of an 'authentic' pseudo-historical reconstruction of
slavery in America in the nineteenth century, the film was
actually shot in Haiti. Although presented as an 'inquiry' into
the horrors of slavery it is in fact totally voyeuristic and exploita-
tive. The blacks are shown to be little more than animals and
the camera gloats at the treatment they receive from whites. The
men are tortured and killed in abundance (and slow motion),
the girls, all young, pretty and generally nude are raped, prostitu-
ted or merely gazed upon.

The film had already been cut by the distributors before submission to the Board, and the censors had no hesitation in demanding the removal of the entire final reel. This presented an
episode in the present in which a negro muses upon the writings
of Nat Turner (who led a slave rebellion involving white killings in the period after the Civil War), and envisaged the practising of Turner's policies today. The rest of the film presented
a more complicated problem. There is no doubt that everyone

on the Board would have liked to have banned the film entirely, but Murphy was not eager to expand the issues upon which 'social undesirability' becomes cause enough for rejection. Harlech's opinion was that the crux of the matter was whether the film was offensive from a black point of view and would harm race relations in this country. A number of black people had been shown *Uncle Tom* already and had expressed a uniform disgust, but for a final opinion the Board decided to call in the Race Relations Board.

The film was seen by two black members of that body, plus the chairman, Mark Bonham Carter. By a 2–1 majority they felt that, repugnant though it was, the film should not be banned, arguing that both blacks and whites were degraded and that therefore the social issue was not directly relevant. Thus, although one member argued forcefully that the film might well stir up racial hatred and lead to violence, the final decision was that only the usual censorship criteria should be used.

One final attempt to resolve the problem remained. There was some suggestion that the film could be rejected under the Race Relations Act. The Board's lawyers were consulted, and they confirmed that the Act did indeed include films under the heading 'written matter', but advised that it seemed quite impossible to implement the Act in the present circumstances. To secure a conviction it is apparently necessary to prove intent to stir up racial feeling on the part of the handlers of the film. In the case of a foreign made film this presents obvious difficulties, for only the distributor or exhibitor can be charged.

Nevertheless, all four examiners who had seen *Uncle Tom* were still keen either that it should be rejected or that such severe cuts should be demanded that the film would not be exhibitable. Though doubtless well-intentioned, it seemed clear that their reaction was not only evinced by the film's treatment, but by the horrors of slavery itself, and that they were making a political decision. The cuts that they requested included many that would not have been necessary in another context, and were designed partly to reduce the impact of the slave-traders' horrific activities. Murphy himself appreciated that this was the sort of occasion when the Board would be criticized whatever decision was made, and was eventually prepared to agree to heavy cuts. The film was finally passed after the removal of thirty-one sections totalling half an hour of film.

In fact, as luck would have it, the film opened in London at the same time as *Last Tango in Paris*, and as a result was almost totally overlooked. Apart from a solitary protest from Mrs Whitehouse, the expected avalanche of criticism did not arrive, and although the film has now been shown quite widely, it has aroused no controversy.

Nevertheless this case does illustrate how the Board does still, on occasions, institute political censorship. Under the general heading of 'offensiveness' and 'tastelessness' it is all too easy to include items of this nature. The banning of the Swedish film *491* in 1966 has already been mentioned. Trevelyan described it as 'a nasty and vicious film, and one which seems to be basically evil'. This description betrays a real fear of the film and suggests that its banning was not just the result of some sex scenes (which could easily have been cut) but of antipathy towards the film's message—that woolly-minded liberalism and idealism is not the answer to delinquency.

Such cases could, of course, be multiplied, but there is no doubt that the Board's record has improved markedly in recent years. It is also significant that the Government is now generally keen *not* to become involved in matters of censorship. Reginald Maudling's ill-advised (and inconsequential) tangling with *A Clockwork Orange* apart, official sources will now rarely pass comment or offer 'advice'. Trevelyan felt that 'successive Home Secretaries were not unwilling to have a way of avoiding being involved in controversy on films'.[31] Robert Carr made no attempt to intervene beyond writing to local authorities recommending them to support the Board. Roy Jenkins' request for a report on *The Exorcist* seems to have been no more than a gesture. This is not to say that there is no communication at all between Soho Square and Whitehall. The Secretary does occasionally see Home Office officials. In preparation for a meeting with local authority representatives in 1972 Murphy had discussions with two Home Office Civil Servants (at Permanent Under Secretary level). On another occasion, prior to a debate in the House of Lords, the Board arranged a film show for guests from the Home Office to give them a better idea of the Board's policies and activities.

The Government has, of course, a perfect right to be kept up-to-date and well-informed in any area of controversy. The Home Secretary needs to be in a position to answer questions that might be asked in the Commons with regard to the various Cinematograph and Obscenity Acts. But the dividing line between the gathering of information and sinister interference is a thin one. A simple request for information may itself be a barely-veiled expression of concern.

The Board is naturally alive to the dangers of any hint of influence from this quarter. Murphy insists that 'I am not conscious of Home Office pressure. The Home Office has always acted perfectly correctly.' One example illustrates his conviction that the Government does indeed go out of its way to avoid any involvement in film censorship. When the American film *Fortune and Men's Eyes*, dealing with homosexuality in prison, was submitted in 1972, the Board decided to seek the advice of the Prisoners' Commission. In error the film's distributors got in touch directly with the Home Office (under whose control the Commission lies). The Home Office refused to involve themselves in any way and the Commission never saw the film.

One recent film in which the Home Office did show a discreet interest was *Manson*, a documentary about the 'family' after their leader's conviction on multiple murder charges. It was certainly not official pressure, however, that led to the Board's rejection of the film, but the personal reactions of Murphy and his examiners, who were 'shaken and disturbed' by the film. Murphy himself has expressed doubts about his own judgement on this occasion. He appreciated that it was a sincere film made with the best intentions as a deterrent to young people, containing no visual violence and only a little sex, and which had been passed for general audiences in America, yet he was quite unable to 'take' it. His decision to reject the film resulted from revulsion at the political and social ideas propounded by the 'family' which he felt were given some degree of attraction by the hedonistic life-style that accompanied them. He himself was not satisfied that it was an entirely 'responsible' judgement.

With no great faith in the decision he encouraged the distributor to apply to the local authorities. The film was passed by the G.L.C. in October 1973 (but rejected by Essex, Berkshire and Surrey), a decision that prompted a lengthy dissenting editorial in *The Times*:

By all accounts the film *Manson* which a subcommittee of the G.L.C. has decided may be shown in London, although it has been banned by the British Board of Film Censors, is a documentary of scrupulous objectivity and a social document of some importance. The G.L.C.'s decision may even so be mistaken. The film deals with the community that gathered in California around Charles Manson, who was convicted in 1971 of seven murders, and examines the attitudes of members of the group who are still at liberty, for the most part simply by allowing them to talk. This detailed study of abnormal psychology was stuff too strong for the censors, who are fairly hardened spectators.

It is legitimate in principle to argue that a film may be a very valuable document for study, and yet too disturbing for general exhibition even to adults. It need not be overtly violent to be potentially dangerous in its effects: the very restraint of the treatment may only tend to make the things described seem bewilderingly prosaic and normal as if the film-maker condoned them by showing them.[32]

Whatever the rights or wrongs of this case, *Manson* has never, at the time of writing, been given a public showing.

In summary, it seems reasonable to accept the conclusions of Paul O'Higgins in his recent book, *Censorship in Britain*, that 'open censorship on political or social grounds appears no longer to be practised by the B.B.F.C., as it certainly was in the 1920s and 1930s, although social and political attitudes still appear to colour some decisions'.[33] Murphy himself is aware that there are circumstances in which political decisions might come to be made. As an example he wonders what decision would have been reached had a well-made pro-I.R.A. film been submitted before that organization was proscribed. While direct politically motivated censorship is rare, the censorship of ideas does continue to take place for, under any system of consensual censorship, it is inevitable that extreme minority attitudes and opinions must be ignored and suppressed.

8

STATUTORY POWERS

THE LOCAL AUTHORITIES hold the statutory powers of censorship. They can accept or reject the decisions of the B.B.F.C. and can impose such conditions as they think suitable regarding the exhibition of any film. As we have seen, relationships between the Board and the authorities have always been uneasy. When the Board was first established most councils were loath to forego their powers so that for some years the Board was supported by only a small number of authorities. The majority continued to favour the establishment of an official Government appointed censor and a conference in April 1916 of local authorities endorsed a proposal by the Home Secretary to set up a new Board containing representatives of the Home Office. This plan eventually came to nothing, and when in 1921 the L.C.C. adopted recommendations that no film 'which has not been passed for "universal" or "public" exhibition by the British Board of Film Censors shall be exhibited without the express consent of the Council',[1] it was clear that the system in operation had been accepted. In 1923 the Home Office circularized all licensing authorities recommending them to adopt the L.C.C. rules which were enclosed in the form of model conditions. Within the next few months most authorities acceded to this request.

There were, however, important exceptions. Manchester has always valued its independence, and it continued to reject the national system relying on a scheme of local censorship in conjunction with the Watch Committee and police that was not to be abandoned until 1953. In January 1932 Beckenham created a local board of nine members which was to see all films to be exhibited within the borough. It even instituted a new certificate, quaintly entitled 'Passed Under Protest', but before long the strictness of its policy brought its downfall. 'The disastrous effect of local censorship on attendance at cinemas spelt ruin for the local traders. Moreover, the refusal of the public to go and see cut pictures made imminent the closing of many cinemas. . . .

Finally, the town itself became divided on the question of censorship. . . . Defeat for the local censorship, which came to an end on 20th July, was thus inevitable.'[2] There was a strong movement for local action at that time: Lincoln, Tipton, Harrow and Barry were considering following Beckenham, but the collapse of that experiment discouraged others.

Dissatisfaction with the system, however, remained. In April 1932 the Birmingham Cinema Enquiry Committee sent a delegation to the Home Office, arguing that 'the present system is working badly and is having unsatisfactory results'. They called for a comprehensive enquiry 'at which evidence can be sifted and cross-examined', and hoped that 'as a result there will probably come out of it recommendations which will be immensely to the improvement of the system'. The Home Secretary expressed sympathy but offered only optimistic forecasts of future trends: 'Undoubtedly the sex element in life has been over-stressed. . . . I think there is a general feeling now that this has been overdone, and there are signs that there is beginning a wholesome reaction in public opinion against this.'[3] In rejecting an inquiry he quoted a report by the Mothers' Union Committee which had found that 'a good deal of the criticism of cinema programmes is exaggerated and not based on careful observation or adequate data'. He was also supported by a Home Office enquiry the previous year, which had established that, of 603 licensing authorities questioned, only 3.5 per cent had had complaints about films in the previous three years. Furthermore, in this period only eight authorities had seen fit to bar a film passed by the Board, and only nine had demanded cuts in certificated films, while, on the other hand 229 had received applications to show films rejected by the Board, of which 85 per cent had been granted (16 per cent subject to special conditions). The evidence thus suggested that the authorities were more liberal than the Board, although these figures are misleading in that 88 per cent of applications concerned the same four films.

After this date criticism seems to have subsided, although some councils retained their independence while others engaged in spells of action—Warwickshire banned 'harrowing' news films in the late thirties, and 'immoral' films in 1960–1, while Oldham rejected 'horror' films during 1946 and 1947. Departures from the Board's certificate over individual films were not uncommon, but these continued to be more often on the side of liberalism. The L.C.C. and Middlesex C.C. were particularly active in this

respect. They created a joint committee to deal with film censorship and this committee was later enlarged to include Surrey
(1930), Essex (1937) and East Ham (1938).

In the years leading up to and during the war there was some
disagreement among certain authorities with the Board's policy
of awarding 'H' certificates, until in 1942 it was decided that
no more 'H' films would be passed while hostilities continued.
There was some consternation in 1949 when *The Snake Pit* was
passed for adults only, for some councils were opposed to this
innovation. The introduction of the 'X' certificate two years later
encountered similar opposition and some authorities at first refused to accept it and demanded to see all 'X' certificated films
before allowing their exhibition.

Generally, however, the licensing authorities took little interest
in such matters and were content to rubber-stamp the Board's
decisions. It was lack of interest also which probably accounted
for their tendency to pass a number of films banned by the Board.
That, at least, is how the Board itself interpreted the situation.
Indeed by the mid-fifties the Secretary was growing increasingly
upset at the extent to which this was happening, especially as,
very often, the authority never even saw the film in question but
relied on the word of the distributor that it was entirely harmless
and unexceptionable. Watkins made some attempt to counter
this tendency by holding meetings with local authorities at which
he explained the Board's point of view and suggested that the
councils were being manipulated too easily by plausible businessmen. This had little effect, however, and a second attempt was
made some years later to 'educate' the authorities. In conjunction
with the County Councils Association and the Association of
Municipal Corporations, Trevelyan arranged a series of 'Conferences on Film Censorship'. At the first of these, held in the
National Film Theatre on 16th November, 1961, members of the
local councils heard addresses by Trevelyan and his President,
Lord Morrison of Lambeth, and also 'a discussion on present
problems in film censorship by the Examiners of the British
Board of Film Censors with the Secretary of the Board, with
illustrations on the screen'. This discussion was divided into
three parts—Violence and Brutality, Horror, and Sex and
Nudity, and was followed by a question and answer session. During this, one councillor expressed his dissatisfaction with local
censorship and pin-pointed its potential weakness: 'next week
our watch committee will be seeing this film. There will prob-

ably be six members of the watch committee present and—I am boasting now—I shall be the only one who has seen many films in his life. What I feel is that the members of the watch committee will in the last twenty years not have seen any films except those which they have had the opportunity to see buckshee. So I wonder whether they are in such a good position to be able to classify a film as "X", "A" or "U".[4]

This is precisely what the B.B.F.C. itself was thinking and hoped to impress on the councillors who attended this conference, and those that followed, in Manchester in April 1963 and in London again five weeks later. However, the conferences seem to have been considered as of doubtful value by the Board who thereafter abandoned their attempts to influence the authorities by these means.[5] In retrospect, it is possible that these meetings did something to stir up the local authority interest in censorship which the Board now finds an embarrassment.

Only a handful of films resulted in disagreement between local councils and the Board during the sixties. One of these was *Fanny Hill* which was refused a certificate in 1965. The distributors applied for local licenses throughout the country, the results of which indicated a low level of consensus among the authorities themselves. At first quite a number agreed with the Board and rejected the film but, by 1968 when the film was finally given a B.B.F.C. certificate, only twenty stuck to this decision. Of the others, seventy-eight had given an 'X' certificate, 153 an 'A' and twenty a 'U'. Alexander Walker has explained this wide divergence of opinion in terms of the inexperience of authorities who are rarely called upon to see films. One of Trevelyan's objections had been 'to a scene in a haystack where Fanny and a young rake are sheltering from the rain. To protect her dress, she asks him to help her off with it and while fumbling behind her she suddenly exclaims that she can feel a mouse in the hay. A few seconds later she cries out that she can feel the mouse again, only now it is bigger.' Walker argued that some local authorities had 'entirely missed the implications of this erection joke. To them a mouse was a mouse. They took Fanny's word for it.'[6] No such ingenuousness can be used to explain a later divergence of judgement when, in 1968, Yoko Ono's *Number Four*, the 'bottoms' film, was thought to be 'X' material by the G.L.C. but 'U' in Birmingham.

The issues involved were also very clear with regard to Joseph Strick's *Ulysses* which was turned down by the Board in 1967.

Once again, when local certification was sought by the distributors, disagreement was found. Seventy-seven authorities rejected the film, while sixty-three passed it uncut in the 'X' category. Six councils banned the film without even seeing it. 'The Board had apparently made available to local authorities the extracts from the script to which it had objected. In Southampton, only these extracts were considered and not the film itself or its script. A storm of local protest at this attitude led to the Public Safety Committee laying down as future policy that, in considering any application to exhibit a contentious film, the committee should obtain the views of the British Board of Film Censors, and should also take into consideration the views and decisions of the Greater London Council and any other corporate body which might have a bearing.'[7]

A similar fate befell Aldrich's *The Killing of Sister George* a couple of years later. The Board demanded the excision of the love-scene, which the distributors were unwilling to accept. The G.L.C. allowed part of the scene, as did a number of other authorities, although others rejected the film altogether. Eventually the Board certificated a modified version.

The modern cinema licence is a fairly standard document based on a model designed by the Home Office. Although there may be small differences between the conditions imposed by different authorities the following clauses are normally included:

(1) No film shall be exhibited unless—
  (a) it has received a 'U', 'A', 'AA', or 'X' certificate of the British Board of Film Censors; or
  (b) it is a current newsreel which has not been submitted to the British Board of Film Censors.

(2) No child apparently under the age of eighteen years shall be admitted to an exhibition at which there is to be shown any film which has received an 'X' certificate from the British Board of Film Censors.

(3) No child apparently under the age of eighteen years shall be admitted to any exhibition at which there is to be shown any film which has received an 'AA' certificate from the British Board of Film Censors.

(4) Notwithstanding the conditions herein before contained, a film may be exhibited, or children, or any class of children, may be admitted thereto if the permission of the licensing

authority is first obtained and any conditions of such permission are complied with.

(5) Where the licensing authority have given notice in writing to the licensee of the premises prohibiting the exhibition of a film on the ground that it contains matter which, if exhibited, would offend against good taste or decency or would be likely to encourage or incite to crime or to lead to disorder or to be offensive to public feeling, that film shall not be exhibited in the premises except with the consent in writing of the licensing authority.

(6) If the licensing authority do not agree with the category in which any film passed by the British Board of Film Censors is placed, they shall be at liberty to alter such category, and, on notice of such alteration being given by the licensing authority to the licensee, the films thereafter shall be treated as having been placed in the altered category and the conditions applicable to the exhibition of films in such altered category shall be complied with.

(7) If, on receipt of a complaint from not less than six persons, the licensing authority request the licensee to exhibit to them any film complained of, he shall do so at such reasonable time and to such persons as the licensing authority may, in writing, direct.

In recent years, until 1971, the policy of all authorities has been to allow the exhibition of films passed by the B.B.F.C. The committees have therefore only been actively involved in considering films not certificated by the Board, but referred to the committee by the producer or distributor hoping to be given permission to show the film locally. The majority of councils, in fact, never receive such applications, for it is uneconomic to refer a film to an area that has only one or two cinemas. Only a dozen authorities regularly receive such applications—the rest are rarely or never involved in censorship at all. Policies regarding such applications inevitably vary. At one extreme Leicester City Council, for example, adopted a policy 'to refuse without viewing, the public exhibition of any film which had been refused a certificate'; at the other, Great Yarmouth's Public Control Committee considered applications 'in conjunction with the observations of the Secretary of the Board and the action taken by other licensing authorities (particularly the G.L.C.). If the G.L.C. and other

authorities have granted local certificates, then Great Yarmouth
Council is normally recommended to do the same.'

Normally, if a council has been approached by a company
it asks the B.B.F.C. to explain its decision to ban the film. The
Secretary then sends a letter outlining the Board's views. It may
include a strong condemnation of the picture, implying that it
really ought not to be passed, or it may be more friendly towards
the film, indicating that, although for one reason or another it
went further than the Board was prepared to allow, there were
grounds for passing it and that the Board did not necessarily wish
to discourage this decision. Many councils apparently find this
letter helpful in performing a job in which many admit that
they have little expertise. The feelings of many authorities were
probably summarized in the words of Hampshire County Council who state that 'the viewing of non-certificated films is not
a task which is relished by Members of the County Council.
The Members have no special skills in the art of censorship and
are able only to exercise mature judgement.'

Although the powers of censorship reside in the District
Councils, these are nearly always delegated to a committee. The
particular committee which is handed this burden varies from
place to place. Usually the Environmental Health Committee
or the Public Protection or General Purposes Committee is
chosen, but it may be the Fire Brigade Committee, Licensing
Committee or even a Committee of Justices. Nor are there any
regulations laid down concerning the composition of this committee. Like all such committees they are made up of those
councillors with a special interest who have volunteered to serve.
Unfortunately film censorship is invariably a small and unconsidered part of the total frame of reference of the committee—
no councillor is serving as a result of his involvement in censorship issues—he takes part as a side-result of his concern over
matters of public safety, road problems and so on. The numbers
in the committee also vary widely. Many are quite large—
Birmingham's General Advisory Committee has twenty-three
members, Blackpool's and Chichester's Environmental Health
Committees twenty and eighteen, respectively. Others are much
smaller: the Environmental Health Licensing Sub-committees
of Leeds and Cardiff are only seven and six strong.[8] Of these
only a small proportion are women—the committees mentioned
above include only fourteen women among their seventy-four
members.

It is, of course, rare for a film to be seen by a full committee.
Certain councillors are more eager than others to fulfil this
duty, and some find it easier than others to make time to attend
viewings. A Labour councillor in Southend has produced figures
to show that 80 per cent of attendances by that city's twelve
committee members had been made by six Conservative members which he accounted for in terms of the arrangements by
which films were shown on weekdays so that 'only the self-
employed, the retired or those who work in Southend can
attend'.[9] In general, it would appear that viewings are attended
by about one-third of all members. The G.L.C., whose committee has a membership of twenty, insists on a quorum of only
five, but states that meetings are normally attended by nine or
ten members. Elsewhere films have been known to have been
seen by only one or two members, but this low level of participation is rare.

An earlier chapter has indicated how in recent years the local
authorities' interest in film censorship has been renewed. The
extensive press coverage of 'controversial' films such as *The
Devils* and *Straw Dogs* alerted many councillors to the increasingly 'adult' nature of the 'entertainment' being offered in
cinemas. Their own powers to influence events were made very
clear and a small, but growing number have made use of them.
Despite the furore *The Devils* was in fact only banned in fourteen places and *Straw Dogs* in ten, but a much larger number
of authorities had become aware of films as a 'problem' and
were prepared to act accordingly in the future. Although Kubrick
had delayed the provincial release of *A Clockwork Orange* for
a year it still met stern opposition from many councils when it
did appear. A series of press reports of acts of violence committed
by young people dressed after the fashion of the 'hero' of the
film did much to spread alarm about the possible consequences
of allowing it to be shown.[10] In fact the most widely publicized
of these incidents turned out to have been perpetrated by a boy
who had not even seen the film and was indeed too young to
have done so. The assertion that the film had increased violence
rather than merely influenced its style was, of course, never supported by evidence. However, local councils were alarmed and
many announced their intention of vetting the film. In February
1973 Hastings became the first authority (and, Brazil apart, the
only place in the world at that time) to ban it. The circumstances
surrounding this decision illustrate how local authority censor-

ship *can* be manifestly unsatisfactory. Apparently, because only short notice of the intended exhibition of *A Clockwork Orange* in Hastings was given, only two members of the Public Health and Licensing Committee were able to attend the viewing. One of these did not see the whole film. It was rejected because it was 'violence for its own sake' and had 'no moral'. The decision was bitterly attacked in the local press, in which an editorial argued that 'it is wrong that the public should be treated like schoolchildren by a handful of fickle councillors whose tastes are not in any way representative of the people they are elected to represent'.[11]

Members of the public, however, were more likely to encourage restrictive policies. In certain areas campaigns were organized to prevent local exhibition of certain films, in others a number of individual protests were sufficient to stimulate the council to action. In Warrington, for example, it has been reported that 'complaints from an angry housewife have led to Warrington's licensing committee drawing up a black list of "X" films that they don't want screened in the town. The list has been sent to the managers of the two local cinemas, but the names of the films are being kept secret because the corporation do not want to give them publicity.'[12] In this case one complaint was sufficient to cause the banning of a number of films, *A Clockwork Orange* included, none of which had been seen by the committee. Such an extreme reaction is rare, but some councils do undoubtedly take account of a very small number of objections. As a north-eastern official has commented, 'as far as "X" films are concerned there has only been one furore in the six years I've been chairman of the committee and that was over *Straw Dogs*. Five people wrote to us.'[13] Elsewhere such concerted opposition might have been enough to ban the film.

A number of authorities followed the example of Hastings and determined to take a look at *A Clockwork Orange*. Among them was Leeds where the Fire Brigade Committee had previously accepted all films passed by the Board. In the course of viewing uncertificated pictures, however, the committee had become aware that, since they saw no films that *had* been passed, they had no standard for making judgements. They therefore resolved to see an "X" film to discover what standards were being maintained. When they saw *A Clockwork Orange*, however, it was agreed by a majority of 9–3 that the film should be banned, because 'it would be injurious to morality, it could

encourage and incite crime, it could cause disorder, it was
thought to be offensive to public feeling, it may be thought to
contain offensive representations of living persons'.[14] Discussion of
this decision was limited by the fact that the chairman of the
committee was seeking re-election to the council, thus barring him
from being interviewed on radio or television.

By the time *Last Tango in Paris* appeared, local councils were
well and truly alerted. The controversies over earlier films and
the wide press coverage of *Last Tango* resulted in a larger number of councils than ever before resolving to see the film before
accepting the censor's decision. Newspaper accounts, many of
which gave a thoroughly unbalanced and sensationalized summary of the film's contents, did much to create the impression
that this was a 'problem' picture, while the Festival of Light
wrote to individual councils condemning the film. In fact the
B.B.F.C. had only considered cutting two scenes and had finally
insisted on the reduction of one, indicating that they had encountered no particular difficulty with the film. Licensing committees up and down the country, however, took their cue from
the press, forsaking their own independent judgement to conclude that a film that had generated so much adverse publicity,
must be suspect and probably pornographic. Thus a Sevenoaks
councillor could condemn it as 'poor quality' and remark that
it 'should be deposited in a vault along with other blue films'
without ever having seen it, while the chairman of the Worcester-
shire licensing committee announced that while he wasn't prepared to prejudge the film, 'it is unlikely we shall allow' it to
be shown.[15]

The various pressure groups were not slow to capitalize on this
situation. A Festival of Light campaigner in London, although
admitting that 'he did not know a great deal about *Last Tango*',
insisted that 'he was getting fed up with that kind of film being
foisted on the public' and approached his local councillor about
getting the film banned. The latter responded that, while he
couldn't judge the film unseen, 'I expect it's a bad film and dare
say if I saw it I would come out against it', a reaction which he
admitted was based on press reports he had read.[16] In Hull, the
council received a petition from thirty-four members of the Union
of Catholic Mothers. After originally banning *Last Tango* unseen, they did eventually view the film but upheld their previous
decision on a 6–2 vote. During the showing, three telegrams had
been read out, all coming from local Catholic organizations. Two

councillors later commented that they had felt it essential to protect 'young people' and 'teenagers'. The 'X' category had, of course, been created for this precise purpose. The chairman of the Environment Services Committee which deals with licensing remarked that his judgement on any film was 'whether I would like my female folk, my daughter, to see it'.[17] In all, *Last Tango* was banned by fifty councils.

The great majority of councils, of course, continued to support the decisions of the B.B.F.C., and where this policy is no longer followed, there are often strong minorities who would welcome a return to former habits. The Teesside General Purposes Committee had viewed *Straw Dogs* 'because of publicity given it by the press' and banned it on the grounds that it could 'incite crime or lead to disorder', and had also seen *A Clockwork Orange*. Some members were heartily opposed to these actions feeling that it was 'illogical and wrong for the committee to pass judgement on films which already had a certificate, especially when only two or three were seen in isolation'.[18] Even the mayor argued that 'to arbitrarily choose isolated films for viewing because things had been said about them was a wrong way of exercising statutory duties'.[19]

It should also be noted that a number of authorities have special clauses in their licences that put additional restrictions on cinema managers. This is very prevalent in Wales where non-conformism insists on special rules for Sunday exhibitions. Until October 1972, for instance, not only were cinemas forbidden to show 'X' films in Llandudno on Sundays, but all children had to be accompanied by adults when attending Sunday films. Newport retains a clause insisting that at least one cinema must show a 'U' or 'A' film on Sundays. This was waived for a short time in 1972 when managers claimed that only 'X' films made money on Sundays, but reimposed a few weeks later. The council apparently wished to disassociate themselves from 'today's complete obsession with sex and violence, which are undoubtedly contributory factors in our moral degeneration', while one councillor's attitude towards the cinema was reflected in his observation that 'the cinema must accept some responsibility for this increase in sex crimes'.[20]

Finally, it is worth pointing out that, notwithstanding the recent controversies and publicity, some local authorities in remote areas where films are not an important element, appear to have a very limited awareness of their role and powers in respect of censorship. These are places that always accept B.B.F.C. decisions and to which no distributor bothers to appeal for a local licence, so that involvement in such issues is minimal. Nevertheless, it is surprising to find enquiries such as the one following which came to the Board from a 'Principal Legal Officer and Deputy Town Clerk' in August 1973: 'I am in some doubt as to the precise powers of my Magistrates Committee with regard to the grant or refusal of permission for the exhibition of certain films within the Burgh. . . . I would be obliged if you could refer me to an appropriate statute and other authority defining the powers of the magistrates in such matters.' Nor is this query by any means unique: the Board continues to receive queries from councils asking if they have the right to reject decisions made by the B.B.F.C.

This ignorance may appear shocking but our system of amateur local government involves councillors in a great deal of work in many very different areas. Censorship is only a tiny part of their job, and not one with which they are necessarily very concerned. It is possible to argue that, since they are supposed to be representative of the 'man in the street', it is right that they should not become too involved in matters connected with the cinema, or go out of their way to acquire specialist knowledge. As the chairman of Sheffield's Licensing Sub-Committee has said: 'I'm no expert on the cinema—and most of my time on the Licensing Sub-Committee is taken up with dealing with licence applications from taxi drivers, people who want to install one armed bandits, and so on. But I don't think it is necessary to be an expert for this sort of job. You don't have to have any special qualifications. Almost anybody would do really. It's just people.'[21]

Nevertheless there are specific regulations to be adhered to. Councils only have the right to ban the exhibition of films according to the conditions laid down in the licence. One or two councils would seem to be going beyond these rights and following a policy that is more restrictive than their powers warrant. It is inevitable that individual councillors should wish to follow a course beyond the strict word of the law and seek to impose strict regulations, but it is more serious if councils' stated policy goes too far. To what extent, for instance, was Oxford City justified in announcing that 'a rather more serious view is taken by the Committee . . . where it is felt that a film in its attitude towards religion is considered likely to be offensive to *some people*' (my italics)? Margate Corporation were clearly defining their powers in very broad terms when they argued that 'there is the feeling that children and the more sensitive-minded young people, together with the majority of adults should be spared embarrassment when visiting their local cinema'. Southend also adheres to an unduly restrictive policy as expressed by the vice-chairman of its Public Protection Committee who has remarked that 'we are against [films] that are likely to corrupt and those that tend to offend the more delicate members of society'. Even more extreme was the comment of one committee member on a certain film that 'this is not the sort of thing the average person would like to see in their home on the TV screen. I therefore propose that it should be banned.'[22] This is undoubtedly over-protection and an infringement of the council's own licensing conditions. As more councils feel impelled to take censorship into their own hands this sort of invasion of liberty is likely to become more frequent.

In the long run, any escalation of this trend towards independence amongst local authorities will undermine the whole structure of censorship as it now exists. In recent years periodic attempts have been made to create a closer relationship and a greater understanding between the authorities and the Board: the conferences organized by Watkins and Trevelyan in their years as Secretary are examples.

Other attempts have been made in the form of committees made up of representatives of all the interested parties. The earliest was the Film Censorship Consultative Committee which was set up by the Home Secretary in 1931, which was supposed to 'direct their attention, in the first instance, to securing greater co-operation, between the local licensing authorities and the British Board of Film Censors'.[23] This committee had some effect at first, but had fallen into disuse by the outbreak of war, and was not resurrected afterwards. A second attempt was made in 1951 when, following suggestions in the Wheare Report, a Cinema Consultative Committee was instituted, made up of representatives of the Board, the various industry associations, the County Councils Association, the Association of Municipal Corporations, the London County Council and the Scottish Licensing authorities. Its terms of reference were similar to those of its predecessor, namely, 'to provide a means of joint consultation between the local authorities responsible for the licensing of cinemas, the film industry and the British Board of Film Censors, on matters arising from the public exhibition of films. The matters of consultation shall include the general standard of films exhibited to the public (and especially to children), the censorship of films and the conditions generally under which films are publicly exhibited.'[24] This committee was active throughout the fifties, but gradually became less so during the following decade, and had not met at all for many years until it was revived late in 1973.

The decline of this committee seems a pity, but it must be accepted that its influence could never be very strong. While the lead given by the local authority associations may be followed by many councils, a large number of others are jealous of their independence and will always refuse to conform to the decisions of a committee of this sort. There remains a wide divergence of opinion about the role that authorities ought to adopt, as can be illustrated by a closer look at the policies of a number of prominent examples.

Before embarking on this course, however, a few words are necessary about the reorganization of local government which took effect from April 1974. Until that date there were 463 licensing authorities including county councils, county boroughs, district councils and, in Scotland, cities. When the two-tier system was introduced in England and Wales there was some discussion as to which level of authority should be given censorship powers. As most other licensing arrangements were to be carried out at district level it was finally decided that it would be more consistent to operate censorship on this level also. As a result the number of licensing authorities in England and Wales rose from 229 to 332. The B.B.F.C. was not happy at having to deal with an even greater number of bodies. It had favoured censorship at county level where, it was argued, there would have been a greater awareness of issues and less domination by a handful of individuals.

As it happened, reorganization coincided with the provincial release of *The Exorcist*. On the first day of their existence the new licensing authorities were faced with a letter from the Festival of Light, protesting at the certification of this film. For a time it looked as though a significant proportion of the new authorities might be planning to pursue a course independent of the Board, a development which deeply worried the C.E.A. In fact *The Exorcist* proved to be a non-event in this respect : although widely vetted it was banned in only half a dozen places.

The C.E.A., in addition, was successfully combating the tendency of some local authorities to impose unduly severe conditions on the exhibition of films—such as that all future programmes should be made known to committees many weeks in advance. The Association made it clear that such stipulations could only lead to closure of cinemas, and indicated that it would not hesitate to use clause 6(i)(b) of the 1952 Cinematograph Act against the authorities—'any person aggrieved by any terms, conditions and restrictions on a subject to which such a licence or consent is granted, may appeal to quarter sessions'.

In practice the new structure has not led to many new problems. The situation is much as before, even to the extent that reorganization has not ensured that all censorship is now carried on at one level. Clause 101 of the Local Government Act allows the setting up of consortia of authorities under agency agreements, and a number (including Surrey, Hertfordshire and Cambridgeshire) have taken advantage of this. A *CinemaTV Today* survey of May 1974 indicated that, with a few exceptions, censorship policy would not be expected to change very much.

The account that follows deals largely (but not solely) with pre-1974 organizations: some of the authorities discussed no longer exist in the same form. The points made, however, remain valid. The same people are still involved, albeit in a slightly different structure. Two areas, of course, were not affected by the new legislation. Scotland's reorganization has yet to come: London's had taken place earlier.

London, curiously, has censorship at top-tier level, i.e. by the G.L.C., but then the capital has always had a rather special place in the system. It was the L.C.C.'s rules which were adopted by the Home Office in 1923 in the form of model conditions, and it is to London that distributors have always turned first when their films have been rejected by the Board. During the thirties the L.C.C. developed its own system of special licences for films which had been denied a national certificate but which the council, embarking on a liberal policy it has followed ever since, deemed to be suitable for exhibition in London. On only four occasions since 1921 has the L.C.C. banned films passed by the B.B.F.C.

In 1965 the Council, as we have seen, rejected the Home Office condition which denied exhibition to matter which 'would offend against good taste or decency' as too broad, arguing that 'the scope of censorship by the licensing authority should be restricted to preventing the kinds of harm which the law seeks to prevent'.[25] Alec Grant, the chairman of the film-viewing sub-committee, felt that it was 'entirely unacceptable . . . that the machinery of prior restraint should serve to prohibit the performance of plays or the showing of films which contain nothing contrary to law'.[26]

Grant's successor, Dr Mark Patterson, although a Conservative, shared his predecessor's approach to censorship. He was also generally dissatisfied with the system and felt that local councils were not the appropriate bodies for dealing with film censorship. He felt that a royal commission should be set up to review the whole situation, 'to establish the facts concerning censorship over communications, and, if control seemed desirable, to form a more appropriate body than the local authorities'.[27] The crisis months of 1971–2 somewhat deflected him from his liberal policy, and he was reported to be tightening up 'marginally' on sex and violence. Swayed by the Festival of Light's campaign, Patterson arranged for the committee to see *The Devils* despite its B.B.F.C. certificate, and it was decided to accept the Board's verdict by only three votes. *A Clockwork Orange* was also seen, with Patterson declaring that 'there is decisive evidence that violence creates violent situations'.[28] The history of *Oh! Calcutta!* more fundamentally undermined Patterson's position, for after his committee had passed a cut version of the film, the full council reversed the decision by a large majority. Patterson described his position as 'uneasy', but this episode had no sequel, although the council did order the sub-committee to review *Last Tango in Paris*. No action was taken to deny exhibition to that film, however, and shortly afterwards elections returned a more liberal Labour dominated council.

During the three years prior to this date (May 1973) the committee had inspected thirty-six films, of which thirteen had been given a local certificate. Under its new chairman, Enid Wistrich, the committee adopted a distinctly more permissive policy. Of the thirty-one films seen up to the end of October 1974 only eight were denied certificates. The press largely attributed this to the personality of the new chairman who, on her appointment, had said : 'I consider I was elected to help deal with London's housing, transport and environmental problems and certainly not to say which films Londoners should see', and had described her job as 'obsolete'. However, this is a simplification, for Mrs Wistrich never used her vote unless there was a deadlock and did not lead discussions. The more liberal attitude towards films was a reflection of feelings within the new sub-committee and council.

Like all such committees, the G.L.C.'s film-viewing sub-committee is made up of members from all parties in proportion to their representation on the full council. All members indicate the committees on which they would like to sit, and the final composition is organized by the party whips in consultation with their leaders. Of a total of ninety-six G.L.C. councillors, twenty serve on the film-viewing sub-committee which meets four times a year for general business as well as on occasions when films are to be seen. Viewing sessions usually take place at the British Film Institute or in the Queen Elizabeth Hall. As we have seen the G.L.C. has been part of a joint committee to censor films since 1923. Whenever a film is submitted to the G.L.C.—and this is invariably the first council to be approached—a viewing session is arranged to which councillors from Surrey, and (pre-1974) Essex and Berkshire are also invited. However, although films are seen by all the committees at once, decisions are taken entirely independently. Following the screening, there is no joint discussion amongst members from different councils : each committee confers separately and makes its own decision by a majority vote. In fact there is little unanimity. In the year ending March 1972, for instance, seventeen films were seen of which Berkshire certificated ten, the G.L.C. six, and Essex four. Surrey banned every one.

In all councils, censorship issues split the members along two dimensions. Age is an important factor. Younger members are more likely to be liberal in this respect and to deny the necessity for councillors to defend the morals of those they represent, whereas older members are less reticent about using their powers. Political party is the other factor. Particularly when censorship is in the news and has become a matter for discussion, there may be a tendency to close ranks and to vote along party lines. The vote on *Oh! Calcutta!* in the full G.L.C. council showed 90 per cent of Conservative members to be against the film, and 70 per cent of Labour councillors to be in favour of certificating it. The film-viewing sub-committee which had become the focus of much attention was even more divided on party lines. In December 1973 three successive votes showed a clear split between the two main parties. When Councillor Bernard Brook-Partridge resigned from the committee in January 1974 on the grounds that he was being corrupted by over-exposure to 'depravity and violence', he also pointed out this split along party lines, commenting that it was 'not a healthy situation'.

Later we will note a similar development in Southend. It may be inevitable that when a council's censorship policy becomes controversial, its committee tends to attract those with strong views on the subject—of both extremes. This can only lead to a situation in which differences of opinion harden into dogma so that the characteristics of individual films become of minor importance. As party representation changes, committees will be liable to swing violently from one policy to another.

In addition, there may be some conflict between the censorship committee and the full council. In London the former has tended to be more liberal than the full body. Whether this is because committee members are more likely to be interested in films than other councillors, or, as Mrs Wistrich believes, because seeing a steady diet of violent and sexy pictures makes the committee less sensitive to such content, the result is that the committee stands in constant danger of having its decisions overturned. This predicament is less severe than it appears since the council seems determined not to ban films passed by the B.B.F.C. As Sir Desmond Plummer has commented : 'Until the Council has better evidence than is so far available, it will, I think, be reluctant to ban a film passed by the Board, although it must of course always preserve its right to do so.'

Meanwhile an increasingly liberal line has been taken. Mrs Wistrich has continued to assert : 'I am against a system of prior censorship . . . by a viewing committee such as our own or the B.B.F.C. It is much better if the producer knows what he can or cannot do within the limits of the law. The only exception I would make is for children. There should still be censorship for them and it should be exercised by the Board of Film Censors.'[29] Her own solution was for the establishment of 'an advisory body similar to that operating in Quebec in Canada' which allows for an injunction preventing the exhibition of any film over which a court case is pending. 'It could advise on whether any film is "acceptable" or whether it might be liable for prosecution through the courts. The court would be the final arbiter and any prosecution would be instigated by the Director of Public Prosecutions.'[30]

On taking over as chairman of the film-viewing committee Mrs Wistrich had reiterated her predecessor's call for a national

enquiry into censorship. When this met the predictably un-
enthusiastic response, the committee set out to gather evidence
of its own. A pilot project was funded at Social and Community
Planning Research to explore public attitudes towards film censorship in London. This was published in March 1974 and encouraged Mrs Wistrich to implore the Home Office and the
B.B.F.C. once more to co-operate on a fuller study, to no greater
effect than before.

At the same time a group consisting of the chairman and vice-
chairman of the committee, an opposition representative and an
Assistant Director-General of the G.L.C. had been carrying out
consultations with many people involved in or interested in
censorship, including the film unions, the press, pressure groups,
the police, the trade associations, the B.F.I. and the B.B.F.C.
In December 1974 details of these discussions were made public
together with an essay by Mrs Wistrich which proposed the
abolition of censorship for adults in London. 'The right of individual adults to decide their own choice of film must remain
paramount, and corresponds to the freedom to read uncensored
books and see uncensored plays. If adults in a free society are
deemed fit to vote and decide the Government of the day, or in
time of war may die in defence of their country and the values
of freedom and democracy, it is consistent that they should also
as adults have the freedom to view the films they wish, subject
only to the laws enacted by Parliament.'[31]

In January 1975 the report was discussed by the council,
together with the recommendation to discontinue censorship for
adults. A decision to accept this proposal would clearly have
far-reaching effects, doing away with the B.B.F.C.'s 'court of
appeal' and, in theory, allowing more 'permissive' films to be
shown in London. In fact, it is not likely that distributors would
take the opportunity to show films that would previously have
been banned. The uncertain mercies of the law ensure a good
measure of conservatism. For the result of the vote in council
see the introduction.

In one area the council has not sought to discard its powers,
for in relation to advertising the G.L.C. has, in fact, become
stricter in recent years. As described elsewhere cinema publicity
is dealt with by an advisory committee which vets all publicity and front-of-house advertising. In the early seventies there
were increasing complaints about advertising on cinema front-
ages, chiefly directed at the Jacey and Classic chains. At that

time independent cinemas such as these were not party to the advisory committee's deliberations. The G.L.C., aware that such advertising was a growing public nuisance, demanded that the Association of Independent Cinemas be included in the advisory committee: failing this the council threatened to take direct control of such matters. The committee was reorganized accordingly and an improvement in posters followed.[32] One unforeseen side-effect of this action, however, was that it was no longer so easy for the public to gauge the nature of films from their advertising. The council started to receive complaints from people who had gone to see films like *The Boys in the Band* and *The Killing of Sister George* unaware of their subject-matter.[33] The G.L.C., which has direct control over publicity of all locally certificated films, decided that all pictures passed in the 'X-London' category must display a synopsis in the foyer outlining the plot and indicating that the film might be offensive to some. *Blow Out* and *Quiet Days in Clichy* were the first films to which this regulation was applied.

Before concluding discussion of the G.L.C. one final point is worth recording. Although this body has seen far more films than any other licensing authority over the years the total number is tiny in relation to the number dealt with by the Board. The councillors involved have many other responsibilities: they haven't the time to see many films. It has been noticeable that whenever the volume of films submitted to the G.L.C. has increased, attendance at viewings has fallen. Mrs Wistrich felt that the council could handle a maximum of two films a month. Other councils, for short periods, have seen more than this but it is clear that they cannot indulge in film censorship on a grand scale.

One other council traditionally had a liberal policy. As the chairman of its committee has written: 'For many years Berkshire County Council has been by far the most liberal in its attitude to film censorship. This state of affairs has been achieved by a committee . . . which has all shades of opinion from those who would ban everything to those who would pass anything.'[34] We have already noted figures which support this claim, and the council, until it lost its powers in the reorganization, consistently passed more films than any other. It even certificated *Trash* when it was first submitted, demanding only two cuts.

Most authorities adopt the same policy as Berkshire—'to accept the certificated decisions of the British Board of Film Censors,

and to view films when the producers or distributors appeal to
the Council against decisions of the Board'—but none have
interpreted it in as liberal a fashion. Surrey's committee takes
a very different view. Led by one or two members who favour
strict censorship, the committee feel that those who live in Surrey
do not necessarily share the same standards as those who inhabit
the capital. They are supported in this by the rest of the council
—when the committee's policy was challenged in 1971 it was
given full backing by the full council. It is also argued that the
public in general are in agreement with what the committee is
doing. A press release in 1970 had encouraged people to write
in expressing their views, the majority of which had been in
favour of strict censorship.

Curiously the council are not happy with the new 'X' certificate, and have wanted to see several 'X' rated films since it was
introduced. The main concern appears to be that, despite the
work of the authority's inspectors, it is too easy for teenagers to
get in to see these films. As a result, both *The Devils* and *Straw
Dogs* were banned in Surrey, as was the cartoon *Fritz the Cat*
which was condemned as 'a sordid mixture of sex, violence and
bad language, and for these reasons it was wholly unsuitable'.[35]

The Borough of Southend-on-Sea has reacted more severely to
the liberalization of the B.B.F.C. than any other council in
Britain. Its unique and much criticized system deserves study at
greater length, for it represents the only attempt thus far to
ignore the Board's decisions altogether as far as the 'X' certificate
is concerned.

Until quite recently Southend had a reputation as a relatively
liberal council. During the late sixties, however, there had been
increasing complaints about films which were interpreted by the
council as symptomatic of a strong feeling that films and, in
particular, film advertising were not being adequately controlled.
Dissatisfaction with the work of the censorship board reached a
peak over one specific case. This was the sex education film
Love Variations which had been turned down by the B.B.F.C.
and consequently referred to the council who also rejected it in
October 1970. Shortly afterwards, however (as described earlier),
Trevelyan had changed his mind about this film and given it a
certificate. The distributors therefore reapplied to Southend for
a licence. It was seen again shortly before Christmas and the
original decision confirmed. This case brought the topic of film
censorship to the fore and suggested to the council that even

films passed by the Board might not be suitable for showing in Southend.

In March 1971 the council made the unprecedented decision that all cinemas in the borough were to give six weeks' notice of any 'X' film to be shown and in June announced that they would demand to see all such films to judge whether or not they measured up to the standards required in Southend. As the vice-chairman of the Public Protection Committee said, 'We are now saying that we cannot trust the British Board of Film Censors to let us know in advance when some pornography is coming'. This decision, besides causing all sorts of problems for local exhibitors, was not welcomed by everyone. The local press condemned the council's plans, although its argument that 'their right, when elected to administer the finances and bye-laws of the borough to the benefit or otherwise of their fellow men, surely cannot carry with it an obligation to tell them what they may or may not view from the back row of the stalls', displayed a total ignorance of the Cinematograph Acts. More importantly, the council itself was split. We have seen how censorship issues tend to divide councils on two dimensions—political party and age. In Southend's case, however, it appears to have become a purely political division. The three Labour councillors have strenuously opposed the uni-lateral approach and one of them has refused to take any part. The Labour group's stand has been helped by the fact that George Elvin, leader of one of the film unions, is a member of the council and in a position to make a powerful lobby.

Despite this opposition, however, the council went ahead with its plans, the chairman feeling that 'it is time somebody stood up and said they did not agree with what is going on. We are determined to see that no undesirable films are shown.' If he thought that his stand would be supported by similar action else-where he was to be disappointed. Even worse, within a very short time it became clear that the system was unworkable. Only three weeks after the decision to vet all 'X' films the local paper was triumphantly reporting that 'Southend's film censors are getting fed up with sex films. There are just too many of them. They ban the Danish-made *Bedroom Mazurka*, but pass another Danish film, *Seventeen*. They are also due to see another film—the third in five days.' One councillor said : 'This is purely volun-tary work and there is only a certain amount of time which can be devoted to corporation affairs.' Two weeks later pressure from the C.E.A. forced the council to relax its rule regarding six weeks' notice, and by October the whole policy of reviewing all 'X' films was being re-thought. Attendances at showings had become very low, and it was clear that a very small group were making all the decisions. The credibility of the system was not increased when the committee demanded to see a film that had already been shown in the town three times before.

In November the council bowed to the inevitable and admitted that it could not continue to see all adult films. Thereafter only a small number were selected for viewing, the choice being dictated, as usual, by press reports and synopses provided by distributors. Southend continued to see more films than other councils—eighty-six by the end of 1973—and showed no disinclination to ban. By June 1972 fifteen films had been rejected, many of which had been exhibited without objection throughout the rest of the country. Meanwhile opposition to the policy had been growing and fourteen councillors, representing all three parties, had called for the end of 'X' film censorship. Although this move was resisted there has been evidence of the emergence of a less restrictive policy. In the following eighteen months only five further films were banned in the town.

Evidently Southend defines its powers under the Cinematograph Act in a much broader way than any other council. The committee argues that the standard of judgement is 'that which would be supported by the bulk of the population', and feels that it has a great deal of local support, although much of this seems to originate from the various church bodies. The chairman states that the main areas of concern are violence and drugs and that there is little censorship of sex or nudity, a policy which does not accord with many studies of public opinion which find little widespread concern over violence. There is also some evidence that the council adopts a highly idiosyncratic approach to these issues. *Slaughter* was apparently passed on the grounds that 'the killing was so wholesale that nobody could take it seriously', while *Straw Dogs* which caused so much trouble elsewhere, was almost accepted for the same reason, and was eventually passed in November 1974. On the other hand *Taking Off* was banned because of its drug scene which was 'plausible because it was well-made. If it had been a cheap budget film people would not have taken it seriously.' Evidently 'serious' films receive the harshest treatment. However one must resist the temptation to make this sort of criticism without a much fuller knowledge of how the committee operates. Councils are, unfortunately, not very keen to discuss their work in specific detail.

It has been suggested earlier that Manchester has for many years adopted an independent policy. In the early years it was one of the leading lights in attempts to establish an 'official' censor. In the twenties Manchester refused to accept the status of the B.B.F.C. and set up its own censorship. Attempts by the Home Office to influence the authority to fall in with the national system were resisted and in 1927 it was stated that exhibitors in Manchester were quite happy with the situation which involved 'a working scheme of local censorship in conjunction with the Watch Committee and Police which has operated successfully since its inception several years ago'.[36] In fact this system survived until the fifties when the B.B.F.C. was finally accepted and censorship was handed over to the police department, although a civilian officer has always been in charge of 'Public Entertainments'.

Manchester was able to follow its own policy because it was the northern centre of the film industry. This meant that all films were shown to potential northern exhibitors in Manchester. In the days of independent exhibitors trade shows were a common and essential part of the structure of the industry, for unless they attended these shows northern cinema owners had little guidance as to the qualities of the films they might book for their cinemas. However, during the fifties, the value of the trade show began to fall. Increasingly as the big circuits took over the independents and obtained a stranglehold on most 'first-run' houses, attendances at the trade shows declined. This put Manchester's censorship system in jeopardy for it was based on the existence of these shows. In fact written into Manchester's licensing conditions was clause 35 which demanded that no films except newsreels or those passed for 'Universal' exhibition by the B.B.F.C. could be 'publicly exhibited at the licensed premises before the expiration of seven clear days after such film has been trade shown in Manchester, and should the Licensing Authority or officers acting on their behalf have any objection to any film that has been trade shown, they shall notify the parties concerned within seven days after the trade show. The parties concerned shall give a reasonable notice to the Chief Constable of all trade shows about to be held in Manchester.'

Unfortunately by the early sixties it was apparent that the only people using the trade shows were the council's three full-time examiners. In 1964 A.B.C. and Rank, the two large exhibition chains, asked for clause 35 to be removed, but in fact only the requirement to see 'A' films was cut out: the necessity to show all 'X' films remained until 1968 when a further appeal by the exhibitors was more successful. The condition was not deleted, and it is still in the licensing conditions but it is regularly waived every year. However it can be reapplied at any time, and in recent years it has been waived only on the understanding that in special cases as defined by the council it can be put into immediate effect.

In any case by this time the council's independence was more apparent than real. In the six years up to the disappearance of the trade show in 1968 the committee had only disagreed with B.B.F.C. decisions on two occasions. The day-to-day running of censorship is handled by an officer employed until 1974 by the police department, but now by the Town Hall. His job is to ensure that the licensing conditions (which are concerned primarily with safety and maintenance) are strictly complied with, and that advertising and posters are acceptable. In addition he sees many films at press shows and reads the trade press. Either he or any member of the committee (formerly the Licensing and Fire Brigade but now the Environmental Services Committee) can ask for a film to be vetted by the committee. The committee itself is usually activated by press reports, leading to the viewing and banning of *The Devils* and *Straw Dogs*. This system can lead to problems for no prior information is available about which films are to be shown in the city. *Trash* was seen, and banned only four days before it was due to open, involving complications for the exhibitor and expense for the distributor. The committee also expressed the wish to see *A Clockwork Orange*. Kubrick himself was unwilling to have the film banned and was prepared to forego exhibition in any area which seemed likely to reach this decision, but Columbia-Warner sent a print to Manchester anyway, and the committee, in fact, passed the film.

As in many other such committees, there is a widespread feeling that all is not well with the present system and that B.B.F.C. certificates are not always 'right' for Manchester. Nevertheless nobody wants to revert to the old method. The problem is compounded by the fact that increasing numbers of both the council and the committee feel that censorship for adults is unnecessary anyway. Until 1970 the council had for some time had a Conservative majority. In that year the city was redivided and a

heavy Labour majority emerged. Among the many new councillors are a large number of younger men and women who are
anti-censorship. The committee is now split down the middle : on
the one hand some councillors want stricter censorship, on the
other a group of liberal 'intellectuals' and younger Labour members want less. In this quandary—at one time three consecutive
decisions were made by the chairman's casting vote—the committee has attempted to seek help from the Board in reaching a
more satisfactory situation. First, they asked Murphy to recommend which certificated films they should see—thus, in effect,
calling for an 'XX' certificate which they could then review.
Naturally Murphy was not keen to accept this, not wishing to
agree that certain of his decisions might be questionable. Later
the committee asked if they could be told which films Lord
Harlech had been consulted about. This also was not a solution
to appeal to the Board; for one thing it does not necessarily
isolate 'difficult' films : Harlech had never seen *Straw Dogs*. All
this illustrates the dilemma of the committee, many of whom
wish to see more films but do not know how to select them.

Another complication is introduced by the fact that, unlike
most councils, Manchester has not delegated its powers of censorship to the committee. The power still rests with the full council
who must ratify all committee decisions. This has led to problems.
Language of Love, for instance, was passed by the committee,
but when one councillor brought pressure on the council, it
reversed the decision. A minimum of six months must elapse
before council decisions can be reconsidered and when this period
had elapsed the film was resubmitted. This time the whole council was invited to see it : seventy attended and the film was
passed.

Until 1974 there was a further source of embarrassment in
that the Manchester police department was in charge of censorship for both Manchester and Salford as a result of the amalga-
mation of police forces in 1968. Salford had always adopted a
less independent stance, accepting B.B.F.C. decisions, but at first
the council took the opportunity to see some films passed by the
Board, following the pattern set by its neighbours. This policy
was soon abandoned, however, following one unfortunate week
when the committee saw two films. One was passed by Salford
but rejected by Manchester, the other received the opposite
verdicts.

There is apparently little pressure from the public in Man-

chester. The few complaints that are received are mostly concerned with the inability of cinema managers to apply the correct
age limitations on admissions. Even the organized pressure
groups have made little headway there, although the council have
received one deputation from the Manchester and Salford Council of Churches which has connections with the Festival of Light.
In general this latter body has had more success in the south-
east and it is perhaps worth studying a case in which their
influence has been substantial. Kent has proved to be a particularly successful area for the Festival, partly because in that
county the council had delegated all its powers of censorship to
the county district councils. Censorship has thus always been
handled by a number of small councils who have evidently been
more susceptible to local campaigns than larger, more remote,
bodies. The case of Tunbridge Wells represents an extreme
example.

Until 1972 the council's watch committee (of seven members)
had never seen films passed by the B.B.F.C. whose decisions had
always been accepted. Early that year, however, *The Devils* had
opened in the town. The local Festival of Light and other church
bodies organized pickets and campaigned vociferously against
the showing of the film. Such was the subsequent controversy
that the committee felt that they ought to see the film. When
they did so, they agreed with the film's critics that it was not
suitable for exhibition in Tunbridge Wells on the grounds that
it was blasphemous. Once a film is showing, however, there is
no way in which the council can insist on its being withdrawn,
for notice is bound to be given of any film that cannot be shown.
Fortunately for the council, the local cinema manager proved to
be amenable and he voluntarily agreed to take *The Devils* off
before the end of its scheduled run. This action provoked opposition from those who were in favour of the film's being shown,
but despite support from 2,500 people this movement was unable to influence the committee, who were now alerted to the
problem of 'X' films and resolved to see more. Surprisingly
Straw Dogs and *The Decameron* were both accepted but another
film fell foul of the committee in a rather extraordinary way.
The council had not heard of the cartoon *Fritz the Cat*, and
had no intention of seeing it until the cinema manager brought
their attention to it, pointing out that it might be an awkward
case. Accordingly, the film was viewed and produced very strong
reactions, being variously described as 'sickening pornographic

trash', 'utterly degrading, pure pornography, and full of drug exploitation' and 'full of sex and sadistic violence'. Defending their decision to ban the film councillors used a number of arguments that are commonly put forward in such situations, and some of which must be debatable. Thus, one councillor put forward the theory that the 'silent majority' must be considered, without suggesting what evidence there was to show that they would support such a decision. Another argued that 'if only one young person is prevented from seeing this film, then the ban will be worth it' disregarding the fact that this is precisely the intention of the 'X' certificate. Even the chairman was drawn to 'make it clear' that the B.B.F.C. was a body 'set up by the film industry, for the film industry' which does not accurately comment on the Board's present status. Whatever the reasons, the council was determined, and only three members voted against the watch committee's recommendation to ban the film.

Despite this general agreement, however, the committee was evidently uneasy about its role as a film censor. By early 1973 it had been decided that it was fairer to accept B.B.F.C. decisions on the grounds that it was unsatisfactory to pick out certain films only to be vetted. The chairman believed that censorship should not really be in the hands of local councils at all, and advocated the institution of an elected body to replace the present board. He considered himself ill-equipped to be a censor and admitted that his committee, seeing only a handful of films, had no adequate standard of comparison. While he regretted the more liberal policy adopted by the Board, he felt that it had not become more permissive than society in general. Oddly, he argued that one of the great difficulties facing councils was that they could not ask for cuts whereas the national censor can. This is quite wrong—councils can and do ask for cuts, although it is not always economically possible for these to be accepted by the distributors. In general the committee apparently had had second thoughts about the wisdom of intervening over films and had resolved that, if a situation like that which arose over *The Devils* occurred again, the committee would ignore it and accept the censor's decision.

In practice, however, things were not so simple. Having given way once the committee found itself unable to stand firm a second time. In May, *Last Tango in Paris* was due to be shown in Tunbridge Wells. The Festival of Light immediately demanded that the council look at it, and the committee promptly abandoned its vowed intentions and agreed to do so. Although it was emphasized that this 'did not necessarily mean it would be banned', few were surprised when it was. The vehemence of the opinions expressed, however, were less predictable in view of what had been said earlier. The film was described as 'nothing more than filth', and 'utterly decadent' with the result that 'a vote in its favour must be for decadence'. The chairman thought it 'so disgusting it should be burned'. Once again protection of children was a major argument. One councillor argued that when *A Clockwork Orange* had been passed, the 'very young' had seen it, and another concluded that 'the only real way to stop children seeing *Last Tango* was by not allowing the film'. It seems that films were to be banned because the Council was failing in its duty to enforce its own licensing conditions. This cannot be satisfactory. Another contentious point was made by the watch committee who said 'it had been argued that the film had been made in the name of art, but it was really in the name of big business'. Again this seems an unfair basis for criticism. It is unusual in a capitalist country to find an industry being criticized for attempting to make money.[37]

Although there are clearly some very different interpretations of the role of local councils over film censorship a number of points can be made about the authorities in general. In the first place there is a widespread suspicion of the B.B.F.C. While few councillors are aware of the precise composition and role of the Board, many appreciate that it was originally set up by the industry and therefore assume that it is primarily an instrument of the industry. This feeling prevails even amongst those authorities that accept the Board's certificates, and feel that it is doing a good job. It would seem unlikely that a more satisfactory relationship can be worked out unless this general belief is dealt with first. One councillor noted that the important point is not so much whether or not the Board actually is too closely connected to the trade, but that a lot of people think that it is.

A small number of authorities carry their distrust of the Board so far as to feel that another body should be established in its place. Surrey and Tunbridge Wells, for instance, appear to favour an elected Board of some sort, while Leeds are unhappy with the present system but have no firm recommendations about how it might be improved. Sevenoaks went to the extent of writing to the Government in May 1973 calling for a review of the situation and demanding that 'Her Majesty's Government be asked to give urgent and early consideration to the question of establishing an independent statutory committee for film censorship in Great Britain instead of leaving the question of film censorship to be dealt with by local authorities (the only bodies with authority to refuse to permit films to be exhibited) and the voluntary Board of Film Censors set up by the film industry'. Even the liberal G.L.C. was moved to recommend closer co-operation between authorities and the establishment by the Government of a royal commission on film censorship.

Whether a greater degree of contact between councils would achieve much is very doubtful. There is at present very little. In certain places, groups of councils have got together to organize communal screenings, but decisions are invariably made entirely independently. Very few councils would favour a system that called for more co-operation, for the majority are either in favour of the burden of censorship being removed from the shoulders of councillors altogether, or else argue that it is precisely the awareness of local standards and feelings that makes the present system ideal. Those in the latter group feel that any national censor is bound to make decisions that are not suited to certain areas : in particular, the Board is frequently castiga-ted as being a metropolitan body, reacting to the needs and mores of London, but unaware of the requirements of other parts of the country.[38] The councillors in Leeds, for instance, feel strongly that an independent group in London cannot judge what is permissible in Leeds. At the same time they are un-concerned that all the councils around Leeds adopt a more liberal policy and accept B.B.F.C. decisions. They maintain that their only concern is Leeds and that the opinions of others are irrelevant. If Bradford is misguided enough to pass films not thought suitable to be shown in Leeds that is entirely their con-cern and of no relevance to councils elsewhere. It follows that Leeds are not at all in favour of the establishment of closer communication links with other councils. On the whole, how-ever, this degree of independence is unusual; most committees admit that they are often floundering in unknown waters and would be grateful for any guidance that might be given.

In general it seems that while most authorities are in broad agreement with policies of the B.B.F.C., a growing number are dissatisfied and feel that it is becoming too permissive. A few blame Murphy for not following the policy of his predecessor, arguing that he is too easily influenced by the industry and allows too much sex and violence on the screen. Despite their claims to be more concerned about violence, when it comes to the point it is still sex that troubles councillors most often : 'if copulation is not allowed in public, why should it be acceptable on film?' In part, this reaction is a reflection of the age composition of committees. Many claim to have a number of young councillors on their committee but this in fact means men and women in their early thirties or, at best and very rarely, late twenties. It is hardly surprising that such bodies should be out of sympathy with a medium whose primary audience is the eighteen to twenty-five-year-olds. Even sexual composition may be a factor, for a great many committees are made up exclusively of men. It has been noted that juries in obscenity trials are more liberal if they include one or two married women in their number, and the same rule might well apply in these cases as well.

Other councils, however, feel that B.B.F.C. policy started to change rather before Murphy's appointment and that Trevelyan's last two years saw the introduction of more permissive decisions. This is probably a more accurate reflection of events, for there is some evidence that the gradual liberalization of the sixties accelerated sharply at this time. Whether this change was consciously planned or a result of the fact that Trevelyan was keen to retire and was actively seeking a successor during this time is not clear. Certainly Trevelyan was 'increasingly tired' and had admitted that a surfeit of sex films had dimmed his enthusiasm for the job. Some councils seem to have believed that he was 'not at his best' in the period before his retirement. The complaint is that Murphy has continued in this vein rather than reverting to the more conservative practices of earlier years.

There is an element of truth in this. Especially at first, Murphy was prepared to go to some lengths to accommodate films which he respected. In other ways, however, as the statistics suggest, Murphy has not shown reluctance to cut and reject. In particular he has resolutely preserved the relative innocence of the 'U' and 'A' certificates and has adopted a very much more restrictive policy in this respect than his predecessor. Yet this sort of concern goes almost totally unnoticed by local authorities who are invariably worried only about the 'X' certificate and what should be allowed in it. This is curious for, in fact, while the councils have a *duty* to protect children they are under no such obligation with regard to adults. The 1952 Cinematograph Act

is quite specific about the councils' role concerning children:
3 (1) provides that—'It shall be the duty of the licensing authorities, in granting a license under the Act of 1909 as respects any
premises . . . to impose conditions or restrictions prohibiting the
admission of children to cinematograph exhibitions involving the
showing of works designated, by the licensing authority or such
other body as may be specified in the licence, as works unsuitable for children'.

However, there is no such clear demand for censorship for
adults. The 1909 Act merely empowers the licensing authority to
grant licences 'on such terms and conditions and under such
restrictions as . . . the Council may by the respective licences determine'. The power to censor films for adults is thus present, but
there is no statutory duty to do so. Any council may decline to
censor for adults if it feels so inclined, thus effectively abolishing
censorship for adults. This is an important point that is frequently overlooked, not least by those who argue that, by not
banning, or at least reviewing, certain 'X' films, councils are in
dereliction of their duties.

This being the case it is odd that councils concentrate their
attention entirely on censorship for adults and are content to
let the B.B.F.C. bear the full onus of protecting children. In
recent years no authority has challenged the Board's award of
a 'U' or 'A' certificate or ever asked to see one, although on a
number of occasions films deemed suited only for adults by the
Board have been passed as suitable for children by local authorities. As we have seen one film that was rejected entirely by the
Board was passed 'A' and even 'U' in certain places. Meanwhile
an increasingly strict watch is kept on the allocation of 'X'
certificates, while a number of councils (encouraged by certain
sections of the public) even tend to blame the Board for the
proliferation of films falling into that category. Time and again
the complaint is made that too many 'X' films are made and
that family films now never appear at the local cinema, as though
this phenomenon was entirely unrelated to the demands of the
market,[39] and was within the powers of the B.B.F.C. to change.
In fact, of course, Britain which represents some 5–6 per cent
of the world cinema market is in no position to influence the
films that are made. Even British films, with only a few exceptions, have to be made with one eye on the requirements for
overseas sale. The censor's ability to affect film production is
minimal.

On one issue there does appear to be near-unanimity amongst local authorities. Almost all feel that club cinemas should be brought within their jurisdiction, and that their present immunity from licensing restrictions represents a serious loophole in the Cinematograph Act. There was a general feeling that it was unfair for some cinemas to escape the restrictions imposed on others, coupled with a distaste for the material shown on these premises. The majority of councils would like to be able to regulate, if not close down, these establishments. The fact that they are increasingly popular, and profitable, makes their threat a growing one and hardens the determination that something be done about them.

It is too early yet to say definitely how local government reorganization will affect film censorship. Although little appears to have changed, the danger remains that a proliferation of small licensing bodies will produce a greater number with little of the experience or knowledge necessary for the job. In recent cases it has been those councils that have never taken any part in censorship before which have been most ready to take independent action. In places with only one cinema it would be quite possible for the local authority to have a considerable influence on the films to be seen there. The chairman of Surrey County Districts Film Licensing Joint Committee has expressed his disturbance at 'the actions being taken by local authorities to carry out their duties as film censors', recommending the advantages of joint committees as a better system.[40]

More licensing authorities means more councillors becoming involved in censorship. Many show a hardly surprising ignorance of the modern cinema. The frequent calls for more 'family' films is one example of a naivety that can be amply illustrated by one, admittedly extreme, example. As a New Year's amusement for his readers, Derek Malcolm, film critic of the *Guardian*, wrote a 'spoof' article satirizing some films of 1973, including *Sloshed Horizon* and *Andrei's Seven Roubles*. One of the year's more brutal offerings, *Magnum Force*, was also parodied:

Magnum Fart (Cinecenta 1, 2, 3, 15 and 93, 'X') is not one for the squeamish.... The story is quite deceptively simple. Clint Eastwood plays Filthy Fred, a revolting policeman who, deciding that the law lets pornographers go free, determines to stop the rot his own way. Accordingly, he locks four of the dirtiest books he can find in a Parisian villa and gases them to death through a hole in the roof in an entirely unprintable manner. Marco Cain, the brilliant young Israeli director, brings a cunning sado-masochistic element of fantasy to the screen by suddenly transmogrifying each book into its leading character, totally nude. Thus Anna Neagle plays Lady Chatterley, Laurence Olivier is 'O' and Tatum O'Neal is Little Emily.[41]

One may or may not share Mr Malcolm's sense of humour, but his intentions seem reasonably clear. Not clear enough, however, for one local authority (representing one of the country's major cities) who wrote urgently to the Board questioning the passing of films of this nature. Few councils, fortunately, operate on this level though there are occasional odd cases such as the Cornish borough which bans films despite the fact that there are no cinemas within its jurisdiction.

Judged overall, however, local authority censorship can be a useful part of the system so long as it remains primarily a court of appeal, offering the B.B.F.C. occasional reminders if and when it is thought to be losing contact with public opinion. When, as has increasingly happened in recent years, councils seek to exert a greater influence, the weaknesses of local censorship immediately become apparent. As we have seen, some authorities have attempted to encourage this sort of intervention and to challenge the status of the B.B.F.C. despite the fact that the vast majority of councils appear to be satisfied with the present system. The County Councils' Association seems to feel that no changes are necessary. In November 1973 a suggestion by Bedfordshire C.C. that the Association should consider the whole question of local censorship was turned down and the implicit criticism of the Board rejected. The Association 'was not convinced that further inquiry into the question of existing film censorship arrangements was warranted at the present time'.[42]

Murphy himself has jocularly remarked that the Board approves of the councils retaining their powers—as long as they don't use them. It might be no bad thing if the spread of local censorship led to a review of the whole system, but it would provide an unfortunate context within which to carry out such a review.

PRESSURE GROUPS

A s w e h a v e seen, both the Board of Film Censors and the local authority committees accept that their main responsibility is to reflect public opinion. Unfortunately there is no simple way of judging the will of a majority which is necessarily silent. Guidance is, however, offered by an increasing number of pressure groups who profess to represent that majority and who express their points of view vigorously and often. In the absence of real knowledge about public opinion, these voices assume disproportionate significance and influence.

The pressure group, as a social phenomenon, has really come into its own in this century. The success of the suffragette movement and, more recently, the influence of the Campaign for Nuclear Disarmament, the Consumers' Association and many others, has stimulated public participation in issues both great and small. The appearance of innumerable campaigns and movements is an encouraging sign that more and more people are willing to take an active part in the democratic procedure. 'If the crossing is dangerous to children, it will be blocked by mothers with babies and prams; if the noise from the motorways is intolerable, the residents will picket the roads until they are rehoused; if families are homeless, they will squat in unoccupied premises; if pay increases too slowly and if management are cavalier, the workers will strike.'[1]

The post-war history of media pressure groups really starts with the debate over the introduction of commercial television in the early fifties, although this was not a campaign that originated from any feeling of public concern. Indeed, as H. H. Wilson has chronicled, the public displayed minimal interest in the matter. Although pressure groups were active on both sides, the National Television Council defending the B.B.C.'s monopoly and the Popular Television Association attacking it, 'the public was generally apathetic and did not attend the public meetings sponsored by either pressure group.'[2]

The campaign did, however, represent the first serious challenge to the status of the B.B.C. which still retained its Reithian aura as the official, 'establishment' channel. The P.T.A. in its effort to attack the wisdom of such a monopoly, used as one weapon in its armoury, a general attack on the Corporation's programmes, arguing that a second channel could provide 'much higher quality and a much greater variety.' One speaker was moved to decry the influence of the B.B.C. because 'it set out unashamedly to make people think, and from that it was only a short step to telling them what to think'.[3]

Ten years later the attack on the B.B.C. was renewed by the Clean-Up T.V. Campaign organized by a Midlands schoolteacher, Mary Whitehouse, and the wife of a local vicar, Norah Buckland. The original impetus derived from Moral Re-Armament, but the movement quickly gained a momentum of its own and a much wider membership. Starting as a small local campaign in Birmingham in May 1964, it grew at a great pace. In June the following year a petition was presented to Parliament signed by 365,355 people 'who are deeply concerned about the low standards of certain broadcasts and, in particular, television programmes which are being screened at the present moment'.[4] In addition, 120,000 signatures were received after this occasion.

The petition affirmed that 'the men and women of Great Britain believe in a Christian way of life; deplore present day attempts to be-little and destroy it and in particular object to the propaganda of disbelief, doubt and dirt that the B.B.C. pours into millions of homes through the television screen; and that crime, violence and illegitimacy and venereal disease are steadily increasing, yet the B.B.C. employs people whose ideas and advice pander to the lowest in human nature, accompanying this with a stream of suggestive and erotic plays which present promiscuity, infidelity and drinking as normal and inevitable'.[5]

In November 1966 the campaign was renamed the National Viewers' and Listeners' Association with Mary Whitehouse as its full-time secretary. During the next few years its influence grew until even the B.B.C., which had always studiously ignored it, was forced to recognize its existence. Its strength has probably lain partly in its adherence to a limited platform. Until recently it has concentrated its attention on television, resisting the temptation to develop wider horizons. As an expression of a genuine concern at the way television was developing during the sixties, the campaign was valuable. It allowed an opinion that would otherwise have gone unheard to be given full expression and contributed in this way to the debate on the future of the medium. The problem is to evaluate the weight which should be attached to such a campaign—naturally the movement is inclined to overestimate the extent to which it reflects public opinion as a whole. This is a matter to which we will return.

Although the campaign is primarily concerned with television and its role in society, it goes without saying that a more general ideology underlies the anxiety expressed over certain programmes and policies. In an American study of a similar campaign in 'Midville', Louis Zurcher and George Kirkpatrick noted that

according to respondents, challenges to the Midvillian life style were apparent everywhere. The mass media reminded them of, and even seemed to give approval to, the fact that the 'new generation' was becoming more forceful and prestigious. Traditional attitudes towards sexual behaviour, work, religion, war, education and patriotism were 'eroding', especially among young people. Attitudes which were associated with the life style of the 'typical' Midville citizen were being threatened, not only by the behaviour of other citizens, the editorials and programmes of the media, and the teachings of contemporary educators and theologies, but even (pre-Nixon-Agnew) by significant acts of the Federal Government. The Supreme Court, the most revered and powerful guardian of 'traditional' American values, even legislated against aspects of the respondents' life styles.[6]

The writers found some statistical support for their contention that the campaign against 'smut' concealed a wider concern, 'to maintain the integrity of their accustomed style of life against the challenges of social change'. In a survey of participants in the anti-pornography organizations they found that 64 per cent reported that 'their opposition in this endeavour was "ultra-liberals" and "young people". Only 27 per cent of the participants, by contrast, saw the opposition to be the "smut-peddlars" themselves.'

Zurcher and Kirkpatrick concluded that 'anti-pornography activity, as manifested in the ad hoc anti-pornography organizations, represents a conflict between rival social systems, cultures and status groups, protest against a changing status system, and a mechanism influencing the distribution of prestige associated

with adherence to certain accepted "basic values"'.[7] In this
country also it is clear that pornography is really only one
symptom of what is thought to be a more general and insidious
disease. The reaction to 'permissiveness' is symbolic of a fear
and distrust of the whole way in which society is changing.
Because these changes are largely made manifest through the
media, it is easy to see why television, cinema, etc. are often
held to be a root cause of unwelcome trends.

The overtly political aspect of V.A.L.A.'s ideology is rarely
expressed[8] but it underlies much of the thinking behind the
campaign, which is founded on nationalism and the confirma-
tion of the family as the basic unit of society. The petition to
Parliament stressed that God must be brought back 'to the heart
of the British family and national life'. Television, and by extension the other mass media, are undermining this vision by
a concentration on 'programmes dealing sympathetically with
homosexuality, lesbians, abortion, venereal disease and drug
addiction'.[9]

The principal weakness of V.A.L.A.'s position from a social
scientific view lies in the evaluation of the extent to which the
media can influence people's attitudes and behaviour. On this
point the Association supports an extremely crude and mechanistic model. It is well illustrated in the following episode, which
according to her own account played a very great part in transforming Mary Whitehouse from schoolteacher into national
campaigner. Apparently some of her pupils had seen a 'Meeting
Point' programme dealing with the topic of pre-marital sex.
The discussion had come down in favour of sex before marriage
for engaged couples, and Mrs Whitehouse had been disturbed to
discover that a number of her pupils had been 'persuaded' by
this argument. 'I know that they were normal, healthy, and with
some degree of personal faith and clean living. And yet, in a
few brief words they had been won over to a sub-Christian concept of living.'[10]

All that we know about the ways in which people react to
messages from television, indicates that no such swift conversion
is likely. As we shall see later, attitude formation is a complex
business in which influence from primary sources such as parents,
friends and teachers is far more important than information
derived from the media. It seems especially curious that an
organization based so firmly on orthodox religious views should
consider that years of socialization in the home, the school, the

Church, can be undermined by 'a few brief words'. It suggests a lack of faith in human character that is not supported by any scientific (or common sense) evidence.

Unfortunately, the campaign pays little regard to the findings of research. Like other such groups, it has a distinctly anti-intellectual bias, as evidenced by William Deedes, speaking at the first V.A.L.A. convention : 'I long for us to break the domination of those sociologists who demand "proof" of the effect of broadcasting before conclusions can be drawn and acted upon, and for us to call upon the lessons of human experience accumulated over the centuries. Every parent, every teacher, every adviser KNOWS and builds on the fact that example teaches, that the visual image is more powerful than the spoken word.'[11] Experience has, of course, also shown that common sense is not always correct. It is a pity that the Association indulges in unsupported assertions of this sort (the random case histories that are sometimes put forward as evidence are hardly conclusive), for there is a serious point to be made.

Few would deny Mary Whitehouse's assertion that 'it's very important that we do stand up and speak out about the things in which we believe, and also say that in our view certain things are not right. As the National V.A.L.A. we don't speak for anybody else but ourselves, we're not trying to impose our view on other people ... democracy only works when people get involved in the forces that are shaping their lives and shaping their society. It's open to everybody in this country to say what they feel about television programmes, as about everything else, and if people don't agree with us, they have all the rights and opportunities we have to stand up and say so.'[12]

This wholly admirable thesis of participatory democracy is occasionally compromised by a tendency to engage in denigration of those holding different views. Mrs Whitehouse has dismissed the opposition as 'largely artificial and sponsored, even "inspired" ', while claiming that her own movement reflects a deep and spontaneous concern 'in the hearts of so many people'.[13]

In fact, far from being organized, V.A.L.A.'s opponents have never really made a satisfactory attempt to state the opposite point of view. TRACK had been founded in 1965 but was hardly heard of again, while COSMO, launched at the same time by Harlow housewife Avril Fox, never acquired the national prominence of V.A.L.A. By 1971 the latter was claiming a membership of 10,000—not a large figure in the circumstances, and one remains sceptical about the importance of the block support of organizations representing 2 million people. But by this time V.A.L.A. was not fighting a lone battle. The events of 1970 and 1971 were the precipitating factors behind the formation of three groups which, in their different ways, were to add their weight to Mrs Whitehouse's attack.

The least well-known of these is the Responsible Society founded in 1971 by a group which included Lord Shawcross, Pamela Hansford Johnson and David Holbrook, whose aim was to make their voices heard 'above the clamour of highly vocal minorities'. To date they have not succeeded. One of the Society's few tangible achievements—the banning of the magazine Forum by W. H. Smith—was, in fact, accomplished without any publicity at all. In spite of (or possibly as a result of) having a fairly broad credo ('freedom and tolerance in sexual matters must be tempered by responsibility and restraint') the group has found difficulty in uniting on common ground. Internal disagreements —Holbrook was asked to resign from the executive committee following a letter to the press—have diminished the potential impact of the Society.

The second pressure group was essentially the creation of one man. In a debate in the House of Lords on 21 April, 1971, the Labour peer, Lord Longford, asserted that 'pornography . . . has increased, is increasing and ought to be diminished'.[14] He went on to suggest that the Government set up a 'far-reaching inquiry' into the problem, but, aware that such a study was unlikely, informed the House that 'a number of us have made plans for an unofficial inquiry of our own'. A committee of over fifty members was gathered with the terms of reference : 'To see what means of tackling the problem of Pornography would command general support'.[15] Longford emphasized that he was leading an inquiry into pornography rather than a campaign against it, but there was no claim that anything other than a highly committed viewpoint underlay the work. As Longford explained in a sermon, at London University's Church of Christ the King, in October 1971, 'We are collecting—we hope we are collecting—evidence to prove our point of view'.

When the report was published in September 1972 it aroused wide comment, but was generally dismissed by the press. It displayed the inconsistencies and contradictions inevitable in a work written by many hands, and its legal recommendations offered no solution to the various intractable problems concerning porno-

graphy and obscenity. Enough has been said and written about
the report to make a lengthy analysis here unnecessary. Most of
the assumptions held by the committee were similar to those
held by the V.A.L.A. There is the same mechanistic concept of
the ways in which readers and viewers are corrupted by the
media, which is proved only by the recounting of a small number
of case histories, most of which clearly indicate a much deeper
problem among subjects than the use of pornographic material.
The subtleties and complexities of the problem are glossed over
in a few unhelpful phrases : 'do people become mentally corrupted because of their addiction to pornography, or do they resort
to pornography because their minds are already inclined that
way? . . . it seems overwhelmingly probable that the initial
impetus may come from one side or the other, and that in any
case there is a continuing interaction'.[16] No basis for this probability is suggested, nor is there chapter and verse given for the
'evidence that "normal" people can become addicted to pornography in certain circumstances'.[17]

None of this is surprising since, despite the presence of a
number of academics and teachers, the committee generally displayed the anti-intellectualism we have noted elsewhere. One
writer bemoaned that 'one of the most insidious tendencies of
recent years is society's increasing reliance on so-called "expert"
opinion in preference to natural common sense'.[18] Nor was the
treatment of expert opinion always scientifically defensible—
the report of the American Commission was curtly dismissed
without adequate attention. Indeed the misrepresentation of
research evidence was one ground for Lord Goodman's claim
that his fellow-peer 'lacked the qualifications in terms of social
investigation to carry out an investigation of this kind . . . to
pretend that this is a report at all, and to convey the impression
that a number of gentlemen have surveyed the evidence, considered the evidence, and arrived at cogent conclusions, is slightly
deceptive, and rather more than slightly deceptive, of the public
at large'.[19]

Most of the report's recommendations are concomitant with
the premise that 'Church, state and family are the three institutions divinely ordained for the preservation of society'.[20] Even
sex education is seen as another weapon in the plan to undermine society: 'family life is threatened by powerful disruptive
forces, some of deliberate revolutionary intent, but largely let

loose by a fashionable but unthinking chorus which has now
given its blessing to a wide range of sex education in schools'.[21]

Concern for the stability of the *status quo* was evident in that
section of the report concerned with the cinema. Summing up
present trends in films the committee wrote : 'The counter-culture
in the U.S. has made effective use of film which both mirrors
and influences that society's polarization; it is clearly a powerful
weapon with which to sabotage social institutions especially
among the young who are now its chief patrons. Nor can the
increasing interest in *cinema-verité*, or documentary realism,
claim merely to reflect behaviour; in many cases the message is
a confusion of truth and fiction—an extreme example, for
instance, was *Beyond the Valley of the Dolls*, essentially based
on the Sharon Tate killings.'[22]

The report's final recommendations concerning the cinema
were : 'The British Board of Film Censors should be no longer
responsible solely to the industry. The President and Secretary
should be appointed by the Home Secretary. The Board should
also include representatives of the industry and the local authorities and suitable members of the public. It should continue to
operate a rating system of the present kind. Under such a re-
constituted Board, the statutory powers of the local authorities
would be retained so long as they wished.'[23]

The statement raises a number of points. First, as we have
seen, the Board is not now 'solely responsible' to the industry.
Secondly, there seems good reason why the Board should be
independent of the Government in order to restrict the possibilities of political intervention. In the third place it is not at all
clear how the new Board is to be constituted. How would members remain representatives of local authorities if they took up
positions with the Board? How would 'suitable' members of the
public be selected? Once on the Board how would they remain
members of the public? How would such a large board as is
apparently envisaged manage to secure a coherent policy?

Meanwhile the feelings that lay behind the Longford report
were also being channelled into the formation and growth of an
organization with more concrete intentions. The genesis of the
movement had been the meeting of a small group in March 1971
'to discuss how the large number of ordinary people who felt
threatened, and who were alarmed by the "efforts aimed at
destruction of family life and love", might be given an opportunity to profess their beliefs'.[24] The Festival of Light, which was

thus launched, has its roots in evangelism. 'The original idea came from a young evangelist missionary, Mr Peter Hill, as a result, so it is said, of a vision : the initial meetings before the first major public event in 1971 were held at the West London headquarters of the Evangelical Alliance. Mr Steve Stevens, the Festival's secretary, is a South African who worked as a pilot in Africa for some years flying missionaries to their stations : one of the first to join the new organizing committee was the Rev. Eddie Stride, one of the best-known evangelicals in the Church of England.'[25]

In September 1971 a series of rallies were held up and down the country, attended by a total of around 200,000 people. At the principal meeting in Trafalgar Square a crowd variously estimated at between 30,000 and 80,000 were present, although the Festival's official history notes that 'it would not be accurate to suggest that the Trafalgar Square crowd truly represented a cross-section of British society. They were obviously almost all committed Christians—mainly drawn from the evangelical tradition.'[26]

The rally issued three proclamations—to Parliament, the media and the Church. That to the media was delivered to the B.B.C., I.T.A., the Newspaper Proprietors' Association, the Advertising Standards Council, the Press Council and the B.B.F.C. It argued that 'the freedom of the individual artist has been emphasized at the expense of a responsible attitude to the rest of society. The vulnerable have been put especially at risk. Extreme viewpoints have been given too much prominence. So have anti-Christian views. Blasphemy has been tolerated.' It urged those controlling the media :

1. To promote and encourage productions which emphasize the value of family life, love in all human relationships, and the responsible use of individual freedom.
2. To discourage the commercial exploitation of violence, dishonesty and sex, the trivializing of the important, and the exaggerating of the trivial.
3. To ensure that their productions do not 'offend public feeling' or 'incite to crime and disorder'.
4. To ensure that public issues are dealt with responsibly and without bias.
5. To respond to the public demand for better means of considering complaints.

The Festival of Light drew together the various strands of opposition to 'moral pollution' : its Council of Reference included Mary Whitehouse, Lord Longford and Malcolm Muggeridge. Not surprisingly its position differed little from the V.A.L.A. and the Longford report, although the range of its proposals is rather wider. Again the family is 'the basic unit of society', while such laws as those legalizing homosexuality and abortion are regarded as making 'the preservation of Christian standards of morality' harder. The proclamation to the Government called on the curtailment of 'encouragement by commercial interests of the abuse of drugs, or tobacco, or alcohol, or sex'.

At times, indeed, the movement has almost implied that sex itself is wicked. Councillor Frank Smith, a leading supporter, has declared that 'books and films encouraging sex should be suppressed', while arguing that the commercialization of sex brings more misery than deaths on the road, cancer or the Vietnam War.[27]

By early 1972 the Festival had established 180 regional organizers and had an estimated following of 1,250,000. From its headquarters in South Woodford a vigorous campaign against permissiveness in the media was waged, some aspects of which have already been noted. Its platform for that year included a call for a statutory Film Council independent of the industry, 'Operation Newsagent' to discourage the sale of offensive material and, in association with the V.A.L.A., a 'Nationwide Petition for Public Decency'. This petition was not finally completed until April 1973 when it was presented to the Government by Mary Whitehouse. Supported by 1,350,000 signatures, it demanded :

1. That the present Obscenity Law be reformed in order to make it an effective instrument for the maintenance of public decency.
2. That the Obscenity Law be amended to cover broadcasting, at present exempt from such control.
3. That special legislation be introduced to safeguard children from exposure to teaching material portraying behaviour which, when performed in public, would constitute an offence against public decency.

An accompanying letter signed jointly by V.A.L.A. and the Festival argued that 'an effective law would be liberating and not repressive, since its purpose would be to defend the freedom of those who have a right to choose *not* to come into contact with material which they find offensive'. Even more contentiously, it was suggested that 'the disturbing increase in violent crime cannot be separated from increasing licentiousness in sexual matters'.[28] Mr Heath's reply expressed the Government's concern at the 'widespread assault on the traditional standards of decency' and admitted that in certain respects existing laws were inadequate. However, no legislation of the sort called for was promised.[29]

More immediately successful was the attempt to draw the attention of local authorities to certain films which the Festival felt to be offensive or even illegal. Many councils received letters encouraging them to review such films and to decide 'whether films released with an "X" should be shown in [their area] without coming before this committee'.

Such a campaign is, of course, entirely acceptable. Indeed, Christians (and others) would clearly be failing in their duties if they did not make their voices heard. Unfortunately, however, the Festival has, at times, resorted to tactics of a more dubious character. One example is the way in which councils have been led to believe that they are being presented with outbursts of strong local feeling when, in fact, the literature has emanated from headquarters in London.

More disturbing is the actual presentation of evidence. In May 1973 literature was sent to local authorities with a covering letter referring to the 'mounting concern throughout the country because of the type of film which is being "passed" by the British Board of Film Censors'. A letter to be distributed to councillors claimed that 'there is reason to believe that a number of films given an "X" certificate by the B.B.F.C. are manifestly illegal at common law' : but no further details of this charge were given. A leaflet of press cuttings about *Last Tango* was also included. The critics' comments were selected in such a way as to imply that the film had been generally condemned by the press— which was very far from the truth. Some quotations were lifted from their context and made to give a very different impression from that intended by their authors.

A letter to the G.L.C. shortly before had entirely misrepresented the results of a *Sunday Times* opinion poll, and had claimed that press reports had 'made very clear' that *Last Tango* was an 'obscene film'. It also attributed Machiavellian tactics to the B.B.F.C. which does 'not wish to ban films' as it had been 'set

up and is financed by the film industry'. The G.L.C. was urged
to stand up for taste and decency on behalf of the people of
London, 'instead of one man, Lord Harlech, who considers himself to be the *final* arbiter of good taste'. Once more the claim
was made that research had shown that the Board had 'granted
certificates to a number of films which are obscene and illegal'.

   This sort of campaign is unworthy of a movement of such
evident sincerity as the Festival of Light, and suggests a degree
of desperation resulting from the inability to maintain the initial
impact and momentum. There is little doubt that support has
declined since the heady days of 1972 although, since no membership statistics are issued, this impression is impossible to verify.
In the face of this situation it appears that the Festival has
decided to try a different approach. Its attempts to harry *The
Exorcist* in the same way as it had *Last Tango* had been markedly
less successful. The film had been banned in only a handful of
places, while there had been few signs of the 'crop of schizo-
phrenics' that had been forecast. Nor had a great deal been heard
of the ten member censorship committee set up in February 1973
'to advise local authorities on controversial films'.

   It was to counter this depression that Raymond Johnston was
appointed the Festival's first full-time salaried president in May
1974. He had previously taught in a university department of
education and clearly intended to create a new role for the
movement with a firmer academic and philosophical base than
it had previously espoused. His interest lay less in attacking
individual films than in reviewing the whole relationship between
the media, morality and society. Symbolically, among his early
plans he included the search for a new name for the campaign.

   Before Johnston's arrival there was little doubt that the movement suffered from holding too extreme a position. There are
obvious limits to the extent to which any campaign based on
Christian evangelism can command popular support. In its first
publicity folder of June 1971 the organizers had stated the
belief 'that there are God-given standards for us to go by in the
'70s, and that there are millions in Britain who want these
standards defined and applied'. However, it is clear that the
definitions proposed by the Festival are not broadly acceptable to
all but a minority of Christians. The Anglican orthodoxy has
shown reluctance to become associated with the campaign and
some clerics have spoken against it in forthright terms. The Rev.
Hester of St Paul's, Covent Garden, for instance, has condemned

it as 'theologically unsound . . . another manifestation of the old Manichaean heresy—that anything that's pleasurable is wrong. Its repressive flavour is, surely, contrary to the spirit of Christ who was above all a tolerant figure.'[30] The Rev. Kenneth Leech has described the Festival as 'the voice of the frightened establishment, afraid for its security and stability. . . . Any idea that God might be involved in the disturbance and in the anarchy is not considered : God is on the side of law and order, in this case He is a true British patriot.' He added the warning that 'at a time when so many evils are attributed to pornography, it surely ought to be recalled that on historical evidence the evil effects of irrational religious movements are infinitely greater'.[31]

The Board of Social Responsibility—an advisory committee of the General Synod of the Church of England—was consulted by the G.L.C. during its enquiry into film censorship, and its attitudes reflected little agreement with the Festival. The Board's representatives 'considered that the present system was satisfactory because it cuts out the worst elements from films and that the British Board of Film Censors was performing a useful function'. They also submitted a paper by the late Ian Ramsey, former Professor of Religion and Bishop of Durham, which, while allowing that censorship is 'justified on some occasions', was generally critical of the whole concept. 'In practice censorship undoubtedly inhibits serious and legitimate criticism, tends to foster repression rather than liberal attitudes' and 'infringes personality and liberty and encourages that kind of paternalism which can so easily degenerate into a patronising and self-righteous condescension'.[32]

Support for the Festival from the Church hierarchy has been significantly limited, leading to the conclusion that theirs is the voice of an extreme wing, hardly representative of 'the ordinary people of Britain' or 'the vast body of public opinion' as they claim. The number who earnestly support the precise line adopted by the movement is probably quite small. Clifford Longley, Religious Affairs correspondent of *The Times*, has attempted to explain the development of the campaign in terms of its evangelical beginnings. 'The Evangelical ethic emphasises strict sexual morality, strict obedience to lawful authority . . . and honest hard work. . . . Evangelicals are therefore, of all Christians, the least tolerant of present changes in contemporary society. They are most suspicious, therefore, of the causes and catalysts of social change, such as the mass media (towards which they are almost paranoid in their sensitivity).'[33]

Yet parts of the message have clearly struck a chord with a much wider section of the population, and the Festival must be taken seriously on these grounds. The Heath Government seemed to accept the campaign as a real reflection of opinion among a sizeable proportion of the public. Festival representations were granted interviews by three Ministers and support was forthcoming from a number of influential Conservatives in both Houses. The Labour Government has proved less sympathetic.

Opponents of censorship have been markedly less successful in organizing themselves, with the result that their influence has been minimal. This is probably a reflection of the fact that they have never felt pornography, obscenity, even censorship, to be major issues : their sympathies and support have been channelled towards wider causes. The National Council of Civil Liberties has, however, opposed censorship ever since its foundation in 1934. Its terms of reference as 'an independent voluntary organization protecting civil liberties and the rights of political, racial, and other minorities in Britain' has naturally led it to become the principal defender of freedom of expression in this country. A body with a more specific programme—the Defence of Literature and the Arts Society—was set up by the publishers John Calder and Marion Boyars in 1968 at a time when serious publishers and booksellers were being threatened by the law. The N.C.C.L. was concerned at the failure of section 4 of the Obscene Publications Act (which states that an offence is not committed if it is proved that 'publication of the article in question is justified as being for the public good on the ground that it is in the interests of science, literature, art or learning, or of other objects of general concern') to protect serious works from prosecution, and conveyed this dismay to the Arts Council. Accordingly the latter convened a conference on 6th June, 1968, which was attended by about ninety people representing twenty-one organizations. The conference passed a resolution that 'a Working Party be set up to investigate the working of the Obscene Publications Acts, 1959 and 1964, and other relevant Acts, with special reference to literature, drama and the visual arts, and to consider such changes including the repeal of any such Acts as in their opinion shall be expedient, and to report back to this Conference with such recommendations as they deem necessary'.[34]

In fact, two sub-committees were established, one to consider reforms to the existing laws, and the other to study the case for repeal. The first found the problems of devising a satisfactory law insuperable and only one report resulted which argued that 'the laws against obscenity, while constituting a danger to the innocent private individual, provide no serious benefit to the public'. The working party therefore recommended that the Acts 'should be repealed and should not be replaced for a trial period of five years or even at the expiration of five years from that date unless Parliament should otherwise determine'.[35]

The basis for this decision was that 'it is not for the State to prohibit private citizens from choosing what they may or may not enjoy in literature or art unless there were incontrovertible evidence that the result would be injurious to society',[36] a conclusion that makes light of the extraordinary difficulties encountered in obtaining and evaluating such evidence. Judging the evidence that was available—and it would appear that the search was neither wide nor thorough—the working party adduced that there were no reliable grounds for suggesting that sexual or violent material has unacceptable consequences for individuals or society.

Apart from the somewhat sketchy nature of the inquiry, there is also, of course, doubt as to how objective the committee was able to be. The report affirmed that it had begun its task 'with the knowledge that reform would be less controversial than repeal and therefore with the hope that it might be feasible. That we have come to the opposite conclusion is certainly not the result of prior intention but of examining the problem with as open a mind as possible.'[37] Evidence was obtained from 'as wide a field as possible, including people and bodies who might represent other points of view', but it must remain questionable how impartial a committee which 'consisted largely of people concerned with the production side of literature and the arts'[38] could be. It would be naive and ingenuous to imagine that such a group could keep an open mind on a topic of such vital concern to itself.

The recommendations were overwhelmingly carried by a reconvened conference in July 1969, but rejected by James Callaghan, the Home Secretary, who felt that the report would 'make the situation worse from the point of view of the average person'.[39] Before leaving the report it should be noted that the committee 'would not seek to interfere with the existing arrangements under which the British Board of Film Censors classifies films into various categories'[40]—though presumably the right to reject films would disappear. No mention was made of the powers of the local authorities in this respect.

The N.C.C.L. which had, throughout the sixties, passed resolutions at annual general meetings abhoring all forms of censorship, welcomed the recommendations at its 1970 meeting and expressed regret that police action during the preceding year had 'created a repressive atmosphere, destructive of civil liberties and good relations between public and police'. The call for the repeal of the Obscenity Acts was repeated, together with a demand for 'the repeal or amendment of other relevant Acts which have been used as a basis for indirect censorship'.

Two years later the Council made its policies explicit in a pamphlet entitled *Against Censorship*, written largely by the lawyers Graham Zellick and Alan Burns. In his introduction Tony Smythe (at that time secretary of the N.C.C.L.) stated that the aim was 'to secure the abolition of virtually all existing constraints' and emphasized the importance of the issue : 'Ultimately all censorship, all restraints on freedom of expression, all attempts to licence words or images can be used to sustain, for better or for worse, the prevailing ethos of society and in particular the power of those who control society. Yet the health of a society depends on new ideas which pave the way for change.'[41] The pamphlet itemized the many problems involved in interpreting the present laws and demolished the alternative formulae suggested by the Society of Conservative Lawyers[42] and the Longford Commission, but relied on the Arts Council Report and the United States Presidential Commission for evidence that abolition is the most satisfactory solution.

In December 1972 a member of the N.C.C.L. committee founded the Campaign for the Abolition of Film Censorship for Adults, the first body to deal specifically with film censorship. A year later membership stood at 620, and the Campaign continued to be run by one person with very limited financial resources. Significantly it has received minimal support from the industry and has never had any financial help from that source. The declared aims of C.A.F.C.A. are 'to organize against any further extension of film censorship, and at the same time, continue the longer term struggle for the total abolition of all film censorship for adults. On the other hand, we are seriously concerned that minors (and in particular the very young) be shielded from seeing films which contain horrific or alarming scenes, and in this respect we would advocate the continuance of the British Board of Film Censors.'

The campaign therefore does not adopt an extreme libertarian position : the initial aim is to have films brought under the Obscenity Laws, although a more radical change is hoped for in the longer term. A system like that operating in Belgium, where there is no censorship for adults, is regarded as ideal, but the campaign seems to be unsure how to achieve this. Its activities to date have been confined largely to collecting press material and publishing a monthly bulletin. As a small group with membership predominantly based in London (about 75 per cent live in the capital) and with few big names to attract publicity, C.A.F.C.A. has a long way to go to counter the influence of its opponents.

Curiously the one celebrity who has given support to the campaign is John Trevelyan, probably one of the most influential persons on the side of liberal opinion. While he has often lent his support to his successor at the Board, his opinions on the role of film censorship have changed markedly since his retirement. In a postscript to his memoirs he has written that he feels that 'the time has come when we should treat adults as adults, and let them choose whether they will see a film or not. There are, and will continue to be, some films that might be harmful to some people, but I believe that this risk is not great enough to justify the continuance of restricting the freedom of adults.'[43] He argues for the abolition of the Obscenity Acts with provisions to protect children, the removal of powers of censorship from local authorities, and the restriction of the B.B.F.C. to its role as a classifier. Quite what events led Trevelyan to this recantation and how he judged that the time for change had now come are not clear, and it might also be suggested that his impartiality must to some extent have been compromised by his (then) position as advisor to a company with extensive cinema interests.

Early in 1974 a new campaign was founded in an attempt to organize efforts to abolish censorship. Launched at a press conference on 25th March the National Co-ordinating Committee Against Censorship was an affiliation of various societies already involved in such activities. Principal speakers at the conference included the secretary of the N.C.C.L. and John Trevelyan. Among its aims were the abolition of film censorship for adults and changes in the obscenity and indecency laws, issues on which the committee claimed that the silent majority 'is largely on our side'.

These then are the opposing points of view. As has been found in America there is probably here also a split in terms of class, age and political and religious conviction among those who are concerned in the debate. American research has shown that anti-pornography groups tend to be 'middle-class, middle-aged, religious, conservative and traditional individuals who felt that their value and norm systems represented the majority of United States citizens (the silent majority) and that these norms and value systems were under attack'.[44] Their opponents tended to be better educated, younger, less religious and more liberal. The problem remains of judging how far these organizations do reflect public feeling. As so often, it is probable that the majority of the population have opinions which are not strongly felt and which lie somewhere between the two extremes. What little evidence there is concerning these opinions will be examined in a later chapter.

CENSORSHIP AND RESEARCH EVIDENCE

I T I S G I V I N G away no secrets to point out that people have always engaged in violent and sexual behaviour and that many forms of both are accepted as 'normal' and legitimate. There is little evidence that twentieth-century man is very different from his forebears in regard to these activities. A glance at any history textbook illustrates the fact that ours is a history of violence; indeed Western European culture has valued aggression more than most, while masculinity is defined almost everywhere largely in terms of power and aggression. As far as sex is concerned, promiscuity has probably been the norm for many sections of the population throughout history. Even Victorian morality applied only to the middle classes: the poor and the rich were 'deviant' in their different ways.

It is perhaps curious, therefore, to find the mass media charged with leading to an increase in violent and sexual behaviour, but it is not entirely illogical. The press, film, radio and television have undoubtedly changed our lives in many ways: who can deny the possibility that they have influenced us in these areas also? If acts of violence and immorality are increasing (and it has not been proved that this is so), the hypothesis that the media bear part of the blame cannot be lightly dismissed.

It is a charge that has been levelled at all the media in turn, from their very earliest days. As long ago as April 1912 the problem was considered important enough to be discussed in Parliament itself. 'On the 22nd April a question was asked in the House of Commons about four boys under 14 years of age who had been convicted of house-breaking. The Chief Constable reported that the boys said that they got the idea from the pictures.'[1] Five years later the Secretary of the B.B.F.C. found himself having to disabuse a committee of 'the impression that stealing and impurity and other evils were the unavoidable results of the cinema-theatre'.[2]

In his essay entitled *The Fear of the Film*, published in 1939, G. K. Chesterton referred to similar claims then being made and added his own trenchant comments:

Long lists are being given of particular cases in which children have suffered in spirits or health from alleged horrors of the kinema. One child is said to have had a fit after seeing a film; another to have been sleepless with some fixed ideas taken from a film; another to have killed his father with a carving-knife, through having seen a knife in a film. This may possibly have occurred; though if it did, anybody of common sense would prefer to have details about that particular child, rather than about that particular picture. But what is supposed to be the practical moral of it, in any case? Is it that the young should never see a story with a knife in it? Are they to be brought up in complete ignorance of *The Merchant of Venice* because Shylock flourishes a knife for a highly disagreeable purpose? Are they never to hear of Macbeth, lest it should slowly dawn upon their trembling intelligence that it is a dagger that they see before them? It would be more practical that a child should never see a real carving-knife, and still more practical that he should never see a real father. It is perfectly true that a child will have horrors after seeing some particular detail. It is quite equally true that nobody can predict what that particular detail will be.[3]

Yet, many years later, similarly unsophisticated conceptions prevail. The *Daily Mirror* in July 1973 reported that 'the terrifying violence of the film and novel *A Clockwork Orange* fascinated a quiet, ex-grammar school boy. And it turned him into a brutal killer, a court heard today.'[4] In fact it transpired that the boy had never seen the film, which didn't deter the prosecution from asserting that 'the prosecution is bound to say the makers of this film have much to answer for'.[5]

In a special series entitled 'The Brainwashers' in April 1972 the *Sunday Mirror* indicted 'film-makers who are growing rich by exploiting violence'.[6] The first article claimed that 'it is a fact that real-life violence is on the increase. It is a fact that the meticulous creation and detailing of violence on our cinema screens is becoming increasingly more blatant. And it is a fact that the two are closely related.' The first statement is contentious to say the least, the third even less easy to substantiate. The basis for the conclusion that 'our investigations have shown that violence can be learned and increased by imitation—by what people see on their T.V. and cinema screens' is not clear, for no evidence was put forward. Even more confusingly it was then argued in one sentence that not only were people being stimulated to imitate violence, they were also becoming inured to it by constant mind-dulling exposure. This irresponsible piece of journalism concluded that 'the cult of violence creeps across the land—and it is monstrous that for reasons of "art" or greed, our film-makers should be permitted to add to its cancerous spread'. Beneath, in large letters, 'Next Sunday: Evil Films that must never be shown in Britain'—except, presumably, in the *Sunday Mirror*.

This sort of article is inexcusable given the plethora of evidence available about the ways in which the mass media are used by their audiences. Research into the 'effects' of the media is subject to innumerable obstacles and objections, but over the years a body of knowledge has been developed that enables certain generalizations to be made.

The most important point is that the mass media cannot be considered in isolation : they must be placed in a social context. When this is done it becomes clear that television, film, etc., are by no means as important in shaping attitudes as are agencies like the family, school, friends, workmates. If the media do have an influence, it is likely to be mediated through these interpersonal relationships. It is only in cases where these other agents offer no strong lead that the media can be important sources of information and attitudes.

As far as adults are concerned there is a good deal of evidence to suggest that opinions are too well rooted to be susceptible to transformation by incidental learning. Studies[7] have shown how individuals interpret messages from the media in such a way that they do not conflict with previously held ideas. The same message can have many, and contradictory, meanings for different people. B.B.C. research[8] has shown how little programmes are able to affect attitudes—or even increase knowledge—even when they are designed to convey a clear message.

Children, with less strongly formed opinions and stereotypes, are naturally more open to influence, particularly if 'they have few guide-lines, lack relevant experience, or if the family and other "primary" agencies in the socialization process have not made their point of view clear or provided the necessary standards'.[9] In the areas of 'the unfamiliar, the uncertain and the unknown', the media may become important as purveyors of values. Eleanor Maccoby has argued that 'there is reason to believe that children's attitudes and beliefs can be shaped by what they see on television, . . . children appear to be using television . . . as one of the sources from which they draw material for organizing and interpreting their experiences'.[10]

Naturally this process has both positive and negative aspects. The media undoubtedly play a useful role in conveying information and knowledge. In the realm of values it is clear that they generally reflect the culture which produces them. In all societies the media are largely owned and run by those who also control most other artefacts and institutions: they are rarely revolutionary forces. It is significant that the B.B.C., while being attacked by some as a nest of subversives and communists, is also 'Aunty', the voice of the establishment.[11] The film industry is almost entirely in the hands of financiers, bankers and giant conglomerate businesses. In the long run the message is bound to be conservative, supportive of the *status quo*. If there is a danger, it is this lack of access to the communications media for large sections of the population, which results in the dissemination of purely middle-class values and ideologies.

When it comes to the study of specific areas—like sex and violence—further complications arise in sorting out the plentiful data. Consider two American commissions which set out to review this literature and draw objective conclusions on which future government policy might be based. The National Commission on the Causes and Prevention of Violence, found that 'the preponderance of available research evidence strongly suggests . . . that violence in television programmes can and does have adverse effects upon audiences'.[12] On the other hand, the Commission on Obscenity and Pornography decided that 'extensive empirical investigation . . . provides no evidence that exposure to or use of explicit sexual materials plays a significant role in the causation of social or individual harms such as crime, delinquency, sexual or non-sexual deviancy or severe emotional disturbances'.[13]

These opposed conclusions *may* be explained by their different subject matters. As likely, however, is an explanation in terms of methodology, for 'effects' studies can be carried out in two different ways, in psychological or sociological terms.[14] The Commission on Violence relied very heavily on psychological research as the basis for its conclusions. This approach consists primarily of laboratory experiments and is most closely associated with the names Berkowitz and Bandura. These psychologists have devised many experiments to show that after exposure to violent material, the level of aggression in children is raised and that if they are in a situation in which this can be expressed, violent behaviour may be displayed.

Sociological research on the other hand, relies on survey techniques and attempts to discover relationships between the use individuals make of the mass media (i.e. what they watch, read or listen to) and their attitudes and behaviour. In general this work has supported the null hypothesis. For instance many sociologists have compared children who had been exposed to a great deal of media violence with those who had not, and found no differences in the criminal violence or aggressive behaviour among the two groups.

Some commentators have concluded from this apparent conflict of results that social science cannot provide the answers to the questions with which we are concerned. This is not the case, for a little consideration will suggest that the two approaches are concerned with quite different problems. Berkowitz has said that his experiments had indicated that 'there may be definite but quite temporary, transient effects', and this is no more than can be concluded from such work. A violent film might for a short while induce aggressive tendencies in individuals with 'weak inhibitions against violence' if the violence had been presented as 'good and proper' in the film. Even then there has to be a suitable 'victim' who is 'somehow associated with the sufferer in the film'. In other words psychology has shown that in certain circumstances media violence *might* be the final stimulus to an already disturbed person.

Speaking at Governor Rockefeller's Conference on Crime in April 1966, the sociologist Joseph Klapper stated that he believed 'very strongly that the kind of aggression manifested in the experiments of Dr Berkowitz and his colleagues has nothing to do with the kind of aggression that this conference has been called to discuss. . . . Feelings of aggression are a normal part of our human life, and an adaptive reaction to one's environment, and their expression in socially approved ways is not our concern.'[15] This is surely correct : too many generalizations have been made from the very specific experiments described by the psychologists.

In particular the relationship between laboratory tests and real-life situations remains problematic.[16]

Sociological surveys seem more germane to our problem. Although far from reliable they do paint a broadly consistent picture—one that challenges the 'common sense' theory that audiences are bound to be influenced by what they see. 'Certainly all over the world, behaviour is observed which would appear to have been learned from the cinema or from television : from children's games to the way people perform their social roles. Particularly noticeable is the influence of American material. This behaviour is imitative and I think there need be little dispute that on that level there is *some* influence. However, the stronger hypothesis, that children and young people, being highly impressionable, are tempted to act out violent and sexual scenes from films is a different matter.'[17] Over the years much research effort has been made on this hypothesis, from the Payne Fund studies of the early thirties onwards. The Payne studies found some evidence in support, but rather less than had been widely feared or expected. As early as 1958 Himmelweit, Oppenheim and Vince, after conducting a detailed study of children and television, felt that the question of the 'effects of violence' had been adequately answered. Comparing children with and without viewing experience they had found 'no more aggressive, maladjusted, or delinquent behaviour among viewers than among controls. Seeing violence on television is not likely to turn well-adjusted children into aggressive delinquents; there must be a predisposition for them to be affected in this way. Nor do children as a whole translate television experience into action. It may happen in extreme cases where children have a strong desire to be aggressive or to perform a delinquent act, and for whom constant watching of programmes with an explosive content may be the last straw. Even in extreme cases, the influence of television is small. The child's emotional make-up and the total of his environmental influences determine his behaviour.'[18] Similar conclusions have been reached in America by Maccoby, Schramm, Lyle and Parker and others.[19]

More recent research at the Centre for Mass Communication Research, Leicester, has confirmed and amplified these impressions. Halloran and his colleagues have noted the possibilities of undesirable consequences—'the difficulties of the frustrated, maladjusted and isolated can be intensified, and already existing deviant behaviour patterns may be reinforced'[20]—but have denied that the media are an adequate explanation for supposed increases in violent behaviour. About television, Halloran has warned that 'if the total problem [of violence] is not correctly diagnosed, if the role of television is not seen within the wider social context, and particularly if television is used as a scapegoat, then the real roots of the problem (and these are unlikely to be found in television) may go untouched'. He concluded that 'it would be a mistake to assume that the main roots of violence can be found in the media'.[21] Elsewhere the Leicester researchers have commented that 'the whole weight of research and theory in the juvenile delinquency field would suggest that the mass media, except just possibly in the case of a very small number of pathological individuals, are never the sole cause of delinquent behaviour. At most, they may play a contributory role, and that a minor one.'[22]

This judgement is not unanimously accepted, however. In America a number of official reports have reached a rather different verdict, although one of the earliest, the United States Senate Sub-Committee on Juvenile Delinquency, was forced to admit that it had been 'unable to gather proof of a direct causal relationship in the viewing of acts of crime and violence and the actual performance of criminal deeds'. It did add, rather lamely that 'it has not, however, found irrefutable evidence that young people may not be negatively influenced in their present-day behaviour by the saturated exposure they now receive to pictures and drama based on an underlying theme of lawlessness and crime which depict human violence'.[23]

The Report of the National Commission on the Causes and Prevention of Violence in the United States was more successful in indicting the media : 'A constant diet of violent behaviour on television has an adverse effect on human character and attitudes. Violence on television encourages violent forms of behaviour and fosters moral and social values about violence in daily life which are unacceptable in a civilized society.'[24] This was, however, no more than a review of the literature by a group of laymen. Social scientists in Britain, Italy and America[25] have drawn much less positive conclusions from the same material.

A more recent American report, at first glance, seems also to condemn the media : 'Survey data, while not wholly consistent or conclusive, do indicate that a modest relationship exists between the viewing of violence and aggressive behaviour'.[26] But the report admits that it lacks proof that this is a causal relationship, and that it is possible that 'the viewing and the aggression are joint products of some other common source'. Furthermore, in answering the question of how much contribution to the violence in society was being made by the exclusive watching of violence on television, the report decided that 'the evidence (or more accurately, the difficulty of finding evidence) suggests that the effect is small compared with many other possible causes, such as parental attitudes or knowledge of and experience with real violence in our society'.[27] This review also, therefore, found the media to be a contributory factor of minor importance.

One serious doubt does, however, remain, for no longitudinal studies have been carried out, and it is quite probable that they never can be. The 'common sense' theory that exposure to violent material over a long period may desensitize viewers has not been put to the test. Even the majority of researchers who deny that the media are an important source of aggressive behaviour, admit that the long-term effects are unknown, and there is some early evidence that tends to confirm fears on this score. Halloran has noted that 'one study indicates that heavy exposure to media . . . violence and aggression leads to an "ideology" which entails the acceptance of the legitimate use of force and aggression to oppose or resist violent behaviour in real-life situations. There is a suggestion from some Swedish work that long-term exposure to media violence is related to a tendency towards the use of violence in problem-solving.'[28] Such findings are far from conclusive but they indicate that concern over media violence is not entirely misplaced. Furthermore, the catharsis theory is now generally (but not altogether) discredited, so there is little reason for arguing that violence on the screen may be reducing aggression among viewers.

What has clearly emerged is that the concepts employed in many studies have been too vague and over-simplified. Terms like 'aggression', 'violence', 'brutalization' and 'desensitization' have been used with too little precision in an effort to pin down some simple causal relationship. This approach originated from the necessity to provide policy-makers with data, rather than from logical scientific requirements. It is now clear that this is inadequate. Recent projects 'indicate that numerous researchers have given up seeking to determine a "pure" effect of violence on the screen, and to catalogue its determinants and variables. They are now seeking less to determine a multitude of cause-and-effect relationships . . . and more to study the sociological and psychological co-ordinates governing the way the spectator uses the violence presented on the screen.'[29]

Another ramification of the loose definition of aggression is the easy way in which commentators often move from media aggression to actual aggression. Thus it is sometimes assumed that exposure to the one will influence attitudes to the other. There is, surely, a basic conceptual confusion here. Except in documentary and news contexts, screen violence is simulated by actors who neither feel the emotions nor suffer the consequences. It seems rash to assume that watching this sort of display can radically affect the audience's feelings and behaviour in terms of 'real' violence. Unlike some 'experts', audiences are generally capable of distinguishing between the two very different manifestations.

It may even be that concern about the generation of aggressive attitudes amongst viewers has been directed at quite the wrong problem. A number of commentators have begun to question the validity of the simple hypothesis that violence begets violence through imitation and, drawing on theories from other disciplines, have asked whether violence might not more likely be a reaction to frustration.[30] A U.N.E.S.C.O. conference on 'The Mass Media in a Violent World' in 1970 stated that the roots of violent behaviour 'are more likely to be found in the frustration engendered by such factors as inequality, social injustice, overcrowding, urbanization and so on . . . the media may add to frustration by encouraging levels of aspiration and status which cannot be achieved'.[31] Halloran has made this point more explicit, arguing for 'the possibility of violent behaviour stemming from the heavy emphasis in the mass media (particularly, but by no means solely, through advertising) on wealth, prosperity and material goods as symbols of success. It is claimed by some that the media not only stimulate but constantly remind people, particularly poor people, of their relative deprivation. Aspirations are encouraged which some people cannot achieve. Frustration and eventually violence may ensue.'[32]

To date, such relatively sophisticated hypotheses have not been tested. We have only the evidence evinced by the straightforward 'effects' studies. While these give a fairly clear picture—that the media are, at most, minor agents as causes of violence, they suffer from certain limitations. They tend not, for instance, to take into account the way in which the violent material is used.

The portrayal of certain types of violence may have beneficial social effects—perhaps by showing the horrifying consequences of such behaviour. On the other hand no studies have been made of the very worst excesses of violence. There is no particular reason to think that greater extremes will affect people in a different way, but the possibility cannot be entirely discounted. There is much concern, in particular over sexual violence, which has become more prevalent on the screen in recent years, and is almost the sole *raison d'être* of many Japanese films.

This brings us neatly to that other *bête noire* of censors and moralists—sex. On this subject the evidence is rather more consistent and conclusive, the verdict of 'unproven' less valid. In the first place there is growing realization among psychologists that the individual's sexual proclivities are established at an early age. This knowledge is reflected in the appreciation that sex-education must be taught to children of much tenderer years than was originally thought. The Psychiatric Department of the Council of Forensic Medicine of Denmark has noted that 'it is commonly known in medical science that sexual leanings are fixed at an early age, probably around 5–6 years old, and are in any case completely established by the end of puberty. It is therefore hardly likely that the reading of "obscene" writings or the sight of films etc. will change the sexual leanings of an adult person.'[33]

Moreover, the vast majority of research has supported the contention that adults, and even adolescents, are unlikely to be influenced by sexual material in the media. Of course there are short-term effects: such material is usually designed to provoke reaction, but this is not widely considered to be evil in itself. It is the possibilities of longer-term influence on attitudes and behaviour which has been the object of concern, and an enormous body of data has been accumulated by social scientists. This evidence has been carefully scrutinized by official or quasi-official committees in five countries, and their conclusions are worth some consideration.

The most famous, of course, is the Commission on Obscenity and Pornography which was established by President Johnson in 1968. This body not only reviewed existing data, but also instituted a great deal of further work which was reported in ten technical reports. Like other research in this field, the technical reports include much work that is of very limited value (and some that is, frankly, ludicrous) and a rather smaller body of useful work. The problem of evaluating the results of this effort is enormous and any conclusions are invariably contested. The majority report has been attacked on the grounds of biased reporting,[34] and there is little doubt that in its presentation of its findings it tends to emphasize that research which supports its thesis to the exclusion of other data. While it is true that the Commission had been established by Congress and was composed of respected establishment figures, it had an undeniably 'liberal' flavour : its chairman was a member of the American Civil Liberties Union.

Among other tasks the Commission was asked to 'study the effect of obscenity and pornography upon the public, and particularly minors, and its relationship to crime and other antisocial behaviour; and to recommend such legislative, administrative, or other advisable and appropriate action as the Commission deems necessary to regulate effectively the flow of such traffic, without in any way interfering with constitutional rights'.[35] As is now well known, the Commission came to the conclusion that there was no evidence, or at least no reliable evidence, that a causal relationship exists between pornography and social problems. Furthermore the majority recommended that 'federal, state and local legislation prohibiting the sale, exhibition, or distribution of sexual materials to consenting adults should be repealed'.[36]

Specific verdicts were that :

—Studies of human sexual behaviour show that established patterns of premarital, marital and extramarital coitus, petting, homosexual activity, and sexual fantasy are very stable and are not altered substantially by exposure to erotic stimuli.[37]
—Experimental studies to date indicate that exposure to erotic stimuli have little or no effect on established attitudinal commitments regarding either sexuality or sexual morality.[38]
—Data provide no particular support for the thesis that experience with sexual materials is a significant factor in the causation of juvenile delinquency.[39]
—In comparison with other adults, sex offenders and sexual deviants are significantly less experienced with erotica during adolescence.[40]

Not surprisingly, the Commission's recommendations were not acted upon. Indeed, President Nixon condemned the report in

no uncertain terms : 'I have evaluated that report and categorically reject its morally bankrupt conclusions and major recommendations. . . . Pornography can corrupt a society and a civilization. . . . Moreover, if an attitude of permissiveness were to be
adopted regarding pornography, this would contribute to an
atmosphere condoning anarchy in every other field—and would
increase the threat to our social order as well as to our moral
principles.'[41]

In fact, the Commission's report differed only in its thoroughness from similar summaries elsewhere. In Denmark, for instance,
the Danish Forensic Medicine Council reviewed medical and
psychiatric data and concluded that, 'as far as the Council is
aware, no scientific experiments exist which can lay a basis for
the assumption that pornography or "obscene" pictures and
films contributed to the committing of sexual offences by normal
adults or young people. On the basis of psychiatric and child-
psychiatric experience it can neither be assumed that sexual leanings, the development of personality, and the ordinary attitude
to sex and to ethical-sexual norms either in children or adults,
can be detrimentally affected by the means in question [porno-
graphic literature, pictures and films].'[42]

In Sweden a Ministry of Justice committee in 1969 has found
'scarce support for a hypothesis of harmful effects flowing from
the reading or viewing of pornographic materials'[43] while simul-
taneous study in Israel has also recommended liberalization of
the obscenity laws, on the grounds that pornography does not
lead to crime nor corrupt morals. The British Arts Council
Report has been discussed elsewhere. As a body with a very
obvious interest in liberalizing the law its conclusions cannot be
given any great weight, but it did gather a certain amount of
evidence to support its contention. It included a summary of
research by Halloran who reiterated that 'the overall tendency
[of media exposure] is to reinforce what is already there rather
than to create or put new things there . . . on the whole well
formed attitudes and values are not likely to be changed by
exposure to the media.'[44]

The most recent review was that of Maurice Yaffé, published
as an appendix to the 'Longford Report'. Yaffé was clearly
unimpressed by much of the work done and reluctant to draw
conclusions. Nevertheless, although hedged about with reservations, Yaffé's account does not contradict other summaries—and
sits uneasily in the context of the rest of the book.[45]

Meanwhile attention has also focused closely on the 'Danish experiment'—to see what results followed from the legalization of pornography in that country. Some early studies were reported in the American technical reports, giving empirical support (albeit of a tentative nature) to the theory that there had been no undesirable consequences following the change in the law. Berl Kutchinsky had studied the incidence of various crimes of a sexual nature over a period of years. Overall he admitted that there were a number of possible explanations for the recent decrease in these crimes, but in the case of two types of offence— peeping and physical indecency towards girls—he was prepared to conclude that 'the abundant availability of hard-core pornography in Denmark may have been the direct cause of a veritable decrease in the actual amount of crime committed'.[46] Richard Ben-Veniste was even more cautious but made the point that it was indisputable that 'pornography of the type disseminated in Denmark apparently has caused no increase in the rate of sex crime'.[47] Kutchinsky's long-awaited book on the subject may produce more positive conclusions.[48]

In general, there appears to be growing empirical evidence denying that the media can have a corrupting influence on otherwise 'healthy' individuals. Certainly, as far as pornography goes there is little support for censorship on the grounds of social harm except, possibly, for children. Research on violence is less easy to interpret, and concern on this score does gain some support. As Halloran has pointed out: 'If only a few susceptible youngsters stand to be harmed if the situation with regard to the portrayal of violence and aggression remains unchanged, then it could be argued that it would be wrong to take the risk'.[49] On the other hand many would demand absolute proof of harm before accepting limitations to freedom of expression. The sociologist Edgar Morin has argued that the 'protection' of children and young people is, in any case, only a rationalization by society of its own fears. He says: 'Examination of the problem of cinemas' possible harmful effects has led us to reject any belief that censorship in this field is the least justified. The real sociological foundations of censorship go much deeper than all the secondary justifications and pretexts that have been put forward.'[50]

There are, of course, other bases for the continuance of censorship. Jonathan Miller has noted 'three classes of principle from which the exponents of censorship draw their arguments: first and foremost is the simple *moral* justification, which asserts that pornography, and indulgence in it, is wrong; that it is the task of the law to prosecute it as one of the forms of vice. Secondly, there is the *prudential* principle which claims that pornography is in some way socially *harmful*, and lastly there is the argument which insists that even if pornography were neither immoral nor harmful, it is at least *offensive* and that the public has a right to be protected against insult, abuse and nuisance.'[51]

The moral justification lies beyond the scope of social research and cannot be dealt with here, but having found only a little support for censorship on the second principle, some evidence on the third should be considered. It may be, as the *Daily Telegraph* has asserted in an editorial, that 'in the last analysis, the criteria on which censorship should be based is not a matter for "experts" . . . such men from time to time need a sharp reminder of the more exacting standards of the public'.[52] On this issue, the data available is even less satisfactory than that we have considered so far.

Measuring the extent to which people are offended by what they see through the mass media is, of course, a highly complex task. Attitudes cannot adequately be understood through the use of simple questionnaire survey techniques. Not only cannot they be reached through such superficial methods; they may, in any case, not be stable or consistent. An individual may, for instance, give a different reaction to a female interviewer questioning him in his home in front of his wife and children from that which he would give to a male interviewer talking to him in a purely male environment.

Care must therefore be taken in evaluating the worth of the various opinion polls which have tried to gauge public reaction. They can give a very rough guide in the absence of harder evidence, but the fact that all paint a generally similar picture is no guarantee that it is an accurate one.

Violence on the screen was the subject of a poll conducted by Public Opinion Surveys in April 1972.[53] A representative sample of the population over the age of fifteen was asked a series of questions, some of which are reproduced in the table below.

In general the survey opposed earlier studies, finding wide concern at the amount of violence on film and television, although it was apparent that younger people were less likely to favour more restriction than their elders—only 57 per cent of teenagers wanted 'stricter rules'. Perhaps the most striking finding of this

TABLE 4   PUBLIC OPINION SURVEY OF VIOLENCE
IN THE MEDIA, 1972

Question	Response	%
Do you think that there is too much violence in films now, or that the amount of violence isn't enough to worry about?	Too much	40
	Not enough to worry about	25
	Don't know	35
Do you think stricter rules should be made to cut down the amount of violence in T.V. and films?	Yes	75
	No	23
	Don't know	2
Which do you think is the more serious worry about T.V. and films—the amount of sex or the amount of violence?	Violence	66
	Sex	11
	Both	17
	Neither	4
	Don't know	2

survey was the relative concern expressed over sex and violence. Seventy-six per cent thought violence to be a greater problem than sexual behaviour in society today, while 83 per cent were more worried about violence on the screen than they were about sex. This relative lack of concern about sex was further reflected in surveys during the next twenty months.

Immediately following the publication of the report of Lord Longford's commission in September 1972, National Opinion Polls studied public opinion on pornography, as represented by a sample of 525 adults over the age of fifteen.[54] This survey found that people 'are prepared to tolerate much of what Lord Longford considered pornographic'. The table below indicates responses to a number of items that might be thought pornographic. As the figures indicate, only one item was considered to be so by a majority of those questioned, although there was more agreement that such things might be offensive. The top four items were all thought to be offensive by a majority of the sample (85 per cent, 67 per cent, 56 per cent, and 50 per cent respectively).

In fact, it was clear that the public was primarily worried about possible effects on the young. Ninety-four per cent thought

TABLE 5 RESPONSES TO THE QUESTION—WHICH OF THE
FOLLOWING DO YOU THINK ARE PORNOGRAPHIC?

	Yes: %
Live performance of sex act in a club	82
Full frontal nudity on T.V.	42
Full frontal nudity in the theatre	38
Descriptions of the sex act in books	38
Full frontal nude pictures in magazines	32
Strip shows	26
Sexy magazines in shop windows	20
Rude, four-letter words on T.V.	18
Rude, four-letter words in books	18
An 'X' sex film on general release	16
Pictures of a woman having a baby	8
Underwear advertisements	1

that pornography was harmful to children, 78 per cent that it
harmed teenagers and only 26 per cent that it harmed adults.
Indeed, only 10 per cent thought that they themselves might
be affected. In addition, as many people were satisfied with film
censorship or wanted it relaxed as were in favour of a tougher
approach.

TABLE 6   ATTITUDES TO FILM CENSORSHIP

Film censorship should be stricter	43%
It should stay as it is	38%
It is too strict now	7%
Don't know	12%

The study concluded with the observation : 'The Longford
Report has clearly pinpointed a general sense of unease about
the public display of sex and a feeling that something should be
done about it. But the survey shows that people are probably
more broadminded than Lord Longford realizes.'
A similar overall impression emerged from an Opinion
Research Centre poll of 1,014 adults carried out in February
1973.[55] The majority (52 per cent of the whole sample, and
68 per cent of those in the fifteen to twenty-four range) thought
the moral climate was about right, although a significant minority

(about a third) thought that Britain was too permissive. Violence was once more the main area of concern, particularly as it affected children. As the table below indicates, people were worried as much by bad language and blasphemy on television as they were by sex and nudity. Responses to the question about nudity suggest that the majority are reasonably satisfied with present safeguards on television, while the survey added that nudity 'arouses little censorious passion' in relation to films, theatre, newspapers or magazines.

Other relevant findings were that sex education had widespread approval (from 78 per cent of the sample, and 96 per cent of young people); that pornographic literature should be sold only if it is not publicly displayed; and that there were regional differences, with the south-east being 'more permissive' than other areas.

The publication of the Cinematograph and Indecent Displays Bill was the stimulus for a further Opinion Research Centre survey later in 1973.[56] This questioned over 900 adults (over the age of fifteen) in an attempt to 'find out what the nation considers indecent'. The findings in general did not offer support to the Bill as it had been drafted—the overall conclusion was that the British are not easily shocked, but that there are quite wide

TABLE 7   OPINIONS ON TELEVISION

			Violence			
	Ex-plicit sex	Nudity	(adult T.V.)	(children's T.V.)	Bad language	Blasphemy
	%	%	%	%	%	%
Should be banned	23	18	14	27	24	23
Should be allowed with more restrictions	26	21	27	37	31	21
Should be allowed with some restrictions	35	40	38	22	26	33
Should be allowed with fewer restrictions	5	6	2	1	2	3

variations around the country, as well as differences of outlook related to sex, education and income.

On the whole it appeared that few people were offended by public displays. Asked whether they had ever been seriously upset by something which they considered indecent on public display, 71 per cent gave a negative response. A further 10 per cent answered 'hardly ever' and 8 per cent 'not very often'. Only 4 per cent and 2 per cent respectively answered 'fairly often' or 'very often'. When asked what they personally would consider as indecent, only the sex act evoked wide agreement (48 per cent of respondents). Nudity (24 per cent), suggestive poses (21 per cent) and sex organs (18 per cent) were regarded as indecent by significant minorities, but breasts, nipples, violence, swearing, homosexuals and cruelty to children were all mentioned by 6 per cent or fewer.

This survey also included two questions specifically about film censorship. As the table below indicates, answers suggested that there was much greater approval of a national than of a local system, with a majority actually expressing disagreement with the present structure of local authority censorship. Although the first question referred only in general terms to 'a national censorship board' few would deny that the responses amounted to a vote of confidence in the B.B.F.C.

TABLE 8   Opinions on Film Censorship

	Yes %	No %	Don't know %
All films shown in public cinemas should be passed by a national censorship board before they can be shown	79	15	6
Local councils should be able to override the censors' decisions and either allow films to be shown which the censors have banned or stop films being shown which the censors have passed	32	57	11

A further question was designed to evaluate public reaction to 'several well-known targets for anti-porn campaigners', but as Table 9 indicates, answers failed to support the claim that the 'silent majority' were in agreement with such campaigns. In addition, it was found that 74 per cent of respondents were of the opinion that adults should be allowed to buy whatever indecent or erotic books or magazines they liked, as long as they were not on public display.

TABLE 9 ANSWERS TO QUESTION—HAVE YOU EVER BEEN SERIOUSLY UPSET BY HAVING SEEN ANYTHING WHICH YOU FELT WAS INDECENT IN ANY OF THE FOLLOWING?

	% saying 'Yes'
Posters	4
Advertisements for films	5
'Girlie' magazines	7
Newspaper pin-ups	6
T.V. plays, variety	14
T.V. advertisements	3
Plays	1
Films	8
None of these	64
Don't know	3

Consistent as these findings may be, they cannot be regarded as conclusive. There is, for example, some evidence that people react differently to actual examples of potentially 'indecent' material than to abstract questions.[57] When the poll presented respondents with three pictures (of a Rodin sculpture, a Leon Bakst nude and a 'Men Only' covergirl), responses were rather more conservative than to other stimuli. The minorities who found them indecent were rather larger than might have been expected. The pictures were found to be 'extremely' or 'quite' indecent by 7 per cent, 30 per cent and 28 per cent of respondents respectively. As these figures indicate the Bakst sketch was considered less acceptable than the sex magazine photograph!

Nevertheless there is at least reason to doubt whether the public is strongly behind the various 'clean-up' campaigns. The majority of those sampled by these opinion polls display some degree of tolerance and adopt a middle-of-the-road approach. In the words of one report, 'the survey shows that the public do not automatically follow Mrs Mary Whitehouse's brand of puritanism, nor do they accept the trendy opinions of the so-called progressives'.

Nor was Mrs Whitehouse offered much comfort by a survey carried out by the Opinion Research Centre for the I.B.A. about the controversial David Bailey documentary on Andy Warhol.[58] 929 people were interviewed, of whom 703 had seen the programme which, as a result of the publicity arising from the court case, had achieved a very high audience rating. Mrs Whitehouse had argued that the programme had 'demonstrated in a remarkable way, how totally out of touch with public opinion is the General Advisory Council of the I.B.A.' The research results hardly supported this assertion.

When asked what they had thought of the programme only 3 per cent had thought it obscene, and only 1 per cent had been offended by the nudity and 1 per cent by the bad language. Given a list of statements to agree or disagree with, 24 per cent pronounced the programme offensive (with 56 per cent disagreeing), while 29 per cent had thought there was too much bad language (44 per cent disagreeing). 84 per cent were agreed that it was all a fuss about nothing.

The sample was also asked whether the programme should have been shown, and the majority (63 per cent) thought that it should. Of those who felt it should not have been broadcast, the vast majority complained that it had been boring and incomprehensible. Only a tiny handful wanted it banned on the grounds of its being pornographic (5 per cent of the sample), obscene (3 per cent) or offensive (2 per cent).[59]

Television has provided another instance suggestive of the difficulties of influencing behaviour and of the high resistance of viewers to shock. During 1974 A.T.V. experimented with the device of showing a visual symbol throughout two programmes which were considered to be potentially shocking. Although quite large proportions of the audiences admitted to finding the programmes 'very disturbing' almost nobody modified their behaviour as a result of the symbol. Only one child was sent out of the room because an adult thought a programme might be unsuitable. Yet 90 per cent of viewers interviewed felt that the symbol was a good idea—as always it is others who need protection.

There are numerous other scraps of evidence about public

opinion, but the overall impression that emerges is of a vote for the *status quo*.[60] Research suggests that the majority wants neither an extension nor an abolition of censorship. As always, however, reservations must be held. Past experience has shown that the public is in favour of change *after* it has been made, but not before. Many liberalizations of this century have been carried through despite widespread apathy or opposition, only to prove popular after the event.

Some of the problems of attitude research are well-illustrated by a small study conducted in Sweden.[61] Four groups of soldiers were shown the controversial film *491*, half seeing a censored version, the others seeing the whole film. In each group, half the soldiers were told they were being shown a censored version, half that they were seeing the film uncut.

The men on whom the film made the least impression were those who saw the uncensored version but believed it to be the censored one. Those, on the contrary, who were shown the censored version, believing it to be uncensored, were the ones most strongly impressed by it. One of the questions asked was 'Do you think this is as near the bone as it is possible to go in a film?' From the answers received it was plain that they had been determined as much by what the men had expected to feel as by what they had actually seen, the proportion of men who thought the film went as far as was allowable being higher among those who, regardless of what version they had actually been shown, believed themselves to have seen the uncensored version.

Findings like this show up the doubtful validity of the concept of absolute standards, and emphasize the difficulties of establishing incontrovertible 'facts' about public opinion. As a small pilot study carried out by Social and Community Planning Research for the G.L.C. concluded: 'respondents' views on censorship in general were not always simple, firmly held or consistent'.[62] Comments elsewhere have indicated the limitations of any approach which assumes the existence of a single homogeneous public. Answers to an American survey (Table 10)[63] exemplify how different sub-groups give different responses. Clearly age and frequency of cinema-going are correlated with considerable differences in opinions about filmed sex.

The B.B.F.C. itself is well aware of the research evidence and

TABLE 10   ATTITUDES REGARDING MOVIES INVOLVING SEX
IN PLOTS OR SITUATIONS

	Total %	Under 30 %	Over 30 %	Frequent movie-goers %	Infrequent movie-goers %
Strong objection	31	13	42	17	35
Qualified approval	63	77	54	72	60
Unqualified approval	6	10	4	11	5

consequently rarely defends its decisions, especially those relating to sex, on the grounds of harm. Although lack of financial resources prevents the Board from instituting research of its own in any systematic way, three very small scale studies have been carried out in recent years. One involved the showing of *Trash* to a group of housewives to gauge their reactions to what was, at that time, a banned film. Although the majority were not offended it was some time before the ban was lifted. On the second occasion, 150 schoolchildren were shown David Hemmings' *The Fourteen* to judge their response to strong language and a fairly 'adult' plot. The study did play some part in the film's being classified as suitable for children. The third study centred on the film *Stardust* which was shown in a public cinema to an audience in Reading. The results confirmed once more that most people are confused about censorship, but even more apparent was the lack of real concern about the subject. Although the showing was widely advertised and featured in the local press fewer than 150 people attended—evidence that the 'silent majority' really has no strong convictions to express.

As a rule, however, the Board is forced to rely on research initiated elsewhere. Until long-term studies have been done, this can never 'prove' the need for more or less censorship. Some protection of children is undoubtedly called for, but how much further this form of defence is necessary remains debatable. All research requires interpretation, and at this stage a good many other variables come into play. Even were the case for or against censorship entirely proven, social mores would ultimately dictate what action would be taken. At present, some degree of censorship of the media is clearly supported by most people.

CENSORSHIP AROUND THE WORLD

BEFORE ANY FINAL judgements can be passed on the British system a few words about censorship abroad will help to provide a context for comparison. In fact the methods and standards adopted vary enormously : the film-maker who contrives to satisfy the requirements of all the bodies who are empowered to examine and alter his work is fortunate indeed. Time and again the dictates of censors result in quite different versions of a film showing in different countries. Reductions and adaptations may even be cumulative so that films become progressively shorter as they travel.

As far as English language pictures are concerned America holds a special position. Its weekly audience of some 20 million (compared with less than 3 million in Britain) ensures that most films are made with that market in mind. In any case, American films still make up a large proportion of the films shown in this country, while many of the rest involve American finance. American censorship regulations, therefore, have a considerable influence on what appears on British screens.

Historically, the American film industry has always been vehemently opposed to all forms of classification, largely on the grounds that, by its nature, it restricts audiences and profits.[1] Justifications for this point of view were usually couched in rather loftier terms, as in 1962 when the M.P.A.A. rationalized that classification 'represents a dangerous infringement of the democratic American freedoms of communication and opinion and of the American tradition of parental responsibility'.

Yet, only six years later, the M.P.A.A. introduced a classificatory system following the breakdown of the Production Code. Twice revised, the categories now in use are :

'G' : General Audiences—All ages admitted.
'PG' : Parental Guidance Suggested—Some material may not be suitable for pre-teenagers.

'R' : Restricted. Under seventeen requires accompanying parent or adult guardian.

'X' : No One Under Seventeen Admitted (Age limit may vary in certain areas).

Fears that the American people would not take kindly to this curtailing of their freedom were quickly dispelled. Research showed that, by 1973, 64 per cent of those surveyed found the categories very or fairly useful (55 per cent in 1972) and only 27 per cent not very useful (36 per cent).[2]

From the start it was clear that the classification system was to be used to curb sex more than violence. As early as January 1969 a commentator anticipated that 'the "G" category will undoubtedly include films in which violence is approved—so long as it's "our side" that does it and wins. . . . I rather suspect that the "G" category is really aimed against the portrayal of sex in films'.[3] Film critic Stephen Farber resigned from the Rating System after only six months, claiming that there was too much concern with 'pubic hair and breasts', and that there were 'overly harsh restrictions for sex; surprising leniency in rating violence'.

This policy was particularly in evidence during the time when Dr Aaron Stern was head of the Rating System. A practising psychiatrist, Stern had originally joined the M.P.A.A. in 1969 as a consultant with the ambitious task of analysing 'all known data about the perceptual responses to audio-visual material'. In July 1971 he undertook a very different role as director of the classifying body. His approach continued the repression of sex while violence was allowed to flourish as never before. Even *Variety*, the American entertainment trade paper, became increasingly alarmed at what Stern admitted to be his weak control of this material. Of one film the paper wrote : 'parents who send their kiddies to this "PG" rated pic will be happy to know that, though it contains a strangling, two suicides, a bloody knife duel, execution with an axe, the hanging of a dog, and the crushing of a man's head, the language is clean and no nipples are shown in the bedroom scenes'.

There is some evidence that this policy is being modified by Richard Heffner (previously a Professor of Communications) who succeeded Stern on the latter's retirement in 1974, but it is unlikely that the very marked contrast between the approaches adopted in Britain and America will be easily diminished. Films rated 'X' here because of their violence continue to be thought suitable for children in America where exposure of breasts or buttocks is often enough to warrant an 'X'.

There are three major explanations for the greater strictness over sex than violence in the decisions of the official censorship Board. The most crucial point is probably that the violent nature of American society demands that film-makers deal with issues of violence more often and in greater detail than appears necessary in this country. Films are bound to reflect the social setting in which they are made.

Secondly, American censorship is a more truly voluntary system. The censors cannot ban a film : the 'X' certificate covers all pictures that the board does not wish to pass in other categories, and companies can 'X' rate films themselves without ever submitting them to the P.C.A. There are, therefore, many hundreds of cinemas which show 'X' films (usually of a sexual nature) that cannot be publicly exhibited in Britain at all. The well-known 'pornographic' films like *Deep Throat* and *The Devil in Miss Jones* are only the most notorious examples of what was a thriving genre following the outlawing of prior censorship by the courts. On the other hand it must be remembered that the 'X' certificate still retains a low reputation in America : a poll in 1969 indicated that 47 per cent of exhibitors wouldn't show 'X' films at all. Some studios have adopted a policy of avoiding the 'X' certificate at all costs, and, unlike the B.B.F.C., the Rating Board feels it has an obligation to advise companies how to cut or re-edit (euphemistically called 'correction') in order to obtain a 'better rating'. Although official M.P.A.A. statements deny that 'X' correlates with 'pornographic', remarks by individuals have often suggested otherwise. One censor has described 'X' films as 'garbage, pictures that shouldn't have been made for anybody, films without any kind of artistic merit, poor taste, disgusting, repulsive'.[4]

Thirdly, there is Roman Catholic pressure which has had an immense influence on the American film industry ever since the thirties. Falling cinema admissions during the depression had turned the industry towards sensational subjects until the 25 per cent of such pictures 'was paying for the industry's losses on the clean 75 per cent which nobody seemed to support'.[5] In 1933 the Legion of Decency was formed to combat this tendency, and within a year it had forced the M.P.A.A. to put teeth into its

hitherto ineffective Production Code. Catholic pressure has been
a major factor in film production ever since.

From 1936 onwards the Legion has reviewed and rated films.
The Legion's reviewers were trained by 'experts in the field of
morality and decency' and imposed strict standards. 'A very
important qualification . . . of a reviewer is . . . appreciation of
wholesome motion picture entertainment. (An open mind is
most essential.) The reviewer's yardstick is *traditional* standards
of morality upon which the sanctification of the individual, the
sacredness of the home and the ethical foundations of civilization necessarily depend.'[6]

Six categories are used for classification. 'A1'–'A4' denote
various degrees of acceptance; 'B' indicates that a film is 'morally
objectionable in part for all'; while 'C' stands for 'condemned',
a rating that, for many years, spelt certain financial ruin. Since
the early sixties the Legion has become markedly more liberal.
Renamed the National Catholic Office for Motion Pictures in
1966 it has adopted a less negative attitude towards films, recommending some and presenting awards to those in which
'artistic vision and expression best embody authentic human
values'. Despite this many highly praised films continue to be
condemned : in 1973 about 20 per cent of all films rated were
assigned to the 'C' category. The standards applied are clearly
very different from those adopted in this country. Horror films
are frequently rated 'A2'—unobjectionable for adults and adolescents—while the *Carry On* films usually merit a 'B'. Condemned
films include many passed in this country, including *Everything
You Always Wanted to Know about Sex*, *Heavy Traffic* and
A Clockwork Orange. Yet *The Godfather was* 'A3'—morally
unobjectionable for adults.

Recent developments arising from the banning of prior censorship and the growth of 'porno-houses' has, to an extent, pulled
the carpet from under the feet of the Catholic Office, but any
producer who wants his film to be widely shown in public
cinemas in America must be aware of the pressure before he
can raise a dollar to finance his production. Rather than risk
trouble later, he will usually adjust his script accordingly. As
Randall has remarked, 'such self-operating influence may have
vitality not only in the executive offices of the major companies,
but also in the minds of some producers at all stages in the
film-making process. When this is considered, then the real
extent of office censorship may be truly remarkable, overshadow-

ing any quantitative indications of influence in overt controversies.'[7]

The National Catholic Office is not happy with the recent operation of classification. In May 1970, at the end of an eighteen-month evaluation of the Rating System undertaken jointly with the Broadcasting and Film Commission of the (Protestant) National Council of Churches, a number of specific charges were made. It was argued that "the public has not yet been sufficiently educated to the true significance of the Code's symbols, that children are being admitted to "R" and "X" rated pictures, that advertising for "R" and "X" rated films is frequently deliberately misleading and that trailers for such pictures are often shown at theatres where "G" and "GP" films are running. Most importantly films are being rated less for their basic values and effect upon the viewers than for such superficialities as language, extent of nudity and explicitness of sexual action'.[8]

If such criticisms are in any way valid, it would seem that the American P.C.A. has even more problems than its British equivalent. At that time it was facing an ever-growing disparity between the standards it was accustomed to upholding and the decisions being made in the courts. Throughout the sixties the Supreme Court, under Chief Justice Earl Warren, had been rapidly eroding many of the bastions of censorship. In 1965 it had found that the practice followed in many cities of requiring all films to be licensed by a Board of Regents or similar body 'failed to provide adequate safeguards against undue inhibition of protected expression'.[9] In 1968 the Swedish *I Am Curious—Yellow* had been seized by U.S. Customs, found obscene by a New York Court, but eventually cleared on appeal. As a result of this decision, and the spectacular financial success of the film, a large number of other foreign films were imported, many of a much more dubious nature, but defended nonetheless on the grounds of their having 'redeeming social values', being 'social documents', or 'possessing educational value'.

As a Californian judge was forced to admit when presented with a film version of Henry Miller's novel:

The court is unable to determine whether or not the film *Quiet Days in Clichy* goes substantially beyond customary limits of candour in the nation as a whole in the depiction or representation of matters pertaining to sex or nudity. Qualified, respectable experts have found that the film *Quiet Days in Clichy* has artistic merit and other social values. I am unable to find that it does not. Bearing in mind the increasing frankness in society in matters pertaining to sex and nudity, and the possible artistic merit of the film, I find that the film appeals to the normal interest in sex and nudity which the average person has in such matters and that it does not appeal to the prurient, i.e. shameful, morbid interest of the average man.[10]

However, in 1968 Richard Nixon had been elected President, and a vigorous effort to reverse the trend of the previous decade began. He and his running mate, Spiro Agnew, had campaigned strongly on a decency and law-and-order ticket, and Agnew in particular was known to be antipathetic towards the mass media and the arts. The complexion of the Supreme Court swifty changed as Nixon appointed men known to be out of sympathy with the liberalism of the Warren era. Nixon's own attitude was made clear in his statement rejecting the Report of the Commission on Obscenity and Pornography: 'The warped and brutal portrayal of sex in books, plays, magazines and movies, if not halted and reversed, could poison the wellsprings of American and Western culture and civilization.... Smut should not be simply contained at its present level; it should be outlawed in every state in the union. And the legislatures and courts at every level of American Government should act in unison to achieve that goal.'[11]

In New York, Mayor Lindsay attempted to take action by cleaning up Times Square which had degenerated into an area of seedy cinemas and brothels. He met rebuff in the courts however, it being ruled that the revoking of licences represents prior restraint and is therefore unconstitutional. One court alone rejected 135 cases of prosecution for obscenity. The campaign was fizzling out, when it was finally killed by the revelation that many of the porn-houses, massage parlours and brothels were in fact owned by respectable members of New York society, including the family of the President's son-in-law. Lindsay's only real success was the banning in the city of the film *Deep Throat* and a large fine for the cinema that had been showing the picture for nine months.

Early in 1973 the President presented an anti-obscenity bill that seemed likely to affect wide sections of the film industry. 'Section 1851' of the Bill threatened prison sentences for anyone who 'transfers, distributes, dispenses, displays, exhibits, broadcasts or lends any material, either verbal or written, that represents any act of sexual intercourse, flagellation, torture or violence; shows any explicit close-up of a human genital organ; or makes any advertisement, notice, announcement, or other method by which information is given as to the manner in which any of the obscene material may be procured'.[12] Although exception was made for products which are 'reasonably necessary and appropriate to the integrity of the product as a whole to fulfil an artistic, scientific or literary purpose, and is not included primarily to stimulate prurient interest', this Bill would obviously have far-reaching consequences.

Shortly afterwards, the Supreme Court, now dominated by Nixon appointees,[13] reversed earlier judgements that the constitution protects obscene material as well as free speech under the First Amendment. 'The court held that juries and courts no longer needed to find that material was "utterly" without redeeming social value before they declare it obscene. Instead they may determine whether the work "taken as a whole lacks serious literary, artistic, political or scientific value". The court also held that local community standards rather than national standards should be used in determining whether material is obscene and therefore not protected by the constitution.'[14] This ruling threw the film industry into panic and confusion. The president of the M.P.A.A. predicted that 'the whole film distribution system would be thrown into disorder if local courts do start taking the initiative and start condemning and banning some Hollywood films'.[15] The President of the Directors' Guild echoed the thoughts of many when he lamented that 'as far as it relates to the film industry [the ruling] seems to be a terrible throwback to the dark days of local censorship'.[16]

Nor were these fears unjustified. In Georgia the State Supreme Court endorsed a guilty verdict passed on a cinema owner charged with obscenity for showing *Carnal Knowledge*, an 'R' rated film that had been among the top ten box-office hits of 1971. Intended prosecutions of other major pictures, such as *Last Tango* and *Paper Moon* were soon announced, while *Heavy Traffic*, due to open in 100 American cities, was restricted to eight locations for fear of court action. A number of projects in pre-production were cancelled because it was thought they might be subject to court actions in the South and Mid-West.

Later events did assuage the extremes of industry paranoia. The *Carnal Knowledge* verdict was appealed to the Supreme Court, where it was decided in June 1974 that the film was not obscene although the right of local juries to use 'average citizen' criteria was confirmed—subject always to the ultimate power of the Supreme Court. In New York State Supreme Court cases against four films were thrown out despite the fact that the judge had no doubt that they were 'obscene' and 'patently offensive'. He argued, however, that he had no way of knowing if they would be so regarded by the majority of people living in the city.

The situation in America remains confused, although it seems likely that the fall of President Nixon has taken some of the steam from the movement for restriction. The decline in the porno-film business evident towards the end of 1974 may also (if it continues) help to improve the public image of the cinema and discourage further legal action. All that is certain is that America has not yet found the answer to the censorship riddle.

Study of the systems operating in the democracies of Western Europe shows a wide variety of responses to film content. During the sixties there was some movement away from censorship but this trend was not consistent or unanimous, while in recent years there has been some swing in the other direction.

Northern Europe has seen most progress towards total abolition. Belgium, in fact, has never had censorship for adults at all, while Denmark and Sweden have always had liberal policies with regard to sexual material. Danish reports on pornography (1966) and film censorship (1967) finally led to the abolition of adult censorship in 1969, a move which was supported by all the major political parties. Provided that a minimum age of sixteen is set, films no longer need to be submitted to prior scrutiny, and the Board of Censors (which consists of a lawyer and members with backgrounds in 'pedagogy or psychology' or with knowledge of child and youth problems) now deals purely with classification.

Sweden retains its censorship, although a very tolerant attitude prevails as far as sex is concerned. As early as 1963 regulations laid down that no cuts were to be ordered in any film that had won, or might be expected to win, recognition as a film of substantial artistic merit. In October of that year, following the passing uncut of Bergman's *The Silence* the Board was asked to comment on the censorship regulations. The majority (but not the chairman) favoured the abolition of censorship for adults, although two months later, following medical advice, the Board rejected Sjoman's *491*; only the fourth film ever to be banned. In fact, the government overturned this ban, and further encouraged a liberal policy when they restored cuts in *They Call Us Misfits* in 1968. A year later a report from a special committee recommended the abolition of adult censorship, but no action has been taken and a firm line is still taken over screen violence. The Board may ban any film which they consider might have 'a brutalizing or harmfully exciting effect or may entice to crime'. Excessive violence has even resulted in 'X' certificates for Mickey Mouse cartoons.

Meanwhile a Dutch committee has also recommended change along Danish lines, at the same time querying whether film censorship is commensurate with the free speech provisions of the European Convention on Human Rights. No answer has yet been provided, nor have the committee's suggestions been put into effect.

However, not even in Scandinavia is there consistency of approach. Norway's State Film Control continues to ban 2–3 per cent of all imported films due to violence or sex, while Finland's traditional conservatism has only recently begun to be eroded. Films like *I Am Curious—Yellow* are still banned, while the Finns also operate an ingenious system whereby the Board of Censors can increase the film tax (normally 10 per cent) on any film which causes problems—no doubt an effective form of discouragement.

Nor is there any agreement within the major Common Market countries. In West Germany, film censorship for purposes other than that of the protection of juveniles is unconstitutional, the fifth article stating simply, 'there will be no censorship', but a form of self restraint exists based on an association (the S.P.I.O.) set up by the industry. This voluntary system is, in fact, very powerful and anyone ignoring it would be boycotted. The S.P.I.O. makes few objections to sex, but cuts out anything that might offend religious sensibilities or jeopardize relations with friendly states or their leaders. The S.P.I.O. also administers a classification system for the various states, which were reluctant to establish their own organizations. In addition, there is a Legal Commission which states whether individual films are liable to prosecution or not, and an 'Inter-Ministerial Committee' at Bonn which pronounces on the suitability of films for release in Eastern Europe.

In November 1973 pornography was legalized in books and magazines, but the cinema was excluded. At the same time exploitation of violence on film was made a legal offence. This law is administered locally and has led to heavy cutting of martial arts films in some areas.

An even more complicated system operates in Italy, where the government can influence the choice of subjects and scripts through the Banca Nazionale del Lavoro which controls the credits for financing films. Under a statute of 1962 all films must be approved by the Ministry of Tourism and Public Performances which appoints a number of panels to ensure that no films are 'contrary to good morals'. Unfortunately, acceptance by the Ministry does not preclude subsequent court action, and in the last few years there has been a sharp increase in such cases. Directors, actors and producers have been taken to court, culminating in the series of trials involving *Last Tango in Paris*. These local actions can be almost interminable : de Sica's *Sex in the Confessional* opened and closed continuously throughout 1974 as it was released by the public prosecutor of Latina and seized by his opposite number in Catanzaro. This intensification of repressive activity is associated with the turn to the right in Italian politics and the emergence of the 'Centre-Right' government. Finally, of course, as in all Catholic countries, there is religious pressure : churches display classifications which include 'not recommended' and 'not permitted', although there are signs of some diminution in this practice.

France has a no less complex arrangement. Censorship is exercised by the Minister of Current Affairs assisted by a commission consisting of eight members from government departments, eight from the film industry and eight others—clergy, academics and public figures. The decisions of the commission—which has no legal definitions upon which to base its work—are not binding on the Minister who can change decisions either way. Producers are bound by law to submit both scenarios and finished films to the commission and no film can be shown without a licence. As in Italy, a licensed film is not immune from judicial action under the Penal Code, while mayors have a residual power to ban films which they consider to be of 'an immoral nature'.

On top of this, as in Italy, the Catholic Church takes a very active interest, pinning up notices in churches and issuing news-letters in which new films are given a 'moral rating'. Needless to say, producers are forced to seek co-operation from religious organizations at an early stage in production, so that few finished films provoke opposition. Cases like Rivette's *La Religieuse*, which was passed by the censors but banned by de Gaulle's Minister of Information following Catholic pressure, are con-sequently rare.

The French government has never felt any inhibitions regard-ing political censorship. 'Even previous to the Fifth Republic, film projects which contained realistic references to religious or military themes, or even to current events in general, were usually squelched.'[17] *Zéro de Conduite* was banned in France for twelve years.

In recent years interventions have ranged from the serious—the complete banning of Kubrick's *Paths of Glory* for criticizing a French general, and of Godard's *Le Petit Soldat* for two years—to the trivial—the cutting of a sequence in *Breathless* in which 'Godard displeased Generalissimo de Gaulle by linking a shot of de Gaulle following Eisenhower on the streets of the Champs Elysees to a shot of Jean-Paul Belmondo chasing Jean Seberg along a sidewalk'.[18] Many films are held up for months or even years (e.g. Malle's *Le Souffle au Coeur*, Jaekin's *Emmanuelle*) for reasons of sex, violence or politics, and such action would probably be more frequent were it not that censorship at pre-production level prevents the making of films with a social or political content. 'Directors and producers are warned that their films might not get final visas and are therefore discouraged in their projects.'[19]

There have been periodic promises of an easing of govern-ment control. In 1970 it was announced that pre-censorship and adult censorship would cease, but the only result of this appar-ently liberal attitude was a renewal of local censorship, led by the mayor of Tours who banned a number of films on the grounds of immorality. André Astoux of the National Cinematographic Centre argues that the Minister of Culture still favours 'an econo-mic, political and moral censorship', an opinion given credibility by the banning in 1973 of a film on contraception and abortion. Entitled *Histoires d'A*, this film had been produced by a reputable consumer group and licensed by the censors, only for the Minis-ter to impose his veto. Giscard D'Estaing has once more promised a relaxation of pre-censorship, but it remains to be seen whether words will become reality.

The Republic of Ireland is another country where the Catholic tradition has resulted in strict censorship of films and books. An Act of 1923 laid down that a film censor was to be appointed by the Minister of Justice to ensure that no film is 'unfit for general exhibition in public by reason of its being indecent, obscene or blasphemous; or because the exhibition thereof in public would tend to inculcate principles contrary to public morality, or would be otherwise subversive of public morals'. An Appeals Board was also created, to be appointed once more by the Minister of Justice. It consists of nine members, the majority from the professions, and including two persons nominated by the Catholic and Anglican Archbishops of Dublin. Since the appointment of Dermot Breen as censor in 1972 a relatively liberal policy has been pursued within the limits set by Irish society—Breen founded and continues to direct the Cork International Film Festival. A complex classification system is used, allowing for films to be restricted to those over twenty-one years old, over eighteen, over sixteen, over fourteen and over twelve unless accompanied, but even the most restrictive category does not yet allow the showing of films like *The Devils* or *I Am Curious—Yellow*.

In less democratic and/or less developed countries, of course, even greater control of the cinema is frequently the norm. Naturally the State maintains a position of authority in countries within the Communist bloc. Although censorship was abolished in Russia following the revolution of 1917, it was re-established only five years later. By the thirties a complex system had been built up through which films were vetted at every stage of their creation, culminating in submission to official censors who could object to 'propaganda directed against the Soviet system', 'pornography', 'non-artistic character' and any film 'divulging state secrets or arousing national and religious fanaticism'.[20] An Arts Council was established in 1944 to supervise film-making and a Ministry of Cinematography in 1946 with overall control of the cinema. Under Stalin the system was extremely strict: between 1930 and 1948 Eisenstein was able to finish only three films, one of which was banned, and was forced to make a humiliating public recantation, admitting that he had forgotten that 'the main thing in art is its ideological content and historical truth'.[21] Less repression is exercised now, although, since the fall of Kruschev, Russian artists have been kept on a tight rein. The State retains full control of the cinema and can prevent the showing of films like Tarkovski's *Andrei Rublev* which do not find official favour.

Similar regimes supervise the film industries in other Eastern European countries. The Polish cinema has continued to produce interesting pictures although many of its younger directors have been forced to move abroad (Polanski, Skolimovski). The Czech cinema flourished briefly under Dubcek but has withered since the Russian invasion. Even the traditionally more liberal Yugoslav industry is now under attack, and efforts are being made to bring it into line with the new 'democratic centralism' that was adopted in May 1974. Dusan Makaveyev and others, after being expelled from the Belgrade Academy, have left the country.

At the other political extreme, fascist countries also impose severe censorship. In Spain some liberalization was allowed during the sixties, to the extent that by 1970 bared breasts were occasionally permitted, but this trend has now been reversed. The Film Order of April 1971 abolished the censorship of scripts, but this led only to even tighter self-censorship and the virtual extinction of art-films. The following year the government announced that it would withhold subsidies from any film lacking 'cultural and social values', although as no subsidies had been paid for some years, the effect of this was not likely to be dramatic. One writer has concluded that 'the gap between the official standards of Spain and the rest of the Western world is now so wide that one estimate suggests that as many as eight out of ten foreign films are now taboo'.[22] Prior to April 1974 conditions in Portugal were similar. In 1970 347 films were presented for censorship of which only sixteen were considered, by government officials, to be suitable for general exhibition. The revolution which removed the fascists from power has brought a much more liberal approach to the mass media.

Outside Europe many countries impose rigid censorship. Pakistan's system is notorious in this respect: 'specifically forbidden is the portrayal of poverty or unpleasant political and social realities, and social criticisms and satires that prove unpalatable in any way to the regime in power or to the establishment are not permitted'.[23] South Africa has a similar policy which results in the mutilation or banning of many imported films (and has led to the growth of a very popular 16mm private

exhibition circuit against which action is now being taken).
Among films rejected by the Publication Control Board are
Taking Off, *A Clockwork Orange*, *Satyricon*, and *Sunday,
Bloody Sunday*, all of which were considered 'immoral and
dangerous'. Miscegenation is, of course, not permitted, and a
major character—the black secret agent—was cut from *Live
and Let Die* by the distributors before it was sent to South Africa,
because of her relationship with James Bond.

Particular attention is paid to films to be shown to black
audiences. One of the censors reported to a Parliamentary Select
Committee on Censorship that 'when a film presents too much
primitive violence, too much sadism, too much bloodletting, it is
withheld from coloured and Bantu audiences. A detective who
has much to do with coloured and Bantu cinemas told me the
Bantu is an imitator. If a Bantu has seen a film in which there
is a lot of shooting, he walks out of the cinema shooting. He
wants to do what he has seen.'[24]

The all-white Board is 'broad in range' except that 'an ultra-
leftist liberal person' cannot be included—he being defined as
'someone who was tinged a little pink'. The Minister of the
Interior has promised stricter censorship legislation in the near
future to keep out 'overseas filth' and 'spiritual smallpox'.

The list of countries with firm controls on films is impressively
long. The Arab states have formed a group to blacklist all film
companies admitting close ties with Israel. So far only United
Artists has owned up to having offices in Israel, and as a result
all the company's films are banned. Egypt rejects all films that
'denigrate the honour and prestige of the Arabic peoples'[25] while
the Lebanon vetoes any that 'have any connection with
Zionism'.

In Brazil there is not only an official board of censors, but
also hundreds of other federal and local authorities with the
power to supervise content. In Iran, *The Cow*, probably the most
important film ever made there, was produced by the Ministry
of Culture and the Arts, and then totally banned by the same
official body for a year. The Khosla committee in India recommended that kissing and nudity might be occasionally acceptable in certain contexts, thus arousing heated controversy which
tended to draw attention from the fact that the committee also
called for harsher measures against sex and violence. New
Zealand bans films like *Fritz the Cat* and *Portnoy's Complaint*
and cuts others such as Loach's *Family Life* under a law which

allows the censor to remove anything which is 'contrary to public order or decency'. Guatemala even denies exhibition to films lacking in 'artistic merit', while state control exists in Mexico, Burma, Egypt, Hong Kong, Iraq, Syria, Thailand, etc.

Even Japan, which at first reacted to the wartime banning of all films except those made in Germany, Sweden and Switzerland by outlawing censorship, has reverted to stringent regulation. In 1972 three 'Roman-Porno' (romance/pornography) films were prosecuted by the police, leading to the creation of new regulations for self-censorship and severe prohibitions on sex and nudity. Even the Production Code Administration was taken to court for permitting the exhibition of objectionable films. Sex-films ('eroductions'—an exclusively Japanese mixture of eroticism and extreme violence) are still made, since they are the only fairly certain money-spinners, but they abide by the rules— pubic hair, for instance, is not allowed. Foreign films suffer accordingly : 'Pasolini's *Decameron* is chaotic because so many scenes are missing; *A Clockwork Orange* is hard to follow because the film goes out of focus (an alternative to snipping) during all nude scenes; *I Am Curious—Yellow* has forty-one scenes blacked out with the title "censored".'[26] In *Woodstock* the censors insisted that the emulsion be scraped off scenes depicting nudity, giving the impression of a sudden firework display.

The general picture is one of worldwide repression of the cinema. Censorship systems inevitably reflect the societies in which they exist. In most places either state control or religious or judicial pressures ensure heavy restrictions. Political changes are often quickly followed by changes in censorship policy—new governments in Argentina and Venezuela, for instance, have introduced more liberal methods—but such swings are usually temporary. There is even evidence that the movement to the right in Denmark and Sweden is leading to a diminution of the freedom of the media in those countries. The liberal trend of the sixties has been halted or reversed in almost all places that it affected.

There is, however, one notable exception to this swing towards tighter censorship, for in Australia the traditionally tough line has been weakened to a remarkable extent. Since the appointment of a Chief Censor in 1928 Australia has possessed one of the firmest and most philistine systems in the world based on the supposition that 'Australians are clean living and clean thinking and . . . do not appreciate the efforts made to titillate their

palates with so-called spice'.[27] Political censorship was not uncommon in the thirties, while Warner Brothers' crime films of
that period were particularly harshly dealt with. Later, horror
films were banned altogether as 'neither entertaining nor cultural'.
Recent banned films include *Viridiana*, Godard's *Une Femme
Mariée*, *The Bofors Gun*, *Pretty Poison* and *Ulysses*. By 1969 one
in three of all feature films imported into Australia had been cut.

The great problem facing the censors was that there was no
law to support their decisions. Films were classified as 'G'—
suitable for children, 'NRC'—not recommended for children, and
'AO'—adults only, but these categories were for parental guidance only. In 1972 the six states were at last persuaded to agree to
adopt a 'B' certificate, barring admission to those under eighteen.

This move followed a swing to the left within the country.
The press had been taking a markedly more liberal position for
a number of years. The Australian Labour Party had, in 1969,
adopted an anti-censorship programme without any public outcry. When Gough Whitlam was voted into power in 1972 he
put his policy into action, and Australia became, almost over-
night, one of the least censorious countries in the world. The
secrecy surrounding censorship was dispelled by the monthly
publication of a list of all 35mm films submitted, detailing the
action taken. While hard-core pornography is still banned and
even the soft-core 'sex and violence' films meet trouble, worthier
efforts inspire little opposition. *Straw Dogs*, *The Devils*, *The
Canterbury Tales*, *Last Tango in Paris*, *Heat* and *Deliverance*,
all cut in Britain, were seen in their complete version in Australia.
Significantly, perhaps, in spite of the speed with which policy
has been altered, there has been very little controversy or conflict.
The 'outback' image of Australia is now clearly, in this respect
at least, out-of-date.

But Australia is an interesting case simply because it has
reversed the general trend. The hope expressed by Neville
Hunnings in 1969[28] that censorship might be coming to an end
judging by worldwide trends of that time, has been soundly
dashed in the years since. In most places censorship seems as
firmly based as ever, strengthened by the turn to the right that
has characterized politics in so many countries in the seventies.
While there is no evidence that those few countries that have
done away with censorship have suffered in any calculable sense,
there is no reason to believe that their example is likely to be
widely followed in the immediate future.

HIDDEN CENSORSHIP

THUS FAR WE have considered film censorship under a very narrow definition of that term. Yet it is at least arguable that this sort of censorship appears relatively trivial if a wider context is taken into account. The whole complex structure of the film industry ensures that there are numerous points in the process whereby films are made and presented to the public when it is hard to distinguish decision-making from censorship. The extraordinary marriage of art and finance demands constant compromise, much of which is ultimately more restrictive on the film-maker than the demands of any censoring body.

Hunnings concluded his study of film censorship in Britain by reminding his readers that, 'films are cut or withheld for reasons other than a censor's or licensing authority's ban. Not only the non-co-operation of public bodies, but also the action of the industry itself may prevent the exhibition of a film, and exhibitors have successfully boycotted a number of films. The hidden "censorship" exercised in the offices of film companies themselves would lead to an examination of the financial control of, and degree of monopoly or oligopoly in, the film industry and thence to a detailed investigation into the whole film-making and financing process.'[1] No such detailed examination is possible here, but a few examples may be given of 'hidden' censorship in order to bring some perspective to bear on the main subject of this study. It must be made clear that the abolition of overt censorship cannot, in the present circumstances, lead to any real liberation of the film medium.

In the first place it is evident that the areas of human activity which are thought suitable for the cinema are strictly limited, while the enormous financial investment involved demands that bankers, financiers and top executives call the tune at this critical point in the production process. Many projects founder because the money cannot be raised.

Although the sources of finance are diminishing as the

252   FILM CENSORSHIP

popularity of the cinema declines, this is not, of course, basically a
new situation. In earlier days the small group of men who ran the
major American studios decided what films their companies
would make. Their interest was primarily in making profits.
Immigrants from Poland and Hungary and Germany, they had
started in America as junk dealers, furriers, pool hustlers and rag
traders. For them 'art' was a dirty word. Louis B. Mayer, head
executive of M.G.M. had ideas about films that were not un-
typical. 'He believed in sacred motherhood and omnipotent
fatherhood, the sanctity of the family over all. The virtuous
should be rewarded, transgressors punished. Beautiful locales,
lush sets, and good, heartwarming stories won over grim problem
dramas. A happy ending was decidedly necessary.'[2]

But the disappearance of the moguls has by no means led to
happier conditions for creative film-makers. Many, in fact,
lament their passing. The British-based American director Joseph
Losey has remarked that 'in the early days of Hollywood, when
there were men like L. B. Mayer, Harry Cohn and Darryl
Zanuck, you were better off any day with them than the people
who run the industry now. They loved films, they were interested
in making them, and they did know something about them.'[3]
Bryan Forbes, who has seen the movie business from many
angles, has written in a novel that only thinly disguises real men
and situations : 'The old guard, monstrous regiment though they
were, had at least understood the basic rules of the game. They
had robbed and cheated and lied and blustered their way through
the halcyon days of Hollywood, carpetbaggers to a man, but
they were at least possessed of a buccaneer's sense of humour
which redeemed some of their worst excesses and they had nerve.
Now they were dead or neutered and in their place we had a
succession of faceless corporate men who were usually too busy
jet-setting their way across the world in search of new acquisitions to actually view the films they made. What they couldn't
understand they destroyed. What made them money, they
squandered.'[4]

Ted Ashley, a recent chairman of Warner Brothers has boasted
that 'every book and every script is read by me first and every
idea is discussed with me before we make a start on anything.
Decisions can be made fast because I have no board of directors
to refer to. I agree the cast, the budget and the story for each
and every film . . . then we have to make an investment decision
to see whether the amount of money which we are allocating to

a particular subject is the right one in terms of the market that is available.'[5]

James Aubrey had similar powers when he was president of M.G.M. from 1971–3 and his approach was encapsulated in his comment that film 'is a business that can work, if it's run like a business rather than as an art form'.[6] Aubrey was the man who tried to stop Losey from entering *The Go-Between* at the Cannes Festival, arguing that it was 'the greatest still film ever made'. As it was it had taken Losey ten years to set up the picture, the budget of which was then progressively chopped from $2 million to $1½ million and finally to $1 million.[7] Experiences like this have made Losey understandably critical of the industry and of the powers of executives to strangle projects at birth.

> The most important kind of censorship is right at the very initiation of a project: one finds there are certain taboo subjects or certain subjects considered to be non-commercial or subjects which haven't a current vogue or are supposed to be worn out. . . . This kind of censorship applies to every director, no matter how money-making he is supposed to be. . . . I know of very few directors who have had full freedom of choice in their selection of subjects. Almost none. So choice boils down to the freedom *not* to make certain subjects which one feels to be potentially vicious or which one feels one 'can't do anything with'. This is the censorship of fear and ignorance, a pressure to conform that applies in almost every country: the conservation of money.[8]

Not surprisingly very few film-makers who hope to continue working are prepared to publish their criticisms openly. Bryan Forbes has done so, at one remove through the narrator of his novel *The Distant Laughter*. There he argues that 'making a film nowadays is a political and economic act before it can dare to have any artistic pretensions. The studio head talks of frozen currencies before casts and in the early stages a succession of grey-faced accountants sit in on all the planning conferences . . . when casts are finally discussed another set of financial advisers come in to quote top and bottom prices on every major star, and even tabulate with alarming accuracy the extra liability for drunkenness, normal and abnormal ill-health, loss of memory, fornication, marital and extra-marital habits and most known varieties of perversion.'[9]

More fundamental factors may also be considered. The most extreme examples occurred during the 'red' scare in America when J. Parnell Thomas and his Un-American Activities Committee contrived to ruin the careers of many Hollywood personalities. McCarthyism caused ripples throughout the industry forcing the studios to study all projected films carefully for any sign of 'pink' ideology or sympathy. To take one instance, a film about the work of the New York City Youth Board's battle against delinquency (a percentage of the profits of which were to go to the city) was cancelled after pressure by local politicians and the press simply because it was to be scripted by Arthur Miller, 'a left-winger at best'. In a triumphant editorial the *New York World Telegram* stated: 'The question was not whether Mr Miller is talented, or whether he could write an unbiased script on the work of the Youth Board. It was simply whether the city should enhance the playwright's prestige and diminish its own by indirectly hiring a man with such a "questionable" political background.'[10]

Britain has never suffered from quite this degree of repression, but it remains true that certain subjects, representing certain viewpoints, are more likely to prove acceptable to those who control the medium than are others which are consequently unlikely to be translated to the screen. Ivor Montagu has described the way in which the system filters out all but a limited range of ideas, maintaining that the essential problem is that 'too much money is involved. Money for production, money to maintain a distribution apparatus, money to own and run theatre chains. Only a certain class of people own and control that kind of money. And nothing not acceptable to such a kind of people can reach the screen accessible to the general public.'[11]

These words were written ten years ago. The intervening decade of uninterrupted recession in the industry has forced a wider range of material on those who control the 'means of production'. The box-office is the ultimate judge, overriding the beliefs of the studio executives. Successive waves of motor-bike films, 'youth' films, 'black' films, sex films and martial arts films have no doubt appalled the businessmen as much as their profits have delighted them.

Yet a high proportion of films continue to fall into the small number of 'genres' on which the cinema has relied for so long. These are the 'safe' subjects with long and satisfactory track records. Anything that falls outside these headings is a shot in the dark, a risk and an expensive risk at that. 'Downbeat' films remain in a tiny minority, rarely receiving full distribution or the whole-hearted backing of the big companies with all that this entails in the way of advertising and publicity.

Even the films that do get made have many obstacles to overcome before ideas become celluloid. In America their progress, if they are being made under the auspices of one of the major companies (which, contrary to popular belief, still dominate film-production)[12] will be under the watchful eye of the censorship department. These were created by the studios to deal with the Production Code when it was first introduced. 'It was necessary to do this in view of the heavy investment which was at stake if and when subsequent rulings of the Production Code Administration compelled producers either to leave out portions of a finished motion picture or to retake parts of it. Accordingly, a method was worked out by which the studio censorship department started to work almost before the studio would acquire any given story, warning the producer of any possible censorship problems and guiding him over the pitfalls.'[13] Thus the Code was being applied to films not only by the official censors, but also by the studio's experts : small wonder that a conservative policy resulted.

More sinister influences than this are at work, however. There is no doubt, for instance, that in America war films have been considerably influenced by the Pentagon. For such films to be made in a realistic fashion, help from the armed forces is often essential. In fact in the years 1948–71 assistance was given by the Pentagon to 41 per cent of all American war films. Russell Shain has shown that films assisted in this way were more likely to glorify war and to show American forces in a favourable light.[14] This is the natural result of the censorship to which the film company must submit if it is to be given the sort of facilities and help which only the Pentagon can provide. 'Before a producer can obtain assistance he needs from the military to make the film his project is subject of a process of review of the office of the Assistant Secretary for Public Affairs that in effect makes the Department of Defence an overseer of the production. . . . If assistance is desired, four copies of the film's script must be submitted for "evaluation and review", and an itemized list of the kinds of assistance needed from the military might be provided. Only after the script is approved are arrangements made to provide shooting assistance.'[15]

Without this help many films using substantial military hardware and personnel (such as *In Harm's Way* and *The Green Berets*) could not have been made on the same scale. Scripts which do not present the armed forces in such a favourable light do not receive support and may never be produced as a result. Hal Ashby's *The Last Detail* was refused assistance by the U.S. Navy who felt it was not going to aid recruitment. In addition permission to shoot outside the Supreme Court was also refused apparently because Chief Justice Berger took exception to the political opinions of star Jack Nicholson.[16]

The extent to which authority will go to protect itself may be gathered from the objections raised to Stanley Kramer's *The Caine Mutiny*. It was suggested that Kramer should 'drop the word mutiny from the title, clean up the Caine, increase the intelligence of the enlisted men, play down Queeg's cowardice, tone down one reference to "the morons who run the Navy" and present Queeg as more a madman than an Annapolis man'.[17] Shain concluded that 'the military did influence its own portrayal by the American film industry . . . the intrusion of the Pentagon into movie-making does raise certain ethical questions and does provide an example of what can happen when a mass medium relinquishes editorial control in return for economic favours'.[18]

In the modern political climate few would be surprised to learn that governments take steps to protect their images as presented by the cinema. Chapter 7 gave an illustration of this while a more recent example is provided by Theodore Flicker's *The President's Analyst*. It has been said that pressure was brought on the company to abandon the project after filming had already begun, but if this is so it was to no avail. The film was finished and accorded a favourable critical reception. But it then encountered unusual distribution difficulties, both in America and elsewhere. In Britain it has hardly been seen. James Coburn has publicly suggested that political manoeuvrings might have had something to do with the 'disappearance' of the film.[19]

On the other hand it might equally be argued that many other films never get shown at all. This is inevitable since some 3000 feature films are produced each year of which the British Board of Film Censors sees about 500. Of these only about 380 are actually exhibited in Britain of which a mere fifty or sixty are selected by the two big circuits for release around the country.

'The rest are sieved out in the ruthless commercial rat-race of a film business which, for all its nods to art, operates with the same cut-throat logic as any industry.'[20] Small wonder then that by 1969, according to David McGillivray in *Films and Filming* 'the number of completed British and American features awaiting an initial showing in this country has accumulated to over 500'.[21] Naturally, most of these films are shelved for the very good reason that they are considered unsuccessful: others, however, appear to be of more than passing interest. Yet of the 300 pictures mentioned by McGillivray in 1969 less than 15 per cent had had any sort of exhibition by the time he wrote follow-up articles in 1973. Then he noted that 'censorship continues to account for very few serious losses'.[22] More frequently it is the distributors who are to blame for the non-appearance in this country of works by Robert Aldrich, Andrej Wajda, Bob Rafelson, Pier Paolo Pasolini, Robert Mulligan, Frank Perry, René Clement, John Huston and many others.

Some apparently forgotten films do turn up years after production. Truffaut's *Mississippi Mermaid*, filmed in 1968, finally achieved a few bookings in 1974. More often, however, the films appear in cut versions to be released as supporting features. Abraham Polonski's *Romance of a Horse Thief*, made in 1971, was seen by the censors two years later so savaged by 're-editing' as to be virtually incomprehensible. But it is not only 'lost' films which suffer this sort of treatment. Jarvie, in *Towards a Sociology of the Cinema* has described how frequently films are altered by executives: 'These men order changes on the basis of their guesses as to public reaction. Their aim: to please the audience, to avoid offending significant minorities within it. Such interference drove Orson Welles, John Huston and Stanley Kubrick from Hollywood. Time and again young directors complain bitterly of changes—*Sanctuary* (Tony Richardson), *Major Dundee* (Sam Peckinpah)—which distort their films, render them meaningless, etc. The complaint is less that the films have been changed, than that they have been changed at someone's speculation or whim, and without consultation with those whose names are upon them as creators.'[23]

The examples of this practice are numerous. Roman Polanski had his name removed from the American version of *Dance of the Vampires* because it had been so severely cut.[24] Arthur Penn has complained that in one scene alone of *The Chase* 'there are six reels of exposed, printed film missing' following re-editing by

Sam Spiegel.'[25] Sam Peckinpah has suffered more than most in this respect. He has described his reactions to the cutting of *Major Dundee*, considered by many to be his masterpiece: '*Dundee* was one of the most painful things that has ever happened in my life ... *Dundee* was a fine film. Possibly the best picture I've made in my life. At two hours and forty-four minutes it was much better than *Ride the High Country*. There's fifty-five minutes gone. And it's wrongly cut. ... It was agony.'[26] Peckinpah was not the only one to be hurt in this episode. Charlton Heston had offered his whole salary ($200,000) to cover the cost of putting in several scenes which had been eliminated from the script. The offer was accepted, the scenes shot ... and then cut by the producer.

Nor were Peckinpah's sufferings over, for a similar fate overtook his film *Pat Garrett and Billy the Kid*. The director's four-hour rough cut was entirely rejected by M.G.M. who re-edited the film down to two hours for American release. The whole structure of the film was altered: it was to have started with the death of Garrett, shot by one of those who had helped him track down Billy. Peckinpah threatened to remove his name from the film, but relented. For Britain a further quarter of an hour was removed by the distributors (and a few seconds by the censors). The version shown here was reduced to a series of only loosely connected set pieces, which nevertheless attracted a number of very favourable reviews.

Joseph Losey has also encountered this problem, although in his case the distributors were not the villains.

Eve has not, as far as I know, been censored anywhere in the world. ... However there is a considerable discrepancy between the version released in France and Italy and the version I completed. ... Twenty-five minutes had been removed from the version that I think should have been *the* version of the picture. There were a great many things in the script from beginning to end which the producer didn't agree with, didn't like or didn't understand. He made it so difficult to shoot these sequences by not making locations and other facilities available, that the conditions of shooting finally made the results inferior in quality, at least so far as I was concerned. Having seen these sequences as shot, inferior as they were, he wanted them in the picture. I did not, so they are not in the picture, even though I think they should have been in, in terms of the original conception if they could have been shot right. There has been another kind of censorship exercised in relation to *Eve* and which is perhaps the bitterest of all. That is the post-synching of the Italian and French versions, which was done without any reference to me, the cutter, the writer or any of the actors concerned excepting Jeanne Moreau in her own role in French. Whatever the producers didn't like or didn't understand they either left out or distorted or changed or added and this was true also with the sub-titles in French over the English version.[27]

A later Losey film, *A Doll's House*, was killed as a commercial proposition by the distributor in Britain and by exhibitors in America. Here the director had been promised 'an eight weeks advertising campaign, six weeks minimum in the West End, and special handling in twelve University towns. None of these promises had been fulfilled. There were no bookings in the U.S.A., where Jane Fonda, who stars in the picture, was effectively banned on eight major cinema circuits.'[28]

It is hard for an outsider accustomed to 'auteur' theory and the deification of the director, to appreciate how little power over the final stages of film-making a director often has.[29] Jack Gold has described the problems that this presents : 'There's a general system where the director has the right of first cut, but after that the producer and distributor can do what they like. Unless you have sympathetic producer who is going to fight for you against the distributor it's a terrible situation, because you shoot with cutting in mind. I shoot a scene knowing that I want it cut in a certain way. But otherwise, after your first cut, there's nothing you can do about it.'[30] Even if this stage is successfully negotiated, of course, there is no certainty that the film will be shown. Gold's *The Bofors Gun* was made for Universal who had a special deal with Rank. 'It's not just that Rank had first refusal on the film, they own it to the extent that, if they refuse to show it, then Universal cannot say : "Right, we're going off somewhere else", unless Rank agree. We made the film. It got its censor's certificate. We showed it to Rank. There's one man at Rank who has the final say as to whether it goes on release or not, and he said "No".'[31] As a result, *The Bofors Gun* was hardly shown until it finally surfaced on television in November 1973.

Of course, many films are rejected by the two big cinema circuits. It was rather surprising therefore that the 'banning' of

Hitler—The Last Ten Days by A.B.C./E.M.I. whose chairman, Bernard (now Sir Bernard) Delfont, thought it 'utterly boring' and unlikely to be a commercial success, received widespread publicity. There were indications, in the press that the decision had involved less straightforward considerations. Delfont admitted that, as a Jew, 'my emotions have played a part in my judgement about not showing' *Hitler.* He also apparently objected to a hero being made out of a villain, an objection that could surely be raised against vast numbers of pictures shown in A.B.C. cinemas. In any case the decision whether to show a film or not is not usually taken by Delfont, who hardly helped his case by discussing another film turned down by his company apparently because 'there are things in it which I don't like. One of them is a scene showing the burning in effigy of Churchill.'[32] *Hitler* eventually went out on the Rank circuit.

David Pirie has gone so far as to doubt whether 'a commercial film is in any sense as its director intended it to be'. His examination of the English Gothic Cinema gives support to his suggestion, no case better than that of *Murders in the Rue Morgue,* which, in the director's final cut, Pirie considered to be a 'surreal masterpiece'. Unfortunately, on completion the film was flown straight to America to be cut and re-edited. Additional footage was inserted and a red filter imposed on all the dream sequences 'so that the structural confusion which was the film's whole *raison d'être,* no longer existed . . . the result was a travesty which contains only the remotest traces of what was originally intended'.[33]

This sort of treatment is far from unique. Donald Cammell and Nicolas Roeg had continuous problems with Warner Brothers over their film *Performance.* Warners, who at first saw it as an *Easy Rider* ahead of its time with sex, violence, drugs, and pop music, had a change of heart midway through the shooting schedule when they threatened to close the production down. Somehow the film was finished and a rough cut produced in February 1969. Warners, however, were by now strongly opposed to this 'decadent movie', disliking the violence and pornography —'even the bath water is dirty'. Six months' silence was finally broken when the company was taken over by Kinney, who produced a final cut early in 1970. Before release, according to Cammell, extensive cuts were demanded by the distributors and fifteen minutes were removed from the early part of the film. Recutting was finished in April and the film submitted for censorship. 'John Trevelyan asked, among other minor points, for the removal of intercut shots of Chas' girl friend clawing his back inserted into the flogging sequence. He said he could not countenance an explicit statement of Chas' sado-masochism. Cammell pointed out that deletion of this piece of character development would make the scene gratuitously violent. This Trevelyan accepted. Then, says Cammell, Warner Brothers Distributors exercised their own censorship and removed the intercutting anyhow.'[34]

Distributors' interference can go further than this however. Keith Irvine has reported the history of a famous French film in America. *The Wages of Fear*, directed by Henri-Georges Clouzot, had won the Grand Prix at Cannes in 1953 and had been chosen as film of the year by many British critics. But the version that was shown in America 'was not the film that Clouzot made'. The distributors, 'having heard that the film was "anti-American", that it dealt with homosexuality, and that it expressed "dangerous thoughts" ', had cut twenty-two minutes. In so doing they had entirely altered the social background against which the drama unfolds : 'shots establishing the poverty of the indigenous population had been cut . . . in the mutilated version the truckdrivers are just unemployed drifters, for the sequences that showed they were not responsible for their fate have been deleted. . . . Most typical of all is the elimination of references to unions. That "the company" and "the union" are groups with conflicting interests is evidently a controversial concept and therefore an invitation to the scissors.'[35]

Yet this case seems trivial in comparison with Universal's handling of Peter Hall's *Three Into Two Won't Go*, for there very much more than cutting was involved. As Hall indicated in a long letter to *The Times*,[36] the whole story had been radically changed by the addition of material shot in America by the studio. Entirely new scenes and characters had been introduced which turned the plot completely upside down. What had been a slightly subversive story about the dishonesty and double standards of a marriage, became instead a predictable and safe soap opera in which a probation officer rescues a young girl who has strayed from the straight and narrow. Both Hall and the screenwriter Edna O'Brien insisted on the removal of their names from this version.

Few cases are as blatant as this, but many films suffer to some extent, often for no better reason than the necessity to allow time for the 'candy break' which is now a greater source of profit

for many exhibitors than revenue from admissions. Many long
films are heavily cut on these grounds. Even American pictures
which are usually made to the required length are affected.
Lost Horizon and *The Lady Sings the Blues*, for instance, were
considerably shorter here than they had been in the States.
Bogdanovich's *Targets* was trimmed by fourteen minutes to make
it short enough for a supporting feature. But, according to John
Baxter, 'the real losses are in European films, many of which
are slightly reduced by the local distributors to extend sweet-buy-
ing time. *The Garden of the Finzi-Continis*, *The Discreet Charm
of the Bourgeoisie*, *The Decameron* and *Fellini's Roma* were all
between four and twenty minutes shorter in London than in
other European capitals.'[37]

For general release, of course, the films are liable to be cut
even further. Ten years ago *Sight and Sound*'s Arkadin was
complaining that 'the general assumption of the average suburban or provincial film-goer these days seems to be that he will
automatically be seeing at his local something cut down from and
inferior to what he might see in the West End'.[38] As an example
he cited two films running 136 and 113 minutes that had been
paired as a double bill and cut by almost an hour.

One could, of course, continue at great length along these lines.
In fact, Doug McClelland has written a book consisting entirely
of an accumulation of such tales.[39] Among the 650 examples are
many of what are now considered to be the finest films of all
time, but which can now rarely be seen as their makers intended.

In some instances sheer length forced reductions in completed
films. Howard Hughes shot 3 million feet of film (some 500
hours) for *Hell's Angels*, while William Wyler's cutting of *The
Collector* from its original four hours meant the complete disappearance of co-star Kenneth More. *High Noon* was an over-
long failure until the removal of half the footage and the use of
a song to bridge the inevitable gaps turned it into a classic. Other
cutting, however, is less understandable.

Some forty-five minutes (according to Welles, the whole heart
of the picture) were removed from *The Magnificent Ambersons*,
while scenes neither written by nor directed by Welles were
added. The 1936 version of *Lost Horizon* was originally edited
to sixteen reels but director Frank Capra removed two after a
disastrous preview. The film was acclaimed by the critics but, on
general release, twelve minutes more disappeared 'that rendered
meaningless and confusing several scenes and story points'. Re-

release in 1942 saw further deletions, while the 1952 version was shorter still. The film was later heavily cut by the television companies. Hitchcock's *Spellbound* had dream sequences designed by Salvador Dali, but these were severely cut by producer David Selznick. Don Siegel's *Invasion of the Body Snatchers* not only had all the humour removed, but also suffered the addition of a prologue and epilogue, shot by the director against his will. Two Fritz Lang films of the thirties were released as a double bill with the inevitable cuts to reduce running time to three hours. Years later the two were re-edited into one picture playing only ninety minutes. *King Kong* was reduced in length on three separate occasions in 1938, 1942 and 1952 before being restored to something like its directors' intentions. Even Disney's *Fantasia* was at one time cut from two hours to eighty-two minutes.

Most tragic of all, perhaps, was the case of French director Max Ophuls who in 1955 completed his 'masterpiece' *Lola Montez*. This was then 'cut by panicky producers from 143 minutes' running time to 110, then ninety-three, and finally, for the U.S., seventy-two minutes, with its unorthodox narrative technique "simplified" of its recurrent flashbacks so that what was left of the story was told chronologically, robbing the picture of its whole point'.[40] According to David Robinson, this 'mutilation by the distributors certainly hastened Ophuls' death'.[41]

It is interesting to note that two films which were at the centre of censorship controversies in this country had already been subjected to cutting in America. In an attempt to reduce the brutality of *Lady in a Cage* scenes had been removed which left one sub-plot entirely unresolved. The film still caused outrage in America and was banned altogether in Britain.

The Chapman Report was the subject of many complaints when the B.B.F.C. ordered a number of cuts which badly affected the continuity. Few realized that the picture had already been 'edited' by Darryl Zanuck to the anger of director George Cukor. The latter commented: 'It was my idea to get four rather appetizing girls, to counteract the vulgarity. You had Claire Bloom, for instance, playing a rather high-minded woman who did ignoble things; but in the cutting they removed whatever they thought wasn't lurid, so that the justification for her was cut out, and it became the conventional, sensational thing.'[42]

As if problems with company executives and distributors were not enough, films can also be censored by their audiences.[43] This follows from the practice of the 'sneak preview', whereby a new production is thrust upon an unsuspecting audience who are asked to rate it. Depending on their judgement the film may be considerably altered before final release. In America this method of finding out a film's potential is apparently almost standard practice. The most famous example is, of course, Huston's *The Red Badge of Courage*, the history of which has been described by Lillian Ross in her book *Picture*.[44] Throughout its production the film had been the pawn in various personality struggles within the studio. Huston himself appeared to lose interest as soon as shooting had finished. The studio cutter was largely supervised by producer Gottfried Reinhardt, who was torn between the desire to make a 'great picture' and the need to turn out a 'commercial success'. He was completely bewildered when a version that had been applauded by studio executives and critics alike was received with distinct animosity by a preview audience which consisted largely of teenagers. Following this 'disaster' editing was taken over by the studio production head who finally produced a version which retained almost nothing of Huston's original conception.

A similar fate befell 20th Century Fox's expensive *Dr Dolittle* in 1968. At the preview only 101 of the 169 present rated the film 'excellent', whilst as many as twenty-seven wrote it off as no better than 'fair'. Extensive cutting and re-editing followed which failed to prevent the film contributing towards the studio's massive losses.[45]

Of course, the audience affects films in other ways—as in all mass media there is a feed-back component, and every producer and director has an image of the audience he wishes to attract and communicate with,[46] but ultimately it is the random straw-poll which counts most. Many a film has been buried for ever after disastrous previews, for it is usually economic sense for a studio to write off a film against tax rather than waste time and money promoting a picture that is unlikely to be a success.

There is also feedback, of a sort, from television to film. Films were never designed to be shown on the small screen, and indeed certain developments in the cinema, particularly with regard to the shape of the screen, were a specific response to competition from television. The cinema concentrated heavily on larger and larger screens in order to capitalize on the limitations of the newer medium in this respect. Whereas films had usually been shot on an aspect ratio of 1.33 : 1 (that is to say, producing an image 4 units wide by 3 units high), technological developments made possible the use of various wide-screen ratios. Cinerama and Cinemascope both had ratios of about 2.5 : 1 and many other methods were utilized during the 1950s, such as Panavision, Vistavision, ToddAO and so on.

Today, however, the need to be able to sell films to the television companies means that few films are now shot in true wide-screen ratios. The competition has now become an important buyer of old (and new) films, and film-makers have had to adjust to its requirements. Wide-screen production meant that when such films appeared on television they either left blank spaces at the top and bottom of the picture or involved 'scanning' —selecting which part of the image to show since all cannot be squeezed on at once. Pressure from television means that most films are now shot at 1.33 : 1. For cinema presentation they are 'masked' or 'cropped' so that the upper and lower sections are not shown. Only the central part of the image is projected, resulting in a ratio of 1.85 : 1, or 1.66 : 1. The result of all this is that the director has to have two ratios in mind when he is lining up a shot. He must be aware of what will appear on the screen in the two different ways his film will be shown.[47]

Those productions that continue to use true wide-screen techniques may fall prey to another danger. Rather than use a scanning machine television companies now 'prefer to obtain what they call "rationalized" prints, which have been adapted for television showing by reducing them to standard ratio while re-cutting to achieve the scanning effect. The danger of this may readily be appreciated. Such prints can later find their way back into the cinema and pass as originals, while the true original goes permanently out of circulation.'[48]

Television has also affected the cinema in other ways. In this country the independent television companies frequently cut films in order to fit them into the available slots. Harold Pinter was moved to complain that *The Pumpkin Eater* for which he had written the script was 'mutilated' when shown by London Weekend Television. 'Twelve minutes were cut from it, including one important sequence and two quite crucial scenes.'[49]

In America this practice is even more common and the care with which this 'editing' is done very much less. The situation has now been reached when directors deliberately pad out their films in the knowledge that the television companies will later take pieces out. 'Nobody cuts to the bone in film-making: there is foresight in all aspects of the production. Some directors put in extra footage to allow for the T.V. version to cut bits out. Every out-take [scene shot, but not used] is filed away so that if need be, it can replace a dubious passage in a film sold to T.V. later on.'[50]

Oddly enough, the very opposite is also done by television companies in order to stretch 'short' films to fit the 100-minute slot. In 1970 *Sight and Sound* reported : 'It has been traditional for films to be cut for television screening; the notion now being pursued by Universal in Hollywood is that films should be added to.' The article quoted *Variety* in stating that 'in at least six titles scheduled for release to T.V. during 1970–1 . . . stars are being brought back—in one case three years after the original was completed—to shoot additional scenes, entirely new characters are being written in and shot, and out-takes added'.[51]

The cinema is even being forced to take account of the tighter censorship restrictions demanded by television. Rudy Wurlitzer, screen-writer of *Pat Garrett and Billy the Kid,* has commented how 'the sexual innuendoes and a lot of the language have been cut out of the film, severed by the studio. The reason why they cut it out is television. They're going to make the cost of the film back on a T.V. sale, they hope. And the censorship is much heavier on T.V., so you have to shoot a T.V. version. Ideally from their point of view, you shoot a movie version and a T.V. version, but it's an impossible thing to ask a director to do. So it's a real problem. . . .'[52] Ironically it is now said that one reason for the increasing use of bad language in American films is that directors are deliberately adding it to prevent their films being immediately sold to television.

In America, one critic has predicted that the reluctance of T.V. networks to broadcast 'R' and 'X' rated films may lead to the Rating Board being asked to cut films for junior categories.

'R' and 'X' movies will probably be resubmitted to the Board several years after their initial release, and the Board will supervise the cuts necessary to bring them into 'GP'. Recently *Last Summer*, first rated 'X', then re-edited for 'R' in 1969, was re-edited again for a 'GP' in preparation for a T.V. sale. Visconti's *The Damned*—the first 'X' movie to appear on television—was sold to C.B.S. after 25 crucial minutes were deleted. Even with the cuts stations in a few cities—Washington and Baltimore among them—refused to play the film because of its original 'X' rating. Some studios shoot covering footage for films during production in order to have the theatre and television versions prepared simultaneously. In several more years it may well be impossible to keep track of all versions of the same film, and future film historians may find themselves looking at badly watered-down versions of the best adult films being made today.[53]

If all this seems a little far from our immediate subject, the point to be made is that the pressures that decide what appears on the screen are various and powerful. The creative men on any production have a host of obstacles to overcome if their conception is to prevail. In this country the greatest obstacle is undoubtedly the system of distribution and exhibition, whereby a handful of men effectively decide what films will be given national release and be allowed the chance to make money. Occasionally the authority of the powerful few can be challenged. Ken Loach's *Kes* was originally shelved, but eventually released after concerted complaints from the critics and others. But such cases are rare. One cannot but give serious consideration to Peter Watkins' contention that the system has 'effectively nullified most of the critically serious film that has ever apeared in this country'. In particular, he argues that any form of political cinema in this country is impossible, for 'anything on film even vaguely smacking of things political is anathema of the highest and most repellent form'.[54]

Here I have discussed only a few problems and a few cases. The vast majority of films that are banned, interfered with, or never made at all, leave no record behind them. The films considered here all involve well-known, reputable directors. The less famous are more likely to suffer and are less able to fight for their work. As Roger Manvell has noted : 'Everywhere the pressures on the film-makers are considerable—to conform commercially, to conform to the censorship, to conform politically, to conform socially and not offend pressure-groups with particular influence. Above all, perhaps, the pressure on him is to be consistently successful, never to make a film which will send him back to square one in his career, or ditch him altogether.'[55] When considering the work of censors and their influence on film production, we must at least be aware of these other pressures— some of them a good deal more pervasive and insidious.

As with all forms of mass communication, the concept of freedom of expression has a very limited application. The Press

Barons jealously guard their own freedom of expression while systematically withholding it from others. As the number of national newspapers dwindles, so the whole concept becomes more illusory. If the workers who actually operate the presses express themselves in the only way at their command, by preventing publication of certain issues or parts of an issue, they are roundly condemned for preventing freedom of expression. In the same way the cinema largely speaks in one language, compromised only by the fact that the wider public can all too easily choose not to listen at all. Film production represents such an enormous financial gamble with not a penny recovered until long after the investment has been made that it is inevitable that the banker and financier follow a cautious policy. As Manvell has gloomily commented: 'If most of the achievement in all but the most recent British films has been on the conservative, or academic levels, the reason for this is . . . that the creative men and the financial interests on which they are dependent have managed to find in this kind of film their largest measure of common ground'.[56] The official censors cannot be apportioned any significant degree of blame for the nature of film production in Britain and Europe. The whole structure of the industry and the society in which it operates are much more important, if less easily changeable, factors.

THE FUTURE OF CENSORSHIP

T H E   R E A D E R   W I L L , no doubt, have his own opinions on censorship, few of which will have been significantly altered by what he has read here. It is only hoped that he may have a slightly firmer grasp of the facts. In this final chapter I would like to examine some of the changes that have been postulated and to make some recommendations of my own based on a personal analysis of the system.

As we have seen throughout, dissatisfaction with film censorship is by no means a recent phenomenon. Charles Oakley, in his study of the British cinema, noted the early appearance of 'self-appointed social reform organizations' who, in the twenties, attacked the Board 'for not using scissors on lingering kisses'.[1] By 1932 a Home Office spokesman was forced to explain to the Commons that he was 'aware that there were signs of growing uneasiness in the public mind as to the tone of many films now exhibited, and he welcomed this evidence of public opinion because he believed that the pressure of public opinion could alone bring about an improvement. There was, however, some confusion of thought in the idea that a change of the system of censorship would provide a remedy. ... He had no reason to believe that any alternative system so far proposed would produce better results or command support.'[2]

Government policy has changed little in the intervening years. Official statements continue to express faith in the present arrangement and to deny that any reform is necessary. They are less inclined, of course, to deal in any depth with the various criticisms that are made.

It is clear that the B.B.F.C. is the crucial body. It makes judgements on all films to be shown publicly in this country, and 99 per cent of its decisions are accepted and given effect. It is all too easy to underestimate the widespread support that the Board appears to enjoy from local authorities and the public, and to pay undue attention to the various minorities who condemn it.

Nevertheless, few would argue that the present system is perfect or ideal.

A frequent complaint directed at the Board is that it is a creature of the film industry. This line of attack arises from the way the Board originated, set up by the industry to protect itself from the growing threat of inconsistent local decisions. It is sustained by the knowledge that the Board is financed by distributors and producers and administered by a trade organization. All of this is true, yet the final conclusion does not bear examination. The real role of the Kinematograph Manufacturers' Association has already been seen to be of little significance and in fact new articles of association drawn up in 1974 specifically deny the K.M.A. any rights to interfere with policy.

It is true that certain individuals in the film industry fail to appreciate that the independence of the Board is of fundamental importance and continue to believe that it ought to be more observant of their wishes. But the financial structure of the system gives the Board a very real independence from pressure from any one source. It is vulnerable only if the whole industry unites to influence decisions, an unlikely development since the trade organizations continue to support the Board.

In certain respects, of course, the relationship between the Board and the industry must involve some degree of co-operation. The censors are naturally loath to take action that might further endanger the survival of an already struggling industry. There is some danger that they may be tempted to go too far in attempting to help pictures that they consider to be worthy. Murphy was castigated on these grounds over *A Clockwork Orange*, about which he wrote to local authorities in glowing terms, defending his decision to pass the film. One commentator evinced this as evidence that the Board was too closely involved with the industry arguing that it was no part of the censor's job to eulogize films in this way. Murphy felt that he had to explain his decision and that this could only be done by expounding his reactions to the film. The episode clearly indicates the narrowness of the path the censor must tread.

Another dilemma further illustrates the ambiguity of the relationship with the industry. Occasionally the Board is presented with a film that falls naturally into one category but which would almost certainly be more commercially successful in another. This may happen with horror or sex films that are relatively 'weak' by current standards, but which require an 'X' certificate to avoid total oblivion. Trevelyan admitted that 'sometimes we were generous, perhaps wrongly, in letting a company have an "X" certificate for a film which they could not sell in any other category',[3] but, as a rule, the Board is very reluctant to comply with such requests. This can, unfortunately, spell ruin for some commendable films, as happened to Nina Companeez's charming *Faustine* which survived a bare four days in the West End with an 'AA' certificate.

In the final analysis it is the overall record of the Board that presents the most convincing evidence of its independence. In its early days the Board was clearly composed of members who considered themselves to be (probably correctly) of superior intellect and sensibility to the totally commercially-oriented producers and distributors of the time. A very condescending air is apparent in the annual reports and in the quite frequent 'warnings' issued to film-makers not to overstep the mark. From the first the Board was by no means prepared to be a servant of the industry, an attitude that has never been relaxed. There is no doubt that, until recently, the Board has taken a firmer line than the local authorities. Many films banned by the Board have been passed at local level without councillors being accused of collusion with the industry. Even now that a more liberal approach has been adopted, complaints concerning the censors' activities arise as often from within the industry as from outside it.

The charge of political censorship is less easily discounted. All censorship has political implications, and while the Board is careful to avoid explicit political interference, it is inevitable that a point of view is taken. There is little doubt that films encouraging anarchy, for example, would be banned or heavily cut on one pretext or another. Whether this is defensible in a democratic society is debatable. All that can be said is that there is only one way to banish political censorship and that is by abolishing censorship altogether. Even if that task were achieved, problems of editorial and financial control would still ensure the dominance of certain modes of expression.

Whether or not the Board accurately reflects public opinion is, of course, hard to decide. Self-styled defenders of the 'silent majority' of all persuasions have never offered much evidence to support their claims to be more than small but energetic pressure-groups. The films at the centre of controversy have, almost without exception been very popular at the box-office, while there have been few appeals for a relaxation of standards. The real problem is that the cinema as a mass medium has undergone enormous changes since the war, which have not been matched by modifications in the system of censorship.

In the inter-war years the cinema was pre-eminent as the medium of entertainment for the family. Football and the public house offered alternative attractions for men, but the cinema had no competitors as a cheap form of amusement for the family as a whole. It was therefore logical that films should be vetted to ensure that they were suitable for the public. Exhibitors could rely on regular patrons to attend irrespective of the programme, secure in the knowledge that no film would fall outside the bounds of the perennially safe and successful genres.

Greater affluence, the car, television, the erosion of the traditional working class and a revolution in social behaviour completely altered this situation. By the fifties the cinema was firmly established on the downward slide that has seen admissions fall to a tenth of the immediate post-war figures. Now film is almost a minority medium. Most people go to the pictures once or twice a year when a particularly attractive (or well publicized) programme is featured. only the younger audience remains faithful to the cinema, generally favouring a diet of 'adult' films ranging from the intellectually stimulating to the meretricious.

The censorship system has made few movements to accommodate this changing situation. The 'X' and 'AA' categories have been introduced, and the allowable range of subjects and treatment greatly widened, but the fiction is acepted that the cinema should still cater for the family audience which deserted it long ago. Films continue to be tailored to a public that now no longer attends while the fact that the cinema now has a new audience, smaller, more discriminating and less shockable, is not sufficiently allowed for. The clear distinction between the public cinema where anyone is entitled to admission on payment, and the members-only club cinema is maintained, despite the fact that the modern cinema has more in common with a club than with the picture-houses of earlier decades. Few now go to films entirely ignorant of their content. The decline of the suburban 'local' has virtually eliminated the casual cinema-goer, while modern publicity techniques ensure that the vast majority of the population is well acquainted with forthcoming attractions.

Under these circumstances a strong case can be made for suggesting that censorship practices should evolve to be more suited to current conditions. This criticism applies more to the local authorities, who have little knowledge of the cinema and its audiences, than to the B.B.F.C. which is well aware of these developments. Yet, in certain respects, the Board itself has become anachronistic.

Back in 1912 the censors seem to have been envisaged as a group of gentlemen keeping a watchful eye on the potentially villainous activities of the film industry. O'Connor, in 1917, was clearly satisfied that breeding and education were adequate qualifications for members of the Board whose main aim was to protect the vulnerable masses from exploitation. Today, as we have seen, the Board professes a less paternalistic and more complex purpose, but the process by which members are selected has changed little over the years. No specific qualities or experience are required. The only real expertise possessed is that gained after appointment through doing the job itself. The Board remains, in effect, a conscientious but unqualified body with no special skills at grappling with the legal, psychological and sociological problems that constitute such a large proportion of its role.

In addition, the continuance of the traditions of secrecy at the Board seem out of step with the demands of modern society, besides contributing unnecessarily to the distrust which is felt at the Board's activities. It is assumed that the public would be deterred from seeing films which were known to have been cut, but the case is far from proved. The removal of scenes from *The Devils*, *Straw Dogs*, etc. were amply documented, yet the films were considerable commercial successes. On the one hand it can be argued that it is manifestly unfair to delude the public into believing that it is seeing an unexpurgated version when cuts have actually been made (no publisher would be allowed to get away with this); on the other, there is reason to believe that some sections of the potential audience might be encouraged to know that they are being protected from the full barbarities of the original.

Nor is the secrecy surrounding examiners really defensible. It might well be thought that they should be public figures, openly exposed to the feelings of people from all backgrounds, rather than cocooned in their own restricted environments. The fear that the press might be able to 'manipulate' them to give good copy right be realised at first, but examiners should be able to look after themselves in this respect. Surely the days when the Board could safely operate behind closed doors are over.

A similar point could also be made with regard to local

authority committees which are generally loath to reveal much about their actions. When they do, they too often reveal an inadequate grasp of the issues. This is not surprising for councillors fulfil an arduous task, much of it concerned with problems of more immediate moment and relevance for their electorate. Censorship is usually little more than an irritant, a chore that few have the time or the inclination to take as seriously as might be wished. As a result the vast majority of councils play no part unless called upon, and thankfully accept the decisions of the B.B.F.C. Those few that do intervene generally have only a superficial understanding of the situation, for the job of censoring is not one for which many councillors have a special talent. It is far removed from the other problems with which they are more familiar. It is usually only those councillors who have strong feelings on the matter who take an active part, and it does not necessarily follow that their opinions reflect those of the people whom they represent.

It can safely be assumed that no councillor has ever been elected as a result of his views on censorship. Local elections are not fought on this sort of platform and nobody would wish that they were. But, this being the case, it is hard to defend the right of councillors to censor films. It is a right that fell to them by accident and no one, before or since, has produced a logical justification. Councillors are clearly not a cross-section of the public nor, despite the claims of some, are they really in a position to know the opinions of their local population.

Furthermore, councillors do not have information available to allow them to be adequately informed participants in the censorship process. In fact, they rely largely on the same sources of information about potentially controversial films as everyone else —i.e. the press. Yet the press itself may be a crucial factor in elevating a film to 'controversial' status, for press comments on the appearance of a new sensation are essentially self-fulfilling prophecies. 'The passive view of news, as simply a selected account of past events' is an inadequate conceptualization that underestimates 'the active part which news presentation may itself play in the ongoing course of events'.[4]

The cinema is covered by the press in two ways. First, it provides news stories of a sort which are popular with editors for a number of reasons. Newspapers must maintain high circulations to survive, and many have fallen by the wayside in recent years. Most of those still in existence are struggling. In such circumstances it is natural that 'news-value' tends to be associated with stories that have a known appeal, one result of which has been the emphasis on the sensational. The spectacular success of Rupert Murdoch's newly risen *Sun* has indicated how this sort of 'news' can work wonders for a declining circulation.

At the same time, competition from television and radio has reduced the importance of the press as a reporter of news. A new role must be sought, either as a commentator on and analyst of stories already in the public consciousness, or as a bearer of the sort of news that the electronic media have neither the time nor the inclination to cover.

The debate on permissiveness in modern society supplies the right sort of copy, and films that have encountered censorship problems, whether real or imagined, have particular appeal—no shortage of conflicting and often extreme opinions, personalities and stars, ready access to eye-catching pictures and so on. Inevitably such reports tend to be less than sober and objective, for it is essential to make the story as 'strong' as possible. Meanwhile producers and distributors are often only too happy to play along in order to guarantee publicity, while there is no difficulty in finding people shocked and outraged enough to give the account credibility.

These sometimes overblown reports provide the statutory censors with much of their information about films. In addition, they may study, in a very random fashion, the comments of the national film critics who can usually be relied on for a less frenzied assessment, but who are also subject to the same sort of pressures as other journalists. At least in part they are entertainers whose columns must have their own intrinsic appeal. As D. A. N. Smith has noted, any reviewer is a performer for 'a good review is only remembered for a fortnight; a reviewer has always to make his reputation afresh'.[5] Objectivity and detachment are not always essential qualities.

Certainly no critic writes with the local authorities in mind. Most have only a very vague conception of their public. John Russell Taylor has said that 'I just express my opinions in much the same way as I suppose I would if I had just come out of a cinema. . . . I do this without any conscious image of my audience.' George Melly used to bear in mind 'the *Observer* reader, whatever that may mean', while Alexander Walker writes 'for myself, in the hope that others will find what I say entertaining and informative'. It is surely unsatisfactory that the comments of these men and their colleagues should come to play such a potentially important part in the process by which the exhibition pattern of a film evolves. The critics themselves are largely unaware of their power in this respect.

As the cinema comes to rely more and more on a small number of heavily publicized productions, press coverage of these films is naturally intense. In a number of cases in recent years, coverage has been such that preconceived ideas have become firmly established before the films themselves have even been seen. *Last Tango in Paris* was an extreme example of publicity reaching the stage when many local councillors felt able to deliver their verdicts on the film without the benefit of having seen it. Such an occurrence must indicate a very serious deficiency in the present arrangements, and leaves no doubt that decisions are being made on inadequate and partial evidence.

Another major problem with local censorship must be mentioned. Local councillors are politicians who must take account of political considerations. An emotive issue like censorship cannot always be isolated from the general rough and tumble of the political scene; now and again it is bound to become entangled in the power struggle going on within councils. This very clearly happened in the G.L.C.'s viewing committee in the latter half of 1973, for instance, when almost all decisions were made on a party basis, with Labour's fourteen members out-voting the six Conservatives.

The underlying trouble is that so many councillors have little interest in and less knowledge of the cinema. The majority are over thirty and, in common with others in this age-group, few are regular cinema-goers, or have much idea of recent developments in the cinema. Very often the rare occasions when councillors are called upon to see a film for censorship purposes are their only contact with the cinema. Such infrequent viewing hardly provides the necessary background knowledge which enables sound decisions to be made. Moreover this ignorance can leave councillors open to the apparently well-informed blandishments of vocal minorities like the Festival of Light.

Some minor difficulties involved in local licensing may also be noted. Professor Harry Street, for instance, has commented that 'it is the practice to make the licence revocable for breach of condition : consequently local authorities have a much wider power to close down cinemas than theatres. Moreover, local authorities (with the laudable exception of the Greater London

Council) do not usually give a licensee the right to appear personally and to be legally represented before them when a licensing decision is taken.'[6] One might also point to a lack of consistency, not only between neighbouring councils but even within one council. Thus, following the local elections of 1973 the new Labour-controlled G.L.C. completely reversed the policy of its Conservative predecessor. Whereas the latter had been threatening to reject films passed by the Board, the new committee embarked on a very liberal policy, certificating several films banned by the Board and a number previously rejected by the council itself.

Before considering alternatives to the present system, a comment on the sort of censorship that is apparently wanted is in order. We have previously noted the elements of superiority and paternalism inherent in all censorship. An extreme version of this was once enunciated by a Daughter of the American Revolution, who declared : 'Nobody knows the world better than I. No woman has had greater educational advantages, has been more in social life, or has travelled more than I. I am able to judge of the temptations that come to the young and the inexperienced. It is the duty of us to protect those who have not had our advantages.'[7] Few would now be so candid, but the same reasoning underlies the protection of children, and most people seem to agree that even adults may succumb to these temptations.

What is more curious is the sort of protection that is demanded, for, despite protestations to the contrary, sex is very much the central issue. Not only have the proponents of strict control always been concerned almost wholly with this aspect, but the obsession is invariably directed at the physical representation of sexual activity, rather than at the problem of the underlying morality. The fact that films are becoming increasingly immoral in the wider meaning of the word is totally disregarded.

Take *Charley Varrick*, for example, one of the most successful films of 1973, released throughout the country without a murmur fo protest. Yet the hero, played by Walter Matthau with his usual charm, organizes a bank-raid that involves the shooting of two policemen and the subsequent suicide of the bank-manager. In the getaway he blows up his unconscious and probably dying wife, and with great deliberation and meticulous planning sets up his accomplice to be tortured and murdered by the Mafia. In the showdown the two Mafia agents are killed and Varrick escapes, after ensuring that his accomplice's body will be mistaken for his own. As so often in such films the women are characterized with considerable contempt. The hero's wife is quickly sacrificed, an executive's personal secretary immediately gives herself to Varrick after he has broken into her room on the trail of her boss, a photographer welcomes the sadistic attentions of the Mafia heavy, while a lady on a camp-site longs for obscene phone-calls and dreams of rape. All the other women are prostitutes.

Charley Varrick is, of course, a highly enjoyable film made with panache and technical skill, but it embodies a very suspect morality. In the old days of the Production Code it is doubtful whether it would have been considered that the hero had received due punishment for his transgressions. But nowadays the film in which the villain is apprehended is becoming almost a rarity. All too often Might is Right and 'law and order' consists in the police outwitting the underworld (or vice versa) at its own foul game. Now all of this may be no more than a true reflection of reality, but it seems odd that the argument over censorship is being fought out on superficial issues of too much flesh here and too much 'perversion' there. Charles Rembar, the American lawyer, once remarked : 'Proponents of sexual censorship must take the position that conformity to sexual convention is more important than honesty, than kindness, than courage. Unless we are ready to embrace censorship with the idea of promoting all virtue—not just one of its meaner aspects—we cannot justify censorship at all.'[8]

This plea for the elevation of the level of the debate must be supported. If censorship is to be maintained it must be based on something more than a fear of sex. It seems strange that such a Puritan outlook is reserved for this one aspect while a blind eye is turned towards the increasing tendency for films to glorify a multitude of more serious crimes and vices.

As we have seen, one of the difficulties involving censorship is in knowing what the public as a whole wants. It is not even clear if a consensus exists at all any more. The Social Morality Council, in a study of broadcasting, commented : 'In British society today there are wide divergencies of view as to what is and is not acceptable human behaviour and what should or should not be portrayed on the screen. Judgements in matters of taste are notoriously subjective and what is acceptable in such matters differs from one social group to another. It is difficult to see how detailed ground rules could be formulated, even were they desirable, which would prevent any scene, word or reference that could conceivably give offence to an individual or social group from reaching the screen.'[9] Nevertheless, the council added that there are 'limits of public tolerance' which are usually respected, commenting that, as far as criticisms expressed by groups such as the V.A.L.A. were concerned, 'we can find no evidence that these represent the true state of popular feeling'. The report concluded that 'it would be a mistake to mollify a small minority simply because they speak loudly'. Unfortunately, the basis upon which this assessment of the strength of the V.A.L.A. was made, was not specified.

At the other extreme, those in favour of a total abolition of censorship are few in number and even weaker in voice. There is little doubt that the vast majority favour the retention of some sort of classification system for children. More popular than total abolition is the suggestion that adult censorship should be done away with. This is, of course, not as simple as it sounds. Even in Belgium, where there has never been a formal system of censorship, cinema managers must comply with the law and beware of police activity—one cinema even employs its own unofficial censor.

The B.B.F.C. could, of course, be disbanded without any difficulty, but local authority censorship can only be abolished by act of Parliament. Even were this achieved, legal sanctions would remain in the shape of the common law and the various statutes discussed earlier. The problems associated with a censorship system based on such vague and complex stipulations hardly require elaboration.

The most widely favoured solution put forward by those who wish a diminution in censorial activity is that the cinema should be brought under the Obscene Publications Act in the same way as art and literature. This would do away with the requirement for committees and would not involve any new legislation. The B.B.F.C.'s function would be reduced to that of a classifying body while decisions on adult films would be left to the courts. The simplicity and apparent equity of this scheme give it an obvious attraction, but a number of problems should be noted.

(1) The obscenity laws are among the least satisfactory on the statute books. The N.C.C.L. concluded that 'the elements of good law include clarity, fairness and certainty. Obscenity law offers none of these. It confuses the public and ... the judges

themselves. Recent obscenity and conspiracy cases have brought the law and legal institutions into ridicule and contempt.'[10] Perhaps not all legal experts would agree with this comment, but there is little doubt that the laws are in many ways unsatisfactory. The definitions put forward are so open to interpretation that the law offers no real guidance about what is permissible. The argument, sometimes suggested, that resort to legal requirements would make it easier for producers and distributors to know where they stand seems naive in these circumstances. Judges themselves are frequently baffled and in disagreement as evidenced by the number of convictions reversed on appeal because the judge had made errors in his handling of the case. Juries, not surprisingly, are frequently unsure of their role, and there is a heavy incidence of 'unexpected' decisions.

In addition, there is evidence of a growing gulf between the judiciary and those serving on juries, in part resulting from the tendency of judges to interpret liberalizations of the law in the narrowest possible terms. Lord Reid, the senior Lord of Appeal, for instance, has commented on the law under which homosexual acts between adults ceased to be illegal that it meant no more than 'if people chose to corrupt themselves in that way it was their affair and the law would not interfere'. In the Birmingham trial in 1974 of five actors who pleaded guilty to performing in 'blue movies', Mr Justice Wien spoke of 'the unnatural and horrible offence of sodomy' and described the films as 'manifestly obscene'. Yet at a later trial the producer was in fact acquitted of conspiring to publish obscene articles by a jury which evidently disregarded the views of the judge. Similar cases were noted earlier. In many ways then the laws relating to obscenity are imperfect and any extension of their scope must cause misgiving.

(2) The American experience, in which the law has played a much greater part in the development of censorship, does not arouse confidence in the law as the most satisfactory answer. There also it has proved an unsuitable instrument with conflicting verdicts and lack of clear guidance. Moreover there is evidence that the law is far more successful in dealing with sex than with violence or other areas of concern. In the United States the laws are rigidly restricted to sexual matters. This is not the case here, but it remains true that they are most suited to problems of this nature. At a time when violence rather than sex is likely to become a major concern, this is a severe handicap.

(3) The courts are bound to encounter the same difficulties as

the local authorities as a result of their limited acquaintance with the cinema. The expertise acquired by a body like the B.B.F.C. with its continuous assessment of films of all types can never be matched by individuals who are occasionally required to deliver a verdict on one film with no real context or knowledge of comparable material. This process of random 'dipping' cannot but produce inconsistent results. Like the local authorities, the law is administered by men and women with little first-hand experience of the cinema; in general they are likely to be out of sympathy with the medium. This attitude was clearly and unequivocally expressed by a judge in the Manchester Crown Court in 1973. Commenting on what came to be called a 'Clockwork Orange' case, he voiced a hope that 'those salacious creatures who appear to dominate what is called show business today are compelled to earn a more respectable and honourable livelihood instead of inciting young persons to violence at the expense of their victims'. His conclusion that 'cases like yours present, in my view, an unassailable argument in favour of the return as quickly as possible of some form of censorship',[11] indicates a profound ignorance of the present system, and of the obscenity laws themselves.

(4) Recourse to the courts also raises problems of time and money. The film industry relies on being able to distribute its product quickly : any delay can severely damage the profitability of many films. The law works in a rather different way. The complexities of obscenity cases tend to make them very costly in any case, while inevitable delay can be commercially ruinous to the company involved. A central problem is that of whether injunctions would be granted to prevent the showing of a film while a case was pending. If this was to be the case, the result might well be that films were written off commercially whether they were found obscene or not (although acquitted films might well profit from the attendant publicity, leading to a situation in which the most successful films were those that had survived an obscenity charge). If no injunction were to be granted, on the other hand, films would have received wide exhibition and collected most of their profits (if any) before the case ever came to court.

(5) Finally, there is a high probability, not always recognized by those who advocate this system, that the uncertainty engendered in the industry by a new form of censorship with which they were not familiar would, in fact, lead to conservatism and,

effectively, to greater restriction. A film represents a vast capital investment with a multitude of hazards : the addition of one more could only lead to even less adventurous policies. The high potential cost of court cases would also represent a heavier burden for the small independent company than for the major backed by the huge financial resources of the parent body. The result might be a further contraction of the industry with fewer outlets for unusual or less commercial films; both sex and 'art' films would probably suffer. While the need to make money might well force the industry to occasional displays of courage (at least on commercial projects), only the financially secure would be able to afford the risk. Alec Grant of the G.L.C.'s licensing committee recognized the possible dangers of legal censorship some years ago when he wrote that 'the absence of any machinery of prior restraint together with the fear of subsequent prosecution may lead some publishers and printers and some managements of theatres and cinemas to impose a self-censorship which is over-cautious. As cinemas and theatres are concentrated in fewer hands than is publishing or printing, there is a danger in the case of films and plays that the absence of prior restraint may lead to more rather than less restriction.'[12] Events since the abolition of the Lord Chancellor's powers over theatrical per-formances have not seriously contradicted this prediction.

Similar problems would arise if the cinema were left to the doubtful mercy of the common law, but this solution appears unlikely unless the obscenity laws were scrapped altogether, a development which, despite the Arts Council recommendations, does not seem imminent.

The other alternative would be to put the B.B.F.C. itself on a statutory basis, thus removing the powers of the local authorities. This would place a very great onus on the Board and would require some changes in its constitution and operation as Harry Street has suggested. 'If the Board were legally recognized, there would be a strong case for widening its membership and ensuring its judicial independence. In order to keep the decisions out of the political arena, it would also be desirable to enact the grounds on which rejection and classification are to be based. Its decisions should be unchallengeable in Parliament and only subject to judicial review if the powers were exceeded. Perhaps such a body should listen to any argument in support of a film made by its sponsors and be required to give reasons for its refusal to comply with the sponsors' requests.'[13]

Such radical changes would clearly reform the Board out of all recognition, and some of Street's recommendations would be quite unacceptable to the Board as constituted at present. In particular, the call for some sort of written Code would be fiercely opposed as contrary to all past practice and present thinking. In any case it must be doubtful whether it would be possible or desirable to create a Board independent and strong enough to wield this sort of power. The concept of censorship is essentially authoritarian and there is some evidence that it cannot be successfully organized on a democratic basis. American and British experience has suggested that the most effective censors have been those determined to run their offices in a fairly autocratic manner. The names of Breen, Shurlock and Trevelyan spring to mind, as men who favoured a concentration of power at the top, to the extent that Breen could exclaim '*I* am the Production Code'. Murphy himself has been forced to abandon most of his attempts at democratization.

Few commentators have argued for such an extension of the Board's powers, and the Board itself does not wish for such a move. Murphy, on the contrary, is in favour of some diminution of his authority in the form of an appeals board similar to those dealing with complaints directed at the B.B.C. and I.B.A. Many people in the industry support this view, feeling that the Board's decisions are too final, the only recourse being the costly and time-consuming process of application to the local authorities. Although similar systems work abroad, there must be doubts as to whether a structure that operates with success in television is necessarily suited to the very different medium of cinema. Television remains an unclassified family medium of relatively low impact and caters to an entirely different kind of audience. In addition, the same problems arise with an appeals board as have already been encountered with other part-time bodies.

What proposals then do offer the possibility of improvements? First, it is essential to accept the new situation in which the cinema finds itself. It cannot be considered any longer as a major mass medium catering for an undiscriminating public. We are already familiar with differing censorship standards for different media, relating largely to availability and popularity. It seems clear that the standards set for the cinema should be re-evaluated to take into consideration these changed circumstances. Furthermore, the recent Cinematograph and Indecent Displays Bill seemed to allow for a distinction between places of public display and places where admission is by payment. It was generally assumed that book and magazine sellers could get around the bill by charging at the door, on the assumption that anyone paying knew what to expect inside. It would not seem unreasonable to argue that cinemas should benefit from this logic, and by reason of their charging for admission no longer be classified as public places.

More specifically it is hard not to agree with the G.L.C. that local authorities are not ideally suited to the role of censor. It would seem sensible to reduce their powers to those originally intended, i.e. to ensure the safety and cleanliness of cinema premises. For reasons that will become apparent they should also continue to impose the certificates issued by the B.B.F.C. through their licensing regulations. Their right to change these certificates or deny exhibition would, however, be withdrawn.

Given the consensus in favour of censorship, a body such as the B.B.F.C. still seems to offer the best solution. The law cannot provide an answer, while the suggestion sometimes put forward that the Government should take a closer interest, must obviously be resisted. The Board, for all its faults, offers experience and independence. Its decisions are no more inconsistent than those which are likely to be arrived at in any other way, and its prestige and character can be improved by one or two changes. First, as previously noted, a question-mark remains over the make-up of the Board. Many similar bodies in other countries demand professional qualifications which have become increasingly relevant as the nature of censorship has changed. Scientific knowledge of the likely reactions of certain sorts of audience to certain sorts of material is more and more necessary, and the Board is signally lacking in this respect. The occasional recourse to 'expert' advice is not always an adequate solution, and can lead to nonsenses of the sort described by Trevelyan, who claimed to have been warned about 'visuals or sound of the ripping of cloth since this was potentially stimulating to men attracted by rape'.[14] It might also be beneficial to limit the terms of office of all appointees to ensure a steady turnover of personnel and avoid the sort of situation that recently arose when four of the six members of the Board retired within a relatively short period, resulting in a largely new and inexperienced panel.

Some reorganization of the role of the examiners is also desirable. The present structure makes impossible the sort of changes which Murphy envisaged but failed to implement. The whole concept of the three-day working week involves elements of a part-time approach. There is an inevitable loss of continuity for examiners who never see all the stages in a film's progress through censorship and who rarely have contact with those who submit films. A four- or five-day week would solve this problem as well as giving examiners a greater sense of identity with the Board. It would also allow them to take over some of the administrative duties from the Secretary who is heavily overburdened in this respect.

The three-day week also means that the examiners rarely meet as a group. Only two are on duty each day, so that the monthly Board meeting is the only regular occasion when the whole Board meets—and then the President is not usually present. In fact, contact between examiners and President is confined almost solely to those occasions when the latter is called in to see a troublesome film. General discussion of censorship matters is often not possible in these circumstances.

There are also features of the formal organization of the Board which militate against total involvement on the examiners' parts. There is no 'examiners' room' for instance : they have no desks, pigeon-holes or filing cabinets. Study of the offices would betray few signs of their existence. These are small points but significant ones. Examiners have few indications of the value of their job. Combined with the anonymity of their role which ensures that they receive little feedback or reassurance, the result is that they operate in a vacuum. The American system has its problems, but a conscious effort is made to make sure that there is job satisfaction for examiners who are assigned a more positive role. They are often detailed to follow films through from first to last while every day there is a meeting or 'huddle' of all members of the administration at which problems are discussed.

The role of the President must also be reviewed. At present he occupies a somewhat ambiguous position, being neither a regular member of the Board nor sufficiently distant to be regarded as an appeals officer. In earlier days, of course, the President played a much larger part and was, indeed, the central figure. Now he is called upon only in cases of wide disagreement among the other members of the Board or on occasions when a film presents a problem that involves a policy decision. Harlech is, in many ways, an ideal President, with a wide knowledge of the arts, a ready grasp of the Board's problems, and the personal charisma and prestige to counter adverse comments from whatever source, but his many and varied interests inevitably limit his involvement at Soho Square. It may well be that the duties of the President have now been reduced too far and that there would be some advantage to be gained from giving him back some of his former powers and creating a more equal distribution of labour. The President would therefore be much more closely integrated into the work of the Board: at present he sees only about thirty films a year in his official capacity. The alternative would be to reinterpret his job so that he becomes an officer to handle appeals, either in his own right, or as the chairman of a small committee, including also, perhaps, the President of the Press Council. Such a body would take some of the pressure off the Board, but it would encounter the old problem of not seeing enough films to know the state of the cinema at any one time.

Given the increased power of the Board under this system, it would have to be more accountable to the public. There is no reason why such a tight veil of secrecy surrounds so much of the Board's activities. Certain facts would remain the business only of the Board and the film companies concerned, but much else could be made public. The revival of the Board's annual reports, dormant for forty years, might be one way of implementing this. A yearly explanation of the Board's policy and decisions, with the opportunity to defend and analyse controversial incidents, could only foster greater faith in and appreciation of the Board's work.

The B.B.F.C. would continue to classify films as at present, but a much greater effort must be made to ensure that certificates are respected. It is impossible to check that only those of the appropriate age are admitted to restricted films, but stricter control should be attempted. All the so-called 'Clockwork Orange' cases and the suicides following visits to *The Exorcist* involved adolescents who should never have been admitted to the films, and the widely known failure of the system at this point is tending to call the whole process into question. It is worth noting that one of the unofficial reasons for the raising of the minimum age for 'X' films from sixteen to eighteen in 1970 was to make sure that no one under sixteen could be admitted to such films. There is some evidence that this hope has not been realized. It is a point of some significance that the Home Office circular and most licensing conditions state only that admittance must be refused to those 'apparently under the age of eighteen years'. The imprecision of this phrase may make the law hard to enforce, but any solution must be at a local level. It is the responsibility of the local authorities to ensure that their licenses are respected but, with one or two exceptions, this part of their duties receives scant attention.

While the Board retains the power to ban films, there is no valid reason for denying these films to those who really want them. Private membership clubs are the most satisfactory answer. The Cinematograph and Indecent Displays Bill sought to outlaw these clubs, but this action was never necessary. All the changes explicitly desired by the Government could have been effected simply by a tighter control on membership rules. Given this, and the right for the local authorities to control safety, cleanliness and front-of-house publicity, there can be few objections to such clubs. On the contrary, they perform a very useful function. Those who wish to see uncensored films can do so without the ordinary public being offended, thus removing some of the onus from the B.B.F.C. who are not eager to be the final arbiter on what can be shown.

Finally, of course, if the less celebrated forms of censorship which stem from the whole monopoly-dominated structure of the industry are to be countered, radical changes are necessary in production, distribution and exhibition. Since such changes are likely only within the context of a total reconstruction of our economy, it can be assumed that they are not likely to be effected in the immediate future. As for the censorship of sex, violence and the rest, it is evident that 'sick' material is only produced when there is a desire and a need for it. The real problem is not how to eradicate such matter from the screen, but how to produce a society in which such needs are less pervasive.

NOTES

Chapter One

1 See *Kinematograph Weekly,* 19th, 22nd and 29th April, 1948.
2 Philip French, 'Violence in the Cinema' in O. Larsen (ed.), *Violence and the Mass Media* (Harper and Row, New York, 1968), p. 59.
3 John Wilcox, 'The Small Knife—Studies in Censorship', in *Sight and Sound,* Vol. 25, 1956, pp. 206–10.
4 There may perhaps be a connection between the two whereby fear of the consequences of events in Ireland is somehow exorcised through the attempt to solve a less intractable problem. Cleansing the cinema provides comfort through the knowledge that something, at least, is being done about one possible cause of violence in society.
5 Neville March Hunnings, *Film Censors and the Law* (George Allen and Unwin, 1967), p. 39. See also, Jeremy Pascall and Clyde Jeavons, *A Pictorial History of Sex in the Movies* (Hamlyn, 1975).
6 Wilcox, *op. cit.,* pp. 208–9.
7 Quoted in Lewis Jacobs, *The Rise of the American Film* (Teachers College, New York, 1968), pp. 62–3.
8 E. G. Cousins, *Filmland in Ferment* (Denis Archer, 1932), p. 272.
9 Low Warren, *The Film Game* (T. Werner Lawrie, 1937), p. 138.
10 Wilcox, *op. cit.,* p. 209.
11 Jacobs, *op. cit.,* p. 156.
12 *Pornography—the Longford Report* (Coronet, 1972), p. 34.
13 *Hansard,* House of Lords, 29th Nov., 1972, Vol. 336, 1293–4.
14 *Ibid.,* 1367.
15 Cinema attendances have declined in Britain from 1,635 million in 1946 to 421 million in 1962 and 142 million in 1973. In recent years the decline has been in the region of 8 per cent per annum.
16 William Fadiman, *Hollywood Now* (Liveright, New York, 1972), p. 12.
17 Bryan Forbes, *The Distant Laughter* (Collins, 1972), p. 63.

Chapter Two

1 Hunnings, *op. cit.*, p. 46.
2 The full title made it clear that it was an Act 'to make better provision for securing safety at Cinematograph and other exhibitions'. Herbert Samuel, Under-Secretary at the Home Office, stated that 'our intention was simply to secure safety in the construction of buildings in which inflammable films are exhibited'.
3 L.C.C. versus Bermondsey Bioscope Co. Ltd., 1911.
4 'One can hardly peruse a daily or weekly paper without reading something in the nature of an attack on moving pictures.' *Bioscope*, 29th Dec., 1910.
5 *Bioscope*, 21st Nov., 1912.
6 Conference notes, 14th April, 1916 (P.R.O. HO 45/10811/ 312397/1).
7 The trade reacted by adjusting its production policy to avoid the 'A' certificate. In 1921 almost 50 per cent of all films fell into this category : in 1923 only 13 per cent did so.
8 *Kinematograph Weekly*, 6th Nov., 1924.
9 Ibsen's *Ghosts* fell into this category.
10 'The B.B.F.C. View', in *The Journal of the Society of Film and Television Arts*, Nos. 43–44, spring–summer 1971.
11 Sir Sidney Harris, 'Notes on the Origin and Development of the B.B.F.C. 1912–52', unpublished typescript, 1960.
12 *The Cinema*, report of the Cinema Commission of Inquiry (Williams and Norgate, 1917), p. 10.
13 B.B.F.C. report for 1923.
14 Rachel Low, *The History of the British Film 1918–29* (George Allen and Unwin, 1971), p. 63.
15 Quoted in Viscount Brentford, *Do We Need a Censor?* (Faber and Faber, 1929), p. 21.
16 Low, *op. cit.*, p. 68.
17 *Ibid.*, p. 65.
18 Throughout the silent era it had been the practice to project two films simultaneously side by side !
19 Dorothy Knowles, *The Censor, the Drama and the Film* (George Allen and Unwin, 1934), p. 258.
20 Audrey Field, *Picture Palace* (Gentry Books, 1973), p. 109.
21 *Hansard*, House of Commons, 1st Nov., 1934. Vol. 293, 339.
22 *Kinematograph Weekly*, 20th April, 1950.
23 *H.M.S.O.*, May 1950, Cmnd. 7945.
24 *Kinematograph Weekly*, 4th Oct., 1951.
25 *The Garden of Eden* (1953) was passed by 285 of the 300 councils to whom it was submitted. Certificates covered the

whole range from 'U' to 'X'. The Board eventually adopted a general policy of awarding such films 'A' certificates.

26 A. T. L. Watkins, 'There is still too much Violence' in *Cine Technician*, Sept. 1955, p. 136.

27 John Trevelyan, *What the Censor Saw* (Michael Joseph, 1973), pp. 54–5.

28 *Financial Times*, 23rd Sept., 1957.

29 Minutes of Meeting, 6th Nov., 1957.

30 B.B.F.C. records.

31 Quoted in Derek Hill, 'The Habit of Censorship', in *Encounter* July 1960, p. 56.

32 John Trevelyan, 'The Censor's Reply', in *Encounter*, Sept. 1960, p. 63.

33 John Trevelyan, 'Censorship and the New Morality', in *The Journal of the Society of Film and Television Arts*, Autumn 1966.

34 *Ibid.*

35 John Trevelyan, 'The Censor's Reply', *op. cit.*, p. 63.

36 Letter from Tony Richardson in *Encounter*, Sept. 1960, p. 65.

37 Gordon McDougall, 'To Deprave and Corrupt?', in *Motion*, No. 2, Winter 1961–2, p. 7.

38 John Trevelyan, *What the Censor Saw*, *op. cit.*, p. 118.

39 David Robinson, 'Trevelyan's Social History', in *Sight and Sound*, Vol. 40, Spring 1971, p. 71.

40 John Trevelyan, *What the Censor Saw*, *op. cit.*, p. 207. Trevelyan has not been the only censor to get involved in the film-making process. Geoffrey Shurlock, head of the American Production Code Administration from 1954 to 1969, commented on the 're-editing' of the opening scene of *Bonnie and Clyde* : 'Well, frankly, I thought we were teaching them how to tell the story in a more intelligent way'. Quoted in Stephen Farber, *The Movie Rating Game* (Public Affairs Press, Washington, 1972), p. 11.

41 Peter Bunzel, in *Life*, 25th May, 1962, p. 86.

42 John Trevelyan, *What the Censor Saw*, *op. cit.*, p. 110.

43 Quoted in David Robinson, *op. cit.*, p. 70.

44 Neville March Hunnings, 'The Silence of Fanny Hill', in *Sight and Sound*, Vol. 35, Summer 1966, p. 135.

45 G.L.C. meeting, 18th Oct., 1965.

46 The G.L.C. was at first opposed to any 'extension' of censorship but was eventually persuaded to adopt the new category. A number of Scottish authorities, however, treat the new 'AA' as a purely advisory classification.

47 See 'The Cinema and the Protection of Youth', Council of Europe, Strasbourg, 1968.

48 The six previous Presidents held office when they were between
the ages of 66 and 70, 68 and 81, 67 and 73, 69 and 80, 70 and
83, and 72 and 77.

Chapter Three

1 Notably the Roscoe Arbuckle manslaughter trials (1921–2), the
mysterious murder of director William Desmond Taylor (1922)
and the death through drugs of matinee idol Wallace Reid
(1923). The divorce in 1920 of Mary Pickford, 'America's sweet-
heart', and the hasty marriage of Charlie Chaplin to sixteen-
year-old Lita Grey shortly before the birth of their child (1924)
were other events that damaged the public image of Hollywood.
The press naturally made the most of such scandals. Kevin
Brownlow has commented on the role of the Hearst newspaper
group in sensationalizing the Arbuckle case and ensuring the
destruction of the comedian's career despite his acquittal—*The
Parade's Gone By* (Secker and Warburg, 1968), p. 559. The
Taylor murder case is said to have sold more papers than the
entry of the United States into the First World War.
2 Alan Reitman, 'The United States', in *Censorship*, No. 1,
Autumn 1964.
3 Jack Vizzard, *See No Evil: Life inside a Hollywood Censor*
(Simon and Schuster, New York, 1970), p. 167.
4 *Time*, 31st May, 1971.
5 *Cinema TV Today*, 28th July, 1973.
6 *Hansard*, House of Commons, 12th March, 1970, Vol. 797, 757.
7 *Hansard*, House of Lords, 21st April, 1971, Vol. 317, 747.
8 *CinemaTV Today*, 7th Jan., 1974.
9 Graham Zellick, 'Films and the Law of Obscenity', in *Criminal
Law Review*, 1971, p. 145.
10 *Guardian*, 25th June, 1974.
11 In December 1974 Maidenhead magistrates cleared *Forum* of
allegations under the Obscene Publications Act.
12 Zellick, *op. cit.*, p. 148.
13 *Hansard*, House of Lords, 21st April, 1971, Vol. 317, 747–8.
14 *Ibid.*, 746.
15 *Guardian*, 13th Nov., 1973.
16 PEST Current Report no. 16, 'Censorship and the Cinema',
Nov. 1973.

Chapter Four

1 *Guardian*, 12th May, 1973.
2 *Language of Love* was finally passed in July 1973 after being
approved by 127 of the 169 local authorities which had been

approached. Ten councils refused to accept this decision and continued to ban the film.

3 *Birmingham Evening Mail*, 28th Oct., 1970.

4 The first major protest was actually caused by the accidental showing during a Disney programme in a London cinema on 30th May, 1971 of the foreign version of the trailer for *Soldier Blue*. The five cuts necessary for the 'U' certificate had not been made in this print which understandably provoked a fierce response from parents.

5 *Guardian*, 12th Aug., 1971.

6 Press release, 30th March, 1972.

7 *Kent and Sussex Courier*, 3rd March, 1972.

8 Fergus Cashin, John Coleman, Nina Hibbin, Margaret Hinxman, Derek Malcolm, George Melly, Tony Palmer, Molly Plowright, Dilys Powell, David Robinson, John Russell Taylor, Arthur Thirkell and Alexander Walker.

9 There were also a number of reviews which disagreed with negative appraisals of *Straw Dogs*. Tom Milne in *The Times* described it as 'undeniably nasty . . . but hardly gratuitous since the film is trying to suggest that the American is degraded rather than raised to the status of hero', while the *Monthly Film Bulletin* felt that '*Straw Dogs* promises to emerge as a classic of the horror film and an indispensible Peckinpah masterpiece'.

10 *Observer* magazine, 28th May, 1972.

11 *Evening Standard,* 16th March, 1972. In fact the programme was a pilot : it was never transmitted.

12 *Ibid.*

13 *The Times*, 15th Jan., 1972.

14 *Evening Standard*, 14th Jan., 1972.

15 *Evening Standard*, 16th March, 1972.

16 It might be noted that the Board continued to reject two films from Rive's own company—*Camille 2000* and *Without a Stitch*. Such lack of consistency between words and action is not unknown in the industry. Sir John Davis, chairman of Rank, also called for stricter censorship while doing profitable business in his cinemas with *Straw Dogs*. At that time Rank did not necessarily accept all films passed by the Board, but this moral stance was abandoned shortly after when managers were advised that future policy was to accept all films with national or local certificates. Even *Trash* had a Rank release. Trevelyan has instanced another occasion when Davis's public statements were not in accord with his private decisions—*What the Censor Saw, op, cit.*, p. 85.

17 11th March, 1972.

18 18th March, 1972.

19 It did have a brief wave of showing in thirteen provincial

situations during the first week of which the film took over £50,000.

20 *CinemaTV Today*, 13th Jan., 1973.

21 Ken Wlaschin, 'Censorship and Cannes '71', in *Films and Filming*, Aug., 1971.

22 *The Times*, 2nd Sept., 1971.

23 *The Report of the Commission on Obscenity and Pornography* (Bantam, New York, 1970), p. 610.

24 By that time the climate had changed to the extent that *Oh! Calcutta!* was passed by most authorities approached. By the end of 1974 only one council had turned it down.

25 This action was defended on the grounds that the cuts were made under the supervision of Morrissey.

26 For a fuller account of the press treatment of *Last Tango in Paris* see Guy Phelps, 'Censorship and the Press', in *Sight and Sound*, Vol. 42, Summer 1973, pp. 138–40.

27 *Sunday Mirror*, 17th Dec., 1972.

28 *CinemaTV Today*, 11th Aug., 1973.

29 *Evening Standard*, 13th Sept., 1973.

30 Bertram Clayton, 'The Cinema and its Censor', in *Fortnightly Review*, Vol. CIX, 1921, p. 223.

31 'In the Picture', in *Sight and Sound*, Vol. 44, winter 1974–5, p. 23.

Chapter Five

1 i.e. the Distributors.

2 *Bioscope*, 21st Nov., 1912.

3 70mm films are charged 15 per cent extra.

4 John Trevelyan, *What the Censor Saw*, op. cit., p. 57.

5 By this stage most films are in the hands of distributors but, occasionally, a producer or director is still handling it, especially if an unfinished print is involved.

Chapter Six

1 *Films Illustrated*, Vol. 1, No. 3, Sept. 1971.

2 Neville March Hunnings, 'Taking the Last Step', in *Censorship*, No. 2, Spring 1965, p. 11.

3 John Trevelyan, *What the Censor Saw*, op. cit., p. 156.

4 *Evening Standard*, 24th Nov., 1972.

5 Stephen Farber, *The Movie Rating Game*, op. cit., p. 36.

6 *The Star*, 28th Dec., 1968.

7 *Evening Standard*, 17th Dec., 1968.

8 John Trevelyan, *What the Censor Saw*, op. cit., p. 103.

9 Ken Wlaschin, 'Cannes '73—an Attack on Taste', in *Films and Filming*, Aug., 1973.
10 *Blazing Saddles* was the subject of much thought at the Board before it was finally decided that fourteen to seventeen-year-olds should be allowed to see the film despite the *risqué* language. The distributors thereupon released it with an 'X' rated second feature which restricted the whole programme to those over eighteen!
11 Carlos Clarens, *Horror Movies* (Panther, 1971), p. 213.
12 David Pirie, *A Heritage of Horror* (Gordon Fraser, 1973), p. 105.
13 Gordon Gow in *Films and Filming*, Jan. 1974, p. 56.
14 Stephen Farber, *op. cit.*, p. 34.
15 Introduction to C. H. Rolph, *Books in the Dock* (Deutsch, 1964), p. 10.
16 At a meeting between the B.B.F.C. and representatives of the industry in Jan. 1973, the latter made three points in favour of allowing 'objectionable' titles: (1) provocative titles attract audiences; (2) they represent the content of the film; (3) audiences for these films are self-selecting. In fact there are few complaints about sex films, apart from odd occasions such as when *Tropic of Cancer* was taken by one person to be a hospital melodrama. The title that has aroused most controversy in recent years was *Sunday, Bloody Sunday*—presumably not the sort of title that the meeting was called to discuss.
17 *Kinematograph Weekly*, 17th Dec., 1953.
18 *CinemaTV Today*, 15th June, 1974.
19 *National Humane Review*, Sept. 1972.

Chapter Seven

1 Ivor Montagu, *The Political Censorship of Films* (Gollancz, 1929).
2 Sir Sidney Harris, *op. cit.*
3 *The Cinema, op. cit.*, p. 244.
4 So concerned were the authorities about this film that quite illegal pressures were exerted by the L.C.C. to prevent the private screening of non-flammable prints, and by Scotland Yard to discourage the distributor from applying to local authorities.
5 Dorothy Knowles, *op. cit*, p. 268.
6 Pabst's *The Joyless Street* (1925) showed the effects of war on a small street in post-war Vienna. 'France accepted the film, deleting two thousand feet and every shot of the "street" itself. Vienna extracted all sequences in which Werner Krauss appeared as the butcher. Russia turned the American lieutenant into a doctor and made the butcher the murderer instead of the

girl. After having run a year in Germany an attempt was made
to censor it. In America it was not shown at all, and in England
once, at a private performance of the Film Society.' Paul
Rotha, *The Film Till Now* (Vision Press, 1949), p. 37.

7 Rachel Low, *The History of the British Film, 1918–29* (George
Allen and Unwin, 1971), p. 66.

8 *Kinematograph Weekly,* 23rd Feb., 1928.

9 Quoted in Derek Hill, *op. cit.,* p. 55.

10 Quoted in Forsyth Hardy, 'Censorship and Film Societies', in
C. Davy (ed.), *Footnotes to the Film* (Lovat Dickinson, 1937),
p. 264.

11 *Ibid.*

12 In 1919 the Board's examiners had wanted to reject *The
Cabinet of Dr Caligari* on these grounds but had been over-
ruled by the President.

13 *Daily Telegraph,* 23rd Aug., 1949.

14 *Evening Standard,* 22nd Aug., 1949.

15 *Daily Express,* 23rd Aug., 1949.

16 *The Times,* 8th Feb., 1950.

17 *Kinematograph Weekly,* 9th Feb., 1950.

18 Ivor Montagu, *Film World* (Pelican, 1964), p. 269.

19 *Film and TV Technician,* Vol. 25, No. 70, March 1959, p. 36.

20 *Films and Filming,* Feb. 1964.

21 John Trevelyan, *What the Censor Saw, op. cit.,* p. 175.

22 Judith Todd, *The Big Sell* (Lawrence and Wishart, 1961), pp.
72–3.

23 *Ibid,* p. 71.

24 John Trevelyan, *What the Censor Saw, op. cit.,* p. 176.

25 J. D. S. Haworth, 'When Should You Censor?', in *Tribune,*
23rd April, 1965.

26 Letters by Trevelyan and Haworth, *Tribune,* 7th May, 1965.

27 *Guardian,* 4th Feb., 1971; *Observer,* 7th Feb., 1971; *The Times,*
5th Feb., 1971.

28 John Trevelyan, *What the Censor Saw, op. cit.,* pp. 187–8.

29 Jack Vizzard, *op. cit.,* p. 183.

30 Quoted in Judith Todd, *op. cit.,* pp. 71–2.

31 *Guardian,* 12th May, 1973.

32 *The Times,* 27th Oct., 1973.

33 Paul O'Higgins, *Censorship in Britain* (Nelson, 1972), p. 90.

Chapter Eight

1 L.C.C. meeting, 20th Dec., 1921.

2 Dorothy Knowles, *op. cit.,* pp. 180–1.

3 Minutes of meeting, 6th April, 1932.

4 Minutes of conference, 16th Nov., 1961.

5 Although Trevelyan has suggested that the conferences were useful in helping to foster confidence in the Board, his admission that he 'never seemed to have the time' to organize further conferences shows that he did not find them indispensable.

6 Alexander Walker, *Sex in the Movies* (Pelican, 1968), p. 163.

7 Paul O'Higgins, *op. cit.,* p. 87. The sending of extracts from the script lifted from their original context is an undesirable practice. Indeed, when the Festival of Light adopted this very tactic in its campaign against *Last Tango in Paris* Trevelyan's successor complained bitterly that this was unfair and dishonest.

8 These statistics refer to committees after the 1974 reorganization.

9 *Southend Standard,* 11th Nov., 1971.

10 Alexander Walker pointed out to me that *West Side Story* had received similar treatment ten years earlier when all teenage groups had been dubbed 'West Side' gangs.

11 *Brighton Evening Argus,* 9th Feb., 1973.

12 *Manchester Evening News,* 3rd May, 1973.

13 *Newcastle Journal,* 8th Feb., 1973.

14 *Yorkshire Evening Post,* 10th March, 1973.

15 *Worcester Evening News,* 23rd Feb., 1973.

16 *Wimbledon News,* 23rd Feb., 1973.

17 *Hull Daily Mail,* 12th, 14th and 17th May, 1973.

18 *Middlesbrough Evening Gazette,* 28th Feb., 1973.

19 *Darlington Northern Echo,* 7th Feb., 1973.

20 *South Wales Argus,* 24th Jan., 1973.

21 *Sheffield Star,* 8th Oct., 1969.

22 *Southend Evening Echo,* 25th Nov., 1974.

23 Home Office circular, 19th Feb., 1932.

24 1951, 44 Off. Gaz. County Councils Assn. (suppt.) 275.

25 Alec Grant, 'Censorship—a Perennial Problem', in *Socialist Commentary,* Oct., 1966, p. 27.

26 *Ibid,* p. 26.

27 *The Times,* 7th March, 1973.

28 Press statement, 1st March, 1972.

29 *The Times,* 27th Oct., 1973.

30 *CinemaTV Today,* 1st Dec., 1973.

31 Enid Wistrich, 'The Future of Film Censorship for Adults', G.L.C. paper, 28th Nov., 1974. For more on her approach to film censorship see her article 'Censorship and the Local Authority', in *Local Government Studies,* Oct., 1974, pp. 1–9.

32 There was one comic side effect to this campaign to clean up front-of-house advertising following the rejection by the B.B.F.C. of a cartoon entitled *Snow White and the Seven Perverts.* The film was submitted to the G.L.C. and given a 'London-X' certificate. The advisory committee, however, promptly rejected the title, acting on the G.L.C.'s own orders to tighten up their

code. As a result the film could be shown, but its title could not be advertised!

33 Both films dealt with homosexuality. Some members of the audience had evidently expected to see a musical and a hospital melodrama respectively.

34 *The Times*, 1st Nov., 1973.

35 *Surrey Herald*, 12th Jan., 1973.

36 *Kinematograph Weekly*, 6th Jan., 1927.

37 *Kent and Sussex Courier*, 9th March, 4th May and 9th Nov., 1973; *The Advertiser*, 28th Feb., 1973.

38 In fact the Board makes some effort to avoid becoming too London-based. Two examiners live outside the capital, in Portsmouth and Folkstone. Murphy is a Glaswegian who has spent much of his career in the north, while Harlech's sphere is cosmopolitan rather than metropolitan.

39 Knight and Alpert quote an Illinois cinema manager explaining how his local public claimed to want family films but actually turned up only when sex films were being shown. 'If I give them what they say they want, I go out of business. If I give them what I *know* they want, I get thrown in jail.' *Sex in Cinema*, Vol. 1 (Playboy Press, Chicago, 1971), p. 19.

40 *CinemaTV Today*, 14th Sept., 1974.

41 *Guardian*, 3rd Jan., 1974.

42 *CinemaTV Today*, 17th Nov., 1973.

Chapter Nine

1 Brian Groombridge, *Television and the People* (Penguin, 1972), p. 95.

2 H. H. Wilson, *Pressure Group* (Secker and Warburg, 1961), p. 178.

3 *Ibid.*, p. 171.

4 Mary Whitehouse, *Who Does She Think She Is?* (New English Library, 1971), p. 68.

5 *Ibid.*, p. 69.

6 Louis Zurcher and George Kirkpatrick, 'Collective Dynamics of Ad Hoc Antipornography Organisations', in *Technical Reports of the Commission on Obscenity and Pornography*, Vol. 5, (U.S. Government Printing Office, Washington, 1970), p. 92.

7 *Ibid.*, p. 87.

8 Occasionally the political perspective becomes explicit as in a speech delivered by Mrs Whitehouse to the International Congress of the Union Internationale d'Action Morale et Sociale in Bonn on 3rd Nov., 1971, when she argued that 'decadence within Western culture plays straight into the hands of those who work towards the destruction of Parliamentary democracy'.

In *Who Does She Think She Is?* she suggests that pornography is a subversive Communist weapon being used to undermine Western morality—see pp. 65 and 127.

9 Mary Whitehouse, *op. cit.*, p. 75.

10 Mary Whitehouse, *Cleaning Up TV* (Blandford, 1967), p. 16.

11 Mary Whitehouse, *Who Does She Think She Is?*, *op. cit.*, p. 181.

12 *Ibid.*, p. 184.

13 *Ibid.*, p. 68.

14 *Hansard*, House of Lords, 21st April, 1971, Vol. 317, 641.

15 *Pornography—the Longford Report*, *op. cit.*, p. 12.

16 *Ibid.*, p. 199.

17 *Ibid.*, p. 42.

18 *Ibid.*, p. 359. Anti-intellectualism is also indicated by the report's reference to T.V., cinema, etc. as 'the entertainment media'.

19 *Hansard*, House of Lords, 29th Nov., 1972. Vol. 336, 1312.

20 *Pornography—the Longford Report*, *op. cit.*, p. 140.

21 *Ibid.*, p. 359.

22 *Ibid.*, p. 265. The sub-committee seems to be in some confusion here : the film is in no way a documentary, or even remotely realistic, and has nothing to do with the murder of Miss Tate and her companions. It might be noted that the sub-committee included nobody with first-hand knowledge of the film industry. It was to have been headed by Sir Bernard Delfont, chairman of E.M.I. and to have included Peter King, then managing director of E.M.I., but both withdrew. The eventual chairman was James Sharkey, managing director of a talent agency.

23 *Ibid.*, pp. 424–5.

24 *Ibid.*, p. 25.

25 Clifford Longley, *The Times*, 9th July, 1973.

26 John Capon, *And There was Light* (Lutterworth, 1972), p. 125.

27 This comment encapsulates two attitudes that were noted by Zurcher and Kirkpatrick in America. First there is the conviction that the problem of pornography has been underestimated, and that it is 'a greater social problem than many others that are currently considered to be more urgent by government officials'. David Holbrook, a signatory to the Longford report, has suggested that the works of men like Ken Russell cause 'immense damage' to people's feelings, the effects of which are 'exactly parallel to those of racial propaganda, and indulgence in pogroms and lynchings'. In his book *The Pseudo-Revolution* (Tom Stacey, 1972) he claims that the 'lewdness of children's magazines today ... should surely be enough to make us realise that in our time we have a mass form of child seduction which far outweighs Victorian child-prostitution in its widespread anti-human effects'. p. 194. Secondly there is a concern that the spread of pornography is undermining the whole ethic of

capitalism. Money is supposed to be one of the rewards for industry and decent behaviour. The American researchers reported that some respondents 'became quite agitated when they learned that local "smut peddlars" were earning rather large amounts of money'. *op. cit.*, p. 104.

28 Letter to Edward Heath, 17th April, 1973.

29 Letter from Mr Heath to Mrs Whitehouse, 8th May, 1973.

30 Quoted in Ian Cotton, 'The Festival of Light : the Authentic Voice of the British Backlash?', in *Nova*, June 1972.

31 *British Weekly*, 4th May, 1973.

32 G.L.C. Arts and Recreation Committee Film Viewing Board, 'Exercise of the Council's Powers of Film Censorship for Adults', 26th Nov., 1974.

33 *The Times*, 9th July, 1973.

34 The Arts Council, *The Obscenity Laws* (Deutsch, 1969), p. 11.

35 *Ibid.*, pp. 36–7.

36 *Ibid.*, p. 35.

37 *Ibid.*, p. 13.

38 *Ibid.*, p. 12.

39 *Hansard*, House of Commons, 24th July, 1969, Vol. 787, 2110.

40 The Arts Council, *op. cit.*, p. 37.

41 National Council for Civil Liberties, *Against Censorship*, 1972, p. 6.

42 The Society of Conservative Lawyers, *The Pollution of the Mind: New Proposals to Control Public Indecency and Obscenity*, 1972.

43 John Trevelyan, *What the Censor Saw*, *op. cit.*, p. 229.

44 Louis Zurcher and Robert Cushing, 'Participants in Ad Hoc Antipornography Organisatons', in *Technical Reports of the Commission on Obscenity and Pornography*, Vol. 5, p. 213.

Chapter Ten

1 Sir Sidney Harris, *op. cit.*

2 T. P. O'Connor in *The Cinema*, *op. cit.*, p. 247.

3 G. K. Chesterton, 'The Fear of the Film', in *Selected Essays* (Collins, 1939).

4 *Daily Mirror*, 4th July, 1973.

5 *The Sun*, 4th July, 1973.

6 *Sunday Mirror*, 23rd and 30th April, 1972.

7 E.g. Philip Elliott, *The Making of a Television Series* (Constable, 1972).

8 B. P. Emmett, 'The Design of Investigations into the Effects of Radio and Television Programmes and Other Mass Communications', in *The Journal of the Royal Statistical Society*, Vol. 129, 1966.

9 James Halloran, 'The Social Effects of Television', in Halloran (ed.), *The Effects of Television* (Panther, 1970), p. 33.

10 E. E. Maccoby, 'The Effects of Television on Children', in Wilbur Schramm (ed), *The Science of Human Communication* (Basic Books, New York, 1963), pp. 126–7.

11 The B.B.C. itself has noted how 'when "permissiveness" is to some a term of abuse, but to others a desirable goal, the B.B.C. inevitably came in for criticism from adherents of both sides. To some of these it could appear over-tolerant, if not "trendy", and yet at the same time others accused it of being too ready to listen to restrictionist views being expressed by a vocal minority.' *B.B.C. Handbook*, 1974, p. 15.

12 National Commission on the Causes and Prevention of Violence, *Statement on Violence in Television Entertainment Programmes* (US Government Printing Office, Washington, 1969).

13 *The Report of the Commission on Obscenity and Pornography, op. cit.*, p. 58.

14 A third method using clinical studies, as pioneered by Frederick Wertham, has little standing in social scientific terms. Random psychiatric cases offer no objective evidence in support of the 'cumulative effect' of screen violence which Wertham asserts to be a 'contributing factor to all kinds of childhood troubles'. He counters this criticism by arguing that 'the ordinary layman doesn't need any science to realise ... that it can't be good for a child, or have no effect on him, if you give him a profusion of slugging, killing, torture, bleeding, branding and so on'. See 'Issues and Perspectives : a Public Confrontation', in O. Larsen (ed)., *Violence and the Mass Media, op. cit.* Malcolm Curruthers and Peter Taggart have established that viewing violence does produce a physical response but they offer no solid evidence for the social implications which they draw. See 'Vagotonicity of Violence : Biochemical and Cardiac Responses to Violent Films and Television Programmes', in *British Medical Journal*, 18th Aug., 1973, pp. 384–9; and 'The Heart's Response to the Portrayal of Violence', in *Medicine, Science, and the Law*, Vol. 13, No. 3, Oct. 1973, pp. 252–5.

15 This and other quotations in the preceding paragraph are taken from Larsen, *op. cit.*

16 Not all psychologists accept the validity of such experimental work. Twenty years ago Marie Jahoda, studying the allegations that 'bad' literature may be a factor in delinquency, reached conclusions with which many would agree today. 'First we have discovered that experts in criminology and psychological theory regard personality as an important and a necessary condition for delinquency. The relevant personality predispositions are formed early in life, long before any exposure to potentially

harmful literature is technically possible. However, personality predispositions are modifiable, for better or worse, by environmental conditions. These modifications can come about by direct or by vicarious experiences. There is evidence from a variety of areas that direct experiences are far more powerful modifiers of human conduct than vicarious experiences.' 'The Impact of Literature', unpublished report to the American Book Publishers' Council, March 1954. Recent, more sophisticated research has failed to support earlier assertions. An American team was able to use a specially written episode in a popular T.V. drama series which was broadcast in the normal way. Viewers in the experiment were then 'presented with temptations in real life similar to those faced by the television character'. Comparison with control groups showed 'no differences in those exposed to our different stimulus programmes'. Stanley Milgram and R. L. Shotland, *Television and Antisocial Behaviour: Field Experiments* (Academic Press, New York, 1973).

17 I. C. Jarvie, *Towards a Sociology of the Cinema* (Routledge and Kegan Paul, 1970).

18 Hilde Himmelweit, A. N. Oppenheim and P. Vince, *Television and the Child* (Oxford University Press, 1958), p. 215.

19 E. E. Maccoby, 'Television and its Impact on Schoolchildren', in *Public Opinion Quarterly*, Vol. 15, 1951, pp. 421–44; W. Schramm, J. Lyle and E. Parker, *Television in the Lives of our Children* (Oxford University Press, 1961).

20 James Halloran, in *The Effects of Television*, op. cit., p. 59.

21 *Ibid.*, p. 62.

22 James Halloran, Roger Brown and David Chaney, *Television and Delinquency* (Leicester University Press, 1970), p. 178.

23 US Senate Committee on the Judiciary, *Television and Juvenile Delinquency* (US Government Printing Office, Washington, 1955).

24 National Commission on the Causes and Prevention of Violence, *To Establish Justice, to Insure Domestic Tranquility* (US Government Printing Office, Washington, 1969).

25 E.g. R. E. Hartley, 'A Review and Evaluation of Recent Studies on the Impact of Violence', Office of Social Research, C.B.S., June 1964, and E. E. Maccoby, 'Effects of the Mass Media', in *Review of Child Development Research*, Vol. 1, 1964. Halloran, in *The Effects of Television*, op. cit., pp. 54–7, and James Wilson, 'Violence, Pornography and Social Science', in *The Public Interest*, No. 22, Winter 1971, offer critiques of the National Commission.

26 Report to the Surgeon General, *Television and Growing Up: the Impact of Televised Violence* (US Government Printing Office, Washington, 1972), p. 16.

27 *Ibid.*, p. 4.
28 Arts Council, *The Obscenity Laws, op. cit.*, p. 70.
29 Andre Glucksmann, *Violence on the Screen* (British Film Institute, 1971), p. 61.
30 The theory that frustration leads to aggression is by no means new. It was raised by Dollard, Doob et. al. in *Frustration and Aggression* (Yale University Press, New Haven) as long ago as 1939.
31 Mary Burnet, *The Mass Media in a Violent World* (Unesco, 1970), p. 36.
32 James Halloran, 'The Impact of Violence in the Mass Media', paper delivered to Unesco Conference, June–July 1970.
33 'Report from the Danish Forensic Medicine Council to the Danish Penal Code Council', in *The Penal Code Council Report on Penalty for Pornography* (Report No. 435, Copenhagen, 1966), pp. 78–80.
34 E.g. by Victor Cline in the Commission Report itself, pp. 463–90. Cline's interpretations have been attacked in their turn.
35 *Report of the Commission on Obscenity and Pornography, op. cit.*, p. 1.
36 *Ibid.*, p. 57. Twelve of the eighteen supported the recommendation; two felt that it was too radical. The Rev. Morton Hill S. J., Rev. Winfrey Link and Thomas Lynch entirely rejected the majority report, as did President Nixon's nominee, Senator Keating, founder of the Citizens for Decent Literature, who refused to participate in discussions altogether. These wrote minority reports criticising the main report and recommending 'commonsense' alternatives.
37 *Ibid.*, p. 232.
38 *Ibid.*, p. 255.
39 *Ibid.*, p. 267.
40 *Ibid.*, p. 286.
41 Press statement, 24th Oct., 1970, quoted in *The Obscenity Report* (Olympia, 1971), pp. 33–5.
42 *Penal Code Council Report, op. cit.*, p. 80.
43 Quoted in the *Report of the Commission on Obscenity and Pornography, op. cit.*, p. 407.
44 Arts Council, *The Obscenity Laws, op. cit.*, p. 65.
45 'Research Survey', in *Pornography—the Longford Report, op. cit.*, pp. 460–98.
46 Berl Kutchinsky, 'Towards an Explanation of the Decrease in Registered Sex Crimes in Copenhagen', in *Technical Reports of the Commission on Obscenity and Pornography*, Vol. 7, *op. cit.*, p. 296.
47 Richard Ben-Veniste, 'Pornography and Sex Crime—the Danish Experience', in *Technical Reports*, Vol. 7, *op. cit.*, p. 252.

48 Berl Kutchinsky, *Law, Pornography and Crime* (Martin Robertson, in press).

49 James Halloran, *The Effects of Television, op. cit.*, p. 63.

50 Edgar Morin, 'Le Problème des Effets Dangereux du Cinéma', in *Revue Internationale de Filmologie*, Vol. 14–5, 1953, p. 231.

51 Jonathan Miller, 'Censorship and the Limits of Permission', in *Against Censorship*, N.C.C.L., *op. cit.*, p. 25.

52 *Daily Telegraph*, 25th Jan., 1973.

53 Published in the *Sunday Mirror*, 30th April, 1972.

54 Published in the *Daily Mail*, 25th Sept., 1972.

55 Published in the *Sunday Times*, 25th Feb., 1973.

56 Published in the *Sunday Times*, 30th Dec., 1973.

57 See also *Report of the Commission on Obscenity and Pornography, op. cit.*, pp. 411–2. Whereas almost 60 per cent of American adults surveyed believed that adults should be allowed to see any explicit sexual material they wished, this proportion was much lower (varying between 29 per cent and 53 per cent) when particular examples were presented.

58 *Broadcast*, 11th May, 1973.

59 This was an open-ended question to which respondents could give several replies, so figures cannot be summed.

60 A survey entitled *Attitudes to Television* by the Australian Broadcasting Control Board (Melbourne, 1970) found that 67 per cent of 544 respondents agreed with the proposition that 'there is still some need for censorship of books and films'. An American study of 2,486 adults concluded that 'there is no such thing as a "contemporary community standard" ', but noted that those who entirely reject pornography are in a minority, although a substantial one. W. Cody Wilson and Herbert Abelson, 'Experience with and Attitudes toward Explicit Sexual Materials', in *Journal of Social Issues*, No. 3, 1973, pp. 19–39.

61 Leif Furhammer, in *The Cinema and the Protection of Youth, op. cit.*, p. 139.

62 Roger Jowell, James Spence and Gulrez Shaheen, *Film Censorship Exploratory Study* (Social and Community Planning Research, March 1974).

63 *The Attitudes of the Movie-Going Public* (report prepared for the M.P.A.A., Jan. 1968).

Chapter Eleven

1 In 1961 Eric Johnston, head of the M.P.A.A., said that : 'In every place where a classification of pictures has been used, the sale of tickets has been retarded.' Quoted in Kenneth

MacGowan, *Behind the Screen* (Dell, New York, 1965), p. 371.

2 *Variety*, 12th Sept., 1973.

3 Hollis Alpert, 'The Movies' New Sex and Violence Ratings', in David Clark and Earl Hutchinson (eds.), *Mass Media and the Law* (Interscience, New York, 1970).

4 Stephen Farber, *The Movie Rating Game, op. cit.*, p. 47.

5 Olga Martin, *Hollywood's Movie Commandments* (H. W. Wilson, New York, 1937), p. 30, quoted in Richard Corliss, 'The Legion of Decency', in *Film Comment*, Summer 1968.

6 Chairman of the Motion Picture Department of the International Federation of Catholic Alumnae (who formed the basis of the Legion's reviewing system), quoted in Richard Randall, *Censorship of the Movies* (University of Wisconsin Press, Madison, 1968), pp. 187–8.

7 *Ibid.*, p. 198.

8 Arthur Knight and Hollis Alpert, 'Sex in Cinema', *op. cit.*, p. 21.

9 *The Times*, 3rd March, 1965.

10 Quoted in Knight and Alpert, *op. cit.*, pp. 17–8.

11 Press statement, 24th Oct., 1970.

12 *Cinema TV Today*, 14th April, 1973.

13 The verdict was reached on a 5–4 majority. On one side were the four Nixon appointees and one Kennedy appointee; on the other three liberal Democrats and one liberal Republican.

14 *New York Post*, 21st June, 1973. See also, 'The US versus Twelve Reels of Film', in *The Sunday Times*, 1st July, 1973.

15 *CinemaTV Today*, 11th Aug., 1973.

16 *CinemaTV Today*, 7th July, 1973.

17 Elliott Stein, 'Suzanne Simonin, Diderot's Nun', in *Sight and Sound*, Vol. 35, Summer 1966, p. 133.

18 Andrew Sarris, *Interviews with Film Directors* (Avon, New York, 1969), p. 202.

19 Michel Ciment, in *International Film Guide, 1973* (Tantivy, 1972), pp. 182–3.

20 Victor Frank, 'Soviet Union', in *Censorship*, No. 1, Autumn 1964.

21 Quoted in Roger Manvell, *The Film and the Public* (Pelican, 1955), p. 252.

22 William Dyckes, in *International Film Guide, 1972* (Tantivy, 1971), p. 238.

23 Alamgir Kabir, in *International Film Guide, 1971* (Tantivy, 1970), p. 216.

24 *Guardian*, 26th Sept., 1973. One of the Board's film viewers told this committee that, of the five members of the Publication Control Board, three (of whom one is deaf) were unable to 'differentiate between the characters' or 'follow the story'.

25 All Marilyn Monroe films were banned after her marriage to Arthur Miller.

26 Donald Ritchie, 'Sex and Sexism in the Eroduction', in *Film Comment*, Jan/Feb. 1973, p. 12.

27 Chief Film Censor Cresswell O'Reilly, quoted in Eric Williams, 'Cultural Despotism—Film Censorship', in Geoffrey Dutton and Max Harris (eds.), *Australia's Censorship Crisis* (Sun Books, Melbourne, 1970), p. 53.

28 Neville March Hunnings, 'Censorship—On the Way Out?', in *Sight and Sound*, Vol. 38, Autumn 1969, p. 201.

Chapter Twelve

1 Neville March Hunnings, *Film Censors and the Law*, op. cit., p. 148.

2 Norman Zierold, *The Moguls* (Avon, New York, 1972), p. 315.

3 *Observer magazine*, 23rd Sept., 1973.

4 Bryan Forbes, *The Distant Laughter*, op. cit., p. 73.

5 *CinemaTV Today*, 26th May, 1973.

6 *Variety*, 10th Nov., 1971.

7 *CinemaTV Today*, 4th Aug., 1973. *The Go-Between* was shown at Cannes where it won the Golden Palm award.

8 *Movie*, No. 6, Jan. 1963.

9 Bryan Forbes, op. cit., p. 40.

10 Walter Goodman, 'How not to Produce a Film', in *New Republic*, No. 133, 1955, p. 12.

11 Ivor Montagu, *Film World*, op. cit., p. 272.

12 See David Gordon, 'Why the Movie Majors are Major', in *Sight and Sound*, Vol. 42, Autumn 1973, p. 194. He argues that 'the movie majors are still the dominant force in film production, in film financing, and in distribution'.

13 Luigi Luraschi, 'Censorship at Home and Abroad', in *Annals of the American Academy*, 1947, p. 147.

14 Russell E. Shain, 'Effects of Pentagon Influence on War Movies, 1948–70', in *Journalism Quarterly*, Winter 1972, pp. 641–7.

15 J. W. Fulbright, *The Pentagon Propaganda Machine* (Liveright, New York, 1970), p. 116.

16 Interview with Jack Nicholson, *Film Night*, B.B.C. Television, 22nd May, 1974. See also *CinemaTV Today*, 12th Jan., 1974.

17 Russell Shain, op. cit., p. 642.

18 *Ibid.*, p. 647.

19 Interview with James Coburn, *Cinema*, Granada Television, 22nd Nov., 1973.

20 John Baxter, 'Unforthcoming Attractions', in the *Sunday Times magazine*, 13th May, 1973.

21 David McGillivray, 'The Crowded Shelf', in *Films and Filming*, Sept. 1969.
22 David McGillivray, 'Dusting the Shelf', in *Films and Filming*, June 1973.
23 I. C. Jarvie, *Towards a Sociology of the Cinema*, op. cit., pp. 90–1.
24 Ivan Butler, *The Cinema of Roman Polanski* (Zwemmer, 1970), p. 117.
25 Joseph Gelmis, *The Film Director as Superstar* (Doubleday, New York, 1970), p. 212.
26 Richard Whitehall, 'Talking with Peckinpah', in *Sight and Sound*, Vol. 38, Autumn 1969, p. 175.
27 *Movie*, No. 6, Jan. 1963.
28 *Guardian*, 1st Aug., 1973.
29 Of course it does not necessarily follow that a director with total independence will always produce a masterpiece, or that studio interference is invariably detrimental, as the career of Arthur Penn illustrates.
30 David Spiers, 'Interview with Jack Gold', in *Screen*, Vol. 10, Nos. 4 and 5, July/Oct. 1969. p. 122.
31 *Ibid.*, p. 123.
32 *Daily Mail*, 11th May, 1973.
33 David Pirie, *A Heritage of Horror*, op. cit., pp. 159–60.
34 Graham Cadwallader, 'Inside Performance', in *Sight and Sound*, Vol. 40, Spring 1971, p. 78. For producer Sandy Lieberson's account see Alexander Walker, *Hollywood, England* (Michael Joseph, 1974), pp. 411–25.
35 Keith Irvine, 'The Film You Won't See', in *The Nation*, Vol. 181, 1955, pp. 109–10.
36 *The Times*, 27th Oct., 1970.
37 John Baxter, op. cit., p. 38.
38 *Sight and Sound*, Vol. 34, Summer 1965.
39 Doug McClelland, *The Unkindest Cuts* (Barnes, New York, 1972).
40 *Ibid.*, p. 139.
41 David Robinson, *World Cinema: a Short History* (Eyre Methuen, 1973), p. 267.
42 Doug McClelland, op. cit., pp. 83–4.
43 There are other possible censors also. The Rank laboratories once refused to process a film by Bob Godfrey in which the Queen was made to appear to sing 'Good Evening, Friends'.
44 Lillian Ross, *Picture* (Penguin, 1962), p. 101.
45 John Gregory Dunne, *The Studio* (W. H. Allen, 1970), p. 235.
46 See Herbert Gans, 'The Creator-Audience Relationship in the Mass Media : an Analysis of Movie Making', in B. Rosenberg

and D. M. White (eds.), *Mass Culture* (Free Press of Glencoe, New York, 1957), pp. 315–24.

47 The differing ratios can lead to problems for censors. *Pal Joey* (1957) was shot in standard ratio (1.33 : 1) to be projected at a wider ratio. The Board saw it as shot, so that in one scene Rita Hayworth's breasts were clearly seen at the bottom of the picture. The distributors, who had seen the picture only in widescreen, denied that such a scene existed until it was proved to them. If during exhibition any projectionist had racked up the film the offending material would have become visible. Since this particular scene occurred at the end of a reel, projectionists, in checking the spots which indicate reel changes, would undoubtedly have spotted the potential of this sequence. More recently, *The Misfits* caused problems. It too was shot in standard ratio to be projected at 1.66 : 1, whilst the Board's equipment at that time could handle only 1.33 or 1.85. For reasons of artistic appreciation the Secretary chose to view at the latter ratio, so that a good part of the film was never actually seen by the Board.

48 Ed Buscombe, 'Films on T.V.', *Screen* pamphlet No. 1, undated, pp. 20–1.

49 The *Sunday Times*, 16th Nov., 1969.

50 American publicity man quoted by Alexander Walker, *Evening Standard*, 29th Nov., 1973.

51 *Sight and Sound*, Vol. 39, Autumn 1970, p. 186. One of these films was Losey's *Secret Ceremony*, a financial disappointment which Universal had somehow sold to U.S. television for $1,250,000 for two screenings. In the meantime nineteen additional pages of script and nearly 300 lines of dialogue had been added which 'exactly reversed the meaning and intention of my film'. See Alexander Walker, *Hollywood, England, op. cit.*, p. 356.

52 Jan Aghed, '*Pat Garrett and Billy the Kid*', in *Sight and Sound*, Vol. 42, Spring 1973, p. 68.

53 Stephen Farber, *The Movie Rating Game, op. cit.*, p. 72.

54 'Open letter from Peter Watkins, English film director, in which is discussed the present repression within British media and its growing intellectual support', March 1970.

55 Roger Manvell, *New Cinema in Britain* (Studio Vista, 1969), pp. 8–9.

56 *Ibid.*, p. 10.

Chapter Thirteen

1 C. A. Oakley, *Where We Came In* (George Allen and Unwin, 1964), p. 102.

2 *The Film in National Life*, report of the Enquiry by the Commission on Educational and Cultural films (George Allen and Unwin, 1932), p. 33.

3 John Trevelyan, *What the Censor Saw, op. cit.*, p. 92.

4 James Halloran, Philip Elliott and Graham Murdock, *Demonstrations and Communication* (Penguin, 1970), p. 145.

5 D. A. N. Smith, 'Reviews Reviewed', in Richard Boston (ed.), *The Press We Deserve* (Routledge and Kegan Paul, 1970), pp. 110–20.

6 Harry Street, *Freedom, the Individual and the Law* (Pelican, 1972), pp. 72–3.

7 Quoted in J. J. Kilpatrick, *The Smut Peddlars* (Elek, 1961), p. 220.

8 Charles Rembar, 'The Outrageously Immoral Fact', in H. Clor (ed.), *Censorship and Freedom of Expression* (Rand McNally, Chicago, 1971).

9 The Social Morality Council, *The Future of Broadcasting* (Eyre Methuen, 1974).

10 N.C.C.L., *Against Censorship, op. cit.*, p. 5.

11 *The Times*, 24th July, 1973.

12 Alec Grant, 'Censorship—a Perennial Problem', *op. cit.*, p. 26.

13 Harry Street, *op. cit.*, p. 73.

14 John Trevelyan, *What the Censor Saw, op. cit.*, p. 161.

INDEX

DATE DUE

NO 30 77			
JAN 28 79			
OC 24 '79			
OC 28 81			
NO 18 81			
DE 17 82			
OC 15 84			
AP 15 85			
MY 2 '86			
AP 15 88			
AP 23		WITHDRAW	
DE 12 90			
MY 3 '91			
MY 20 93			
'98			